POWERFUL LEARNING ENVIRONMENTS:
UNRAVELLING BASIC COMPONENTS AND DIMENSIONS

ADVANCES IN LEARNING AND INSTRUCTION SERIES

Series Editors: **S. Strauss, E. De Corte, R. Wegerif and K. Littleton**

Further details: http://www.socscinet.com/education

Published:

VAN SOMEREN, REIMANN, BOSHUIZEN & DE JONG
Learning with Multiple Representations

DILLENBOURG
Collaborative Learning: Cognitive and Computational Approaches

BLISS, SÄLJÖ & LIGHT
Learning Sites: Social and Technological Resources for Learning

BROMME & STAHL
Writing Hypertext and Learning: Conceptual and Empirical Approaches

KAYSER & VOSNIADOU
Modelling Changes in Understanding

SCHNOTZ, VOSNIADOU & CARRETERO
New Perspectives on Conceptual Change

SMITH
Reasoning by Mathematical Induction in Children's Arithmetic

KOZULIN & RAND
Experience of Mediated Learning

ROUET, LEVONEN & BIARDEAU
Multimedia Learning: Cognitive and Instructional Issues

GARRISON & ARCHER
A Transactional Perspective on Teaching and Learning

COWIE & AALSVOORT
Social Interaction in Learning and Instruction

VOLET & JÄRVELÄ
Motivation in Learning Contexts

Forthcoming Titles

TUOMI-GRÖHN & ENGESTRÖM
Between School and Work — New Perspectives on Transfer and Boundary Crossing

Related journals — sample copies available online from:
http://www.elsevier.com

Learning and Instruction
International Journal of Educational Research
Computers and Education
The Internet and Higher Education
Early Childhood Research Quarterly
Journal of Early Childhood Teacher Education
Learning and Individual Differences

POWERFUL LEARNING ENVIRONMENTS:
UNRAVELLING BASIC COMPONENTS AND DIMENSIONS

EDITED BY

ERIK DE CORTE
University of Leuven, Belgium

LIEVEN VERSCHAFFEL
University of Leuven, Belgium

NOEL ENTWISTLE
School of Education, University of Edinburgh, United Kingdom

JEROEN VAN MERRIËNBOER
Open University, Heerlen, The Netherlands

Published in Association with the European Association for Learning and Instruction

2003

Pergamon
An Imprint of Elsevier Science

Amsterdam – Boston – London – New York – Oxford – Paris
San Diego – San Francisco – Singapore – Sydney – Tokyo

ELSEVIER SCIENCE Ltd
The Boulevard, Langford Lane
Kidlington, Oxford OX5 1GB, UK

First edition 2003

Library of Congress Cataloging in Publication Data
A catalog record from the Library of Congress has been applied for.

British Library Cataloguing in Publication Data
A catalogue record from the British Library has been applied for.

ISBN: 0-08-044275-7

⊚ The paper used in this publication meets the requirements of ANSI/NISO Z39.48-1992 (Permanence of Paper).
Printed in The Netherlands.

110626

Contents

Contributors

Carl Bereiter	Institute for Knowledge Innovation and Technology, Ontario Institute for Studies in Education/University of Toronto, Canada
Mireille Bétrancourt	TECFA, University of Geneva, Switzerland
Monique Boekaerts	Center for the Study of Instruction and Education, Leiden University, The Netherlands
Marcel Crahay	Service de Pédagogie Expérimentale, Université de Liège, Belgium
Erik De Corte	Center for Instructional Psychology and Technology (CIP&T), University of Leuven, Belgium
Pierre Dillenbourg	Center for Research and Support of Training and its Technologies, Swiss Federal Institute of Technology (CRAFT), Ecole Polytechnique Fédérale de Lausanne, Switzerland
Noel Entwistle	School of Education, University of Edinburgh, Scotland
Gijsbert Erkens	Department of Educational Sciences, Utrecht University, The Netherlands
Geneviève Hindryckx	Service de Pédagogie Expérimentale, Université de Liège, Belgium
Jenny Hounsell	School of Education, University of Edinburgh, Scotland
Jos Jaspers	Department of Educational Sciences, Utrecht University, The Netherlands
Ton de Jong	Faculty of Behavioral Sciences, University of Twente, The Netherlands
Gellof Kanselaar	Department of Educational Sciences, Utrecht University, The Netherlands
Vassilios Kollias	Cognitive Science and Educational Technology Laboratory, University of Athens, Greece

Martine Lebé	Institut Sainte Marie, Belgium
Erno Lehtinen	Centre for Learning Research and Department of Teacher Training, University of Turku, Finland
Renate Limbach	Inspectie van het Onderwijs, Utrecht, The Netherlands
Velda McCune	School of Education, University of Edinburgh, Scotland
Jeroen J. G. van Merriënboer	Educational Technology Expertise Center, Open University of the Netherlands, The Netherlands
Alexander Minnaert	Center for the Study of Instruction and Education, Leiden University, The Netherlands
Cécile Montarnal	Ecole Supérieure de Commerce de Grenoble (ESCG), France
Fred Paas	Educational Technology Expertise Center, Open University of the Netherlands, The Netherlands
Jules Pieters	Faculty of Behavioral Sciences, University of Twente, The Netherlands
Maaike Prangsma	Department of Educational Sciences, Utrecht University, The Netherlands
Marlene Scardamalia	Institute for Knowledge Innovation and Technology, Ontario Institute for Studies in Education/University of Toronto, Canada
Hilde Van Keer	Department of Education, Ghent University, Belgium
Jean Pierre Verhaeghe	Department of Education, Ghent University, Belgium
Jan D. Vermunt	ICLON — Graduate School of Education, Leiden University, The Netherlands
Lieven Verschaffel	Center for Instructional Psychology and Technology (CIP&T), University of Leuven, Belgium
Stella Vosniadou	Cognitive Science and Educational Technology Laboratory, University of Athens, Greece

Introduction

Erik De Corte, Lieven Verschaffel, Noel Entwistle and
Jeroen van Merriënboer

Over the past ten to fifteen years the international scene of research on learning and
instruction has witnessed the emergence of important and promising developments.
New theoretical frameworks, design principles, and research methodologies focusing on
the construction, implementation, and evaluation of powerful learning environments
were put forward, coming from three intersecting subdomains within the broader field
of research on learning and instruction, namely instructional psychology, instructional
technology, and instructional design.

In instructional psychology novel perspectives have emerged that emphasize
constructivist, active, and authentic learning, knowledge and skills as (partly) situated,
and the importance of teamwork and collaborative, distributed mental activity. These
perspectives have, for instance, been embedded in the cognitive apprenticeship model
(Collins *et al.* 1989) as a framework for designing learning environments.

The translation of this new conception of learning in educational environments can be
substantially supported by the application of appropriate technology. In this respect
some relevant developments in the domain of instructional technology have occurred.
For instance, the integration of different media in multimedia systems has resulted in
new insights in the complementarity of different symbol systems for learning (Schnotz
2003); research on computer-assisted open learning environments has mapped out the
potential as well as the limits of learner control; and, computer-supported collaborative
learning has shown how technology can facilitate in teams of learners productive
approaches to rich and realistic problem situations.

Instructional design has also not been at a standstill. Coming from a period in which
the focus was mainly on the formulation and validation of proceduralized rules for
achieving rather isolated learning objectives, the attention has shifted towards the
development of design models in which more complex skills and competencies are
paramount and that take into account the layered nature of learning activities (e.g. van
Merriënboer 1997).

Although it is obvious that the developments in those three subdomains of research
on learning and instruction are characterized by similarities and convergencies, there are
still important divergencies. Differences can, for instance, easily be identified in the key
concepts that are prominent in each of the three domains. Therefore, there is a great
need for scientific debate and attempts to integrate, or justify, the contrasting theoretical
frameworks, methodological approaches, and empirical outcomes. It is our conviction

that — if successful — such an endeavor could result in substantial advancement in theory and methodology in the field of learning and instruction in general. It would also promote the elaboration of more valid, research-based principles for the design of powerful learning environments that encourage students to achieve revised educational objectives that focus more directly on conceptual understanding, higher-order cognitive and metacognitive skills, and self-regulated learning. A European research network has been set up to work towards this end. It involves fourteen European research teams, coordinated by the Center for Instructional Psychology and Technology of the University of Leuven and funded for a five-year period by the Flemish Fund for Scientific Research.

The present volume is the first collective output of this European research network, and focuses on unraveling and identifying basic component and dimensions of powerful learning environments. It is based on the presentations and discussions that constituted the "pièce de résistance" of a first meeting of the research network. But all contributions were reviewed, revised and edited in view of their publication in this volume. Part I introduces the three main themes — instructional design, instructional psychology, and instructional technology — through broad reviews, drawing on conceptualizations emerging from ongoing research programmes in Europe and Canada. In Part II three studies are reported that aim at identifying and/or measuring major components and dimensions of novel learning environments in secondary and higher education, while Part III presents three investigations relating to the design and application of advanced technological tools to support inquiry and learning in powerful learning environments. Finally, Part IV focuses on the role of peer tutoring and collaboration to promote conceptual change and intentional learning in different content domains, namely mathematics, science, and reading comprehension.

The chapters in Part I contribute to an understanding of what constitutes a powerful learning environment. Bereiter and Scardamalia suggest that 'immersion' is a prime necessity, implying a planned coherence and alignment in the arrangements made for teaching, and the encouragement of increasingly self-motivated and self-regulated learning directed towards clearly conceived, high-level goals. But the most promising practical arrangements for achieving such an environment are still being actively debated from theoretically disparate positions, as this part of the book clearly illustrates.

Drawing predominantly on cognitive psychology, van Merriënboer and Paas argue that instructional design depends on taking an eclectic view of learning to take account of known individual differences, to ensure that the instructional methods used are aligned to what is known about cognitive architecture, and to plan specific components in the learning environment designed to encourage transfer of learning. They identify three worlds of instructional design — work, knowledge and learning — all having rather different emphases on what constitutes a powerful learning environment. In an attempt to reconcile these differences the authors identify four basic blueprint components: learning tasks, supportive information, procedural information, and part-task practice; they show how these can be integrated within an instructional design model. As students are often required to learn complex material, the blueprint components have to be used in ways that avoid the cognitive overload otherwise created in working memory.

De Corte describes powerful learning environments that enhance transfer, seen in terms of the productive use of previously acquired knowledge and skills in new contexts. He describes three different experiments to illustrate how carefully designed learning environments not only lead to better learning outcomes within the experimental context, but also in subsequent learning. The experimental contexts were set up in teaching topics in primary-level reading and mathematics, and also in business economics at university. All three environments were designed to incorporate some of the main ideas from social constructivism and cognitive apprenticeship, such as initiating active and constructive learning processes in students; progressively developing cognitive and volitional self-regulation; providing socio-cultural supports through interaction and collaboration; and confronting students with challenging, realistic problems, representative of the kind of tasks they will meet in the future.

Lehtinen reviews extensive research into the design and effectiveness of computer-supported collaborative learning (CSCL). He develops the theoretical rationale for CSCL by distinguishing, first, between cooperation (through division of labor) and collaboration (mutual engagement in the task) and indicating the crucial difference in role and participation produced. The development of understanding depends on making thinking 'visible' through collaboratively explored explanations, a process that can be made more powerful through transformative communication based on computer support of various kinds. Much has been claimed for a wide range of different computer-based support for learning, but on its own the computer provides only part of what is required to support learning. It lacks the crucial social dimension that allows discussions to take place between people with strong interpersonal ties, where a special kind of reciprocity can add substantially to the quality and effectiveness of learning. The theoretical rationale is then considered in relation to a review of empirical studies.

In the final chapter in Part I, Bereiter and Scardamalia describe their own attempt to provide a computer-supported learning environment specifically intended to promote collaborative knowledge building. They suggest that most current education typically looks at knowledge in a 'belief mode', with students being expected to accept, and work with, knowledge established by others, and seen as firmly established. They argue that there are crucial soft skills needed to work effectively in the new 'knowledge age', and that these can only be developed by immersion in a classroom context that treats knowledge in a 'design mode'. Knowledge has to be seen as capable of refinement and improvement and, in the environment provided, students are encouraged to interact in an iterative knowledge-building process, supported by a specially designed computer program. The authors use science education as an illustrative example of the difference between belief mode and design mode, showing a progressive shift towards design mode through three widely promoted methods — learning by design, project-based science, and problem-based learning. They conclude, however, that only knowledge building can provide the experience of immersion in an environment that engages students on work that is not context-limited, and which encourages thinking with broad emerging concepts that develop knowledge, and make it understandable.

The three chapters of Part II address research and discussions that focus on attempts at creating learning environments for fostering high-quality learning in students in secondary and tertiary education.

The chapter by Boekaerts and Minnaert deals with a large-scale innovation program in vocational schools in the Netherlands, that aims at designing and evaluating powerful learning environments for fostering students' self-regulation skills. The authors begin with a description of the innovation program, called the Interactive Learning group System (ILS), that involves a set of instructional principles. Two intervention studies using this program are discussed, and lead to the finding that the observed outcomes were not in line with the anticipated effects. A major reason for this finding put forward is the lack of fidelity of implementation of the instructional principles by the participating teachers. This observed inconsistency leads the authors to a discussion of methodological issues relating to the credibility and internal validity of intervention studies, and also to the identification and analysis of some misconceptions they had about the nature of the outcome variables. Taking this into account and using contrasting groups of teachers in terms of the degree to which they adhered to the instructional principles of the ISL, the chapter then explores critically the power of the innovation program to unfold the major components of the ISL learning environment. Finally, some recommendations for future research are presented.

The chapter by Entwistle, McCune, and Hounsell presents work in the early stages of a collaborative research project involving teams from three universities in Britain. The project focuses on approaches for describing existing teaching-learning settings, and on ways of designing more powerful learning environments that enhance the quality of student learning in higher education. Referring to the available literature, especially the work relating to conceptions of learning (such as deep and surface level learning), the authors argue that we have now a rather clear conceptual framework for thinking about students' learning in higher education. Against this background the chapter discusses the development of two questionnaires. The *Learning and Studying Questionnaire (LSQ)* is designed to measure students' orientations and approaches to learning. The *Experiences of Teaching and Learning Questionnaire (ETLQ)* assesses their perceptions of the teaching-learning environment. The chapter reports the extensive analysis of the relevant literature that preceded the construction of the latter questionnaire in view of identifying powerful aspects of learning environments that are likely to foster high-quality learning in students in higher education. The empirical part of the chapter focuses on the factor analysis of the ETLQ leading to the identification of five factors, and on the relationship among those factors and students' approaches to studying as measured by the LSQ. A major question to be answered in the next stages of the project is whether students' perceptions will change as the learning environments will be modified by introducing aspects that are assumed to be "powerful" in fostering high-quality learning.

The chapter by Vermunt explores which kind of learning environments are powerful to foster high-quality learning in students in higher education, resulting in their acquisition of conceptual understanding, higher-order cognitive and metacognitive skills, and self-regulated learning. Based on the available inquiry on student learning, the notion of high-quality learning is first defined. This is followed by a critical review of the case of problem-based learning (PBL) as used since 1976 at Maastricht University in the Netherlands, leading to the conclusion that over the years this method has tended to become a routine, and as such has lost much of its challenging character. Arguing that PBL in Maastricht needs revitalization, but also that it is not the only approach to foster high-quality learning, the author then analyses eight different types of learning environments in terms of the kind of learning they induce, and the degree of self-regulation and independency they foster in students: traditional teaching, assignment-based teaching, classical PBL, PBL with self-directing study teams, project-centered learning, self-directed specialization learning, dual forms of learning, and autodidactic learning. Implications for curriculum development are discussed in terms of sequencing of a variety of the learning environments presented, and major powerful components of these environments are described.

Part III focuses on the role that technological tools can play in powerful learning environments. Well-designed tools should amplify desired thinking and learning processes. Perkins (1992) makes a distinction between five types of tools: (1) *construction kits*, which provide building blocks for designing and constructing artefacts, (2) *information banks*, which provide all kinds of information that may help to perform a task, (3) *phenomenaria*, which present particular objects, events or processes in such a way that they can be studied, (4) *task managers*, which are instruments to plan and perform tasks and receive feedback, and finally (5) *symbol pads*, which allow for the construction and manipulation of symbols. Three chapters discuss the design, use and evaluation of technological tools in relation to different learning processes, respectively learning-by-design, learning from external representations, and dialogical learning.

The chapter by Pieters, Limbach, and de Jong describes an authoring system or construction kit called SIMQUEST for designing and developing a special kind of powerful learning environment, namely simulation-based discovery lessons in science. In particular, it focuses on the effectiveness of an information bank in SIMQUEST for supporting the design process. The information bank presents all kinds of information on discovery learning and the design of discovery learning environments and contains 500 information cards that can be presented just-in-time to teachers-designers. The cards are organized in four categories: (1) definitions (answering what-is questions), (2) examples, (3) considerations, and (4) background information. A multiple case study using a broad range of measurements shows that the purpose and benefit of the information bank are clear to the users, that it is flexible in use, and that the users are satisfied with it. However, the results also indicate the importance of explicitly linking the given information to the specific context for which the teachers-designers develop the learning environment.

The chapter by Bétrancourt, Dillenbourg, and Montarnal describes a learning environment with animated graphics' devices, that is, a phenomenarium to support learning from external representations. In particular, it focuses on the effectiveness of animated and interactive pictures in a multimedia lesson on financial analysis. The reported experiment was conducted as part of a regular course and distinguished three conditions: static pictures that presented all information elements at once; non-interactive animated pictures that sequentially presented the information elements and, finally, interactive animated pictures where learners controlled the display order of the information elements. The results clearly indicate that animated pictures better facilitate the construction of a mental representation of the learned concepts than static pictures and so improve transfer performance. The added value of interactivity is not yet clear. While interactive animated pictures were as beneficial to learning as non-interactive animations, learners' evaluation of their pedagogical value was significantly lower. Possible explanations for this finding include cognitive overload resulting from managing the tool and the use of learning strategies that are facilitated by computer-controlled sequencing of information elements.

The chapter by Erkens, Kanselaar, Prangsma, and Jaspers describes a collaborative writing environment or task manager called TC3 (Text Composer, Computer supported & Collaborative) to support "dialogical learning" by pairs of students. In particular, two specific symbol pads are described that provide shared external representations. First, an *outline* tool helps learners to generate and organize information units as an outline of consecutive subjects in the text; this is expected to result in a better and, therefore, more persuasive argumentative structure of the text. Second, a *diagram* tool helps learners to generate, organize, and relate information units in a graphical knowledge structure with several kinds of text boxes (e.g. information, position, argument pro, argument contra, etc.) and relationships between boxes; it is expected to have positive effects on the consistency and completeness of the argumentation of the text. Furthermore, an information bank was available with advice on how to use the diagram and the outline. An experiment that studied the effects of the different tools as well as several combinations of them, showed that a moderate availability of extra tools has a positive influence on the number of arguments that are exchanged by the learners and also on some aspects of the quality of the produced argumentative text.

Part IV of the book deals with the role of peer tutoring and collaboration for promoting conceptual change and intentional learning in different content domains, respectively physics, mathematics, and reading.

Vosniadou and Kollias start by describing and explaining a set of design principles for the construction of learning environments to promote conceptual change in the area of science, with special attention to the issue of collaboration and the development of intentional learning. According to the authors, conceptual change is required in the learning of science when the concepts introduced through instruction come in contrast with the naive theories that students have constructed on the basis of their everyday experience. Studies of conceptual change have shown that this is a slow and gradual process often accompanied by misconceptions, inert knowledge, internal inconsistencies and lack of critical thinking. Intentional learning is the kind of learning that is goal-directed and deliberate, internally initiated rather than controlled by the environment, and under the conscious control of the learner. Conceptual change can be greatly facilitated by intentional learning because intentional learners are better able to monitor their learning, have greater metaconceptual awareness of their beliefs, and are better able to justify them on the grounds of explanatory adequacy. After having outlined how collaboration in powerful learning environments can lead to conceptual change and intentional learning, a design experiment is presented wherein computer-supported collaborative learning, and more particularly Knowledge Forum, is applied to increase students' ability to take the perspective of other students, to entertain multiple representations, to plan and monitor their learning, to adopt more constructivist epistemologies and to learn to use more sophisticated mechanisms for conceptual change such as analogies, abstractions and models, in the domain of physics.

The chapter of Van Keer and Verhaeghe focuses on peer tutoring as a means to increase the power of a learning environment for primary school children's acquisition of cognitive and metacognitive strategies for reading comprehension. Contrary to many previous studies that have started either from the theoretical perspective of strategic reading instruction or from that of peer tutoring, and that have explored the effects of either explicit reading strategies instruction or peer tutoring, the work presented in this chapter integrates ideas and practices from both research fields, trying to find out if practising reading strategies in tutoring sessions provides a surplus value to explicit strategies instruction. Moreover, whereas past studies on tutoring focused on either cross-age or same-age tutoring, the present studies involve a systematic comparison of both variants. During two successive school years two similar large-scale quasi-experimental studies were conducted to investigate the effects of reading strategies instruction combined with either: (a) teacher-led whole-class practice, (b) same-age, or (c) cross-age peer tutoring activities on second and fifth graders' reading comprehension. Besides providing additional evidence for the value of explicit and systematic reading strategies instruction, the overall results indicate that pupils seem to profit more from participating in peer tutoring with cross-age than with same-age dyads.

Peer tutoring is also the topic of the chapter by Crahay, Hindryckx, and Lebé. Whereas the design studies of Van Keer and Verhaeghe focus on the effects of different forms of cooperative learning and peer tutoring, the investigation reported in the last chapter aims at unraveling the interaction processes that underlie these learning effects. According to the authors, most studies pertaining to peer tutoring interactions are based on the hypothesis that an effective tutor reacts to the tutee's errors, which means that he/she adopts a retroactive regulation strategy. However, a fine-grained analysis of peer interaction among elementary school children in a tutoring situation pertaining to mathematical application problems of the multiplying type leads the authors to the opposite conclusion, namely that the tutors relied strongly on proactive rather than on retroactive regulation strategies. Particularly during the first phase of the peer tutoring session, wherein the children had to correct errors made by the tutee on a previously administered test with multiplication problems, all tutors conducted the exchanges. The tutees, on the other hand, were mainly engaged in performing execution tasks. This interaction mode did not radically change during the application phase of the tutoring session, in which tutors and tutees had to solve together a new set of multiplication problems. This way of acting seemed quite effective, since most tutees made substantial progress from pre-test to post-test. The results are discussed within the perspective of scaffolding theories and of interactive processes likely to promote learning.

As a whole, the chapters of this volume present a varied palet of research work sharing a common objective, namely contributing to unraveling the basic components and dimensions of learning environments that aim at facilitating and enhancing so-called "new learning", a term that is used "to refer to the new learning outcomes, new kinds of learning processes, and new instructional methods both wanted by society and currently stressed in psychological and educational theory" (Simons *et al.* 2000, p. vii). The contributions to the book come from three different perspectives, namely instructional psychology, instructional technology and instructional design, and as mentioned above our European research network aims at confronting and debating theory, methodology and empirical results that have emerged from those three subdomains in research on learning and instruction. This volume is only a first step in that direction. The authors of the different chapters have attempted to focus on the analysis, identification and evaluation of components and dimensions of instructional interventions, and this has resulted in a rich and varied inventory of theoretical and methodological approaches to the design and implementation of powerful learning environments. This inventory constitutes a solid basis for further discussion and inquiry that have the potential at progressively advancing the elaboration and testing of theories of learning from instruction.

We would like to express our thanks to all those who have contributed to the first meeting of the European research network on "Design, development, and implementation of powerful learning environments", and to the production of the present volume. We are especially indebted to the Flemish Fund for Scientific Research for its financial support which made the organization of this first meeting possible, and facilitated the production of this book. Our special thanks go to Raf Canters for his support in the organization of the first meeting of the research network and to Betty Vanden Bavière for her valuable assistance in preparing the final manuscript of this volume.

References

Collins, A., Brown, J. S., & Newman, S. E. (1989). Cognitive apprenticeship: Teaching the craft of reading, writing and mathematics. In: L. B. Resnick (Ed.), *Knowing, learning, and instruction. Essays in honor of Robert Glaser* (pp. 453–494). Hillsdale, NJ: Lawrence Erlbaum Associates.

Perkins, D. N. (1992). Technology meets constructivism: Do they make a marriage? In: T. M. Duffy, & D. H. Jonassen (Eds), *Constructivism and the technology of instruction: A conversation* (pp. 45–56). Hillsdale, NJ: Lawrence Erlbaum Associates.

Schnotz, W., & Lowe, R. (Eds) (2003). External and internal representations in multimedia learning (Special issue). *Learning and Instruction, 13*, 117–252.

Simons, R. J., Van der Linden, J., & Duffy, T. (Eds) (2000). *New learning.* Dordrecht, The Netherlands: Kluwer Academic Publishers.

Van Merriënboer, J. J. G. (1997). *Training complex cognitive skills: A four-component instructional design model for technical training.* Englewood Cliffs, NJ: Educational Technology Publications.

Part I

General Perspectives on Components and Dimensions of Powerful Learning Environments

Chapter 1

Powerful Learning and the Many Faces of Instructional Design: Toward a Framework for the Design of Powerful Learning Environments

Jeroen J. G. van Merriënboer and Fred Paas

Introduction

Powerful learning environments are often defined in a teleological sense as environments for learning that aim at the development of complex and higher-order skills, deep conceptual understanding, and metacognitive skills such as the ability to regulate ones own learning (de Corte 1990, and Chapter 2). These outcomes foster the productive use of acquired knowledge and skill, or, the ability to apply what is learned in new problem situations and thus allow for transfer of learning. In the last decade, research has been conducted on the necessary characteristics of powerful learning environments. These include: (1) the use of complex, realistic and challenging problems that elicit in learners active and constructive processes of knowledge and skill acquisition; (2) the inclusion of small group, collaborative work and ample opportunities for interaction, communication and co-operation; and (3) the encouragement of learners to set their own goals and provision of guidance for students in taking more responsibility for their own learning activities and processes. Furthermore, new information and communication technologies can positively affect powerful learning environments (de Corte 1994; also chapters by Bereiter and Lehtinen). Nevertheless, very little is yet known about the basic blueprint components and the systematic design of powerful learning environments.

The primary goal of this article is to explore and describe the basic requirements for an instructional design model for powerful learning environments. Three basic conditions for the design of powerful learning environments are taken as a starting point. First, instructional design for powerful learning environments must take into account that people learn in numerous different ways, that is, it should take an *eclectic view* of learning (van Merriënboer & Kirschner 2001). Second, instructional design for powerful learning environments must be aimed at *integrated sets of learning goals* or complex learning (van Merriënboer 1997). Such integrated goals allow for the ability to recombine acquired skills, knowledge and attitudes in an effective way to solve new problem situations (i.e. transfer of learning). And third, instructional design for powerful learning environments must yield instructional systems that are fully *aligned with human cognitive architecture* and, in particular, the limited processing capacity of the human mind (Sweller *et al*. 1998). These three conditions reflect a cognitive view on learning. While motivational and social views may provide equally important conditions for the design of powerful learning environments, they fall beyond the scope of this article.

The structure of this chapter is as follows. First, three worlds of instructional design are distinguished: (1) the world of work; (2) the world of knowledge; and (3) the world of learning. It is argued that a reconciliation of those three worlds is necessary to reach a truly eclectic view on learning. Second, this eclectic view on learning is coupled to the issue of integrated learning goals or complex learning. According to our approach, powerful learning environments for complex learning can be described in terms of four basic blueprint components: (1) learning tasks; (2) supportive information; (3) procedural information; and (4) part-task practice. Third and last, the alignment of powerful learning environment with human cognitive architecture is discussed. In particular, the focus is on instructional methods that optimize cognitive load for each of the four blueprint components. The chapter ends with a brief summary and discussion.

How to Reconcile Three Worlds of Instructional Design?

People learn in many different ways. They learn by being told, by comparing and contrasting information, by discussing with others, by looking at other people performing a task, by making and testing predictions, by practicing procedures, by processing feedback, by reading books, by rehearsing and paraphrasing information, by solving problems, by trial and error and by many, many other activities. For the design of powerful learning environments, one should acknowledge that people learn in many different ways — and, in principle, aim to support all those different ways. What is needed is an *eclectic* view on learning. Unfortunately, the field of instructional design has not been very successful in developing design theories and models that take such an eclectic view. Instead, theories and models are typically founded in one philosophical paradigm or "world", stressing particular types of learning and ignoring others. Van Merriënboer & Kirschner (2001; see also van Merriënboer *et al*. 2002) distinguish: (1) the world of work; (2) the world of knowledge; and (3) the world of learning. These three worlds represent fundamentally different perspectives on the two main issues in instructional design, namely, *what to teach* and *how to teach it* (Reigeluth 1999: ix). In the next sections, the basic characteristics of each of the three worlds will be discussed and a proposal is made to reconcile them.

The World of Work

The world of work is currently dominating the field of instructional design. The common answer to the "what-to-teach" question lies in a description of real-life or professional tasks. This world is closely related to social-constructivist views on learning, based on the idea that learners construct knowledge based on their own mental and social activity. Constructivism ideas suggest that in order to learn, learning needs to be situated in problem solving in real-life, authentic contexts (Brown *et al.* 1989) where the environment is rich in information and where there are no right answers (embedded knowledge).

In answering the how-to-teach question, theories within the world of work take the viewpoint that complex knowledge and skills are best learnt through cognitive apprenticeship on the part of the learner within a rich environment (Collins 1988). Experiences are provided for learners that mimic the apprenticeship programs of adults in trades, or teachers in internship. Although it is not possible to immerse the learner to the extent that an internship would imply, the use of simulations and meaningful experiences enable the learner to learn the ways of knowing of an expert. Meaning is negotiated through interactions with others in contexts where multiple perspectives on reality exist (Von Glasersfeld 1988). Reflexivity is essential and must be nurtured (Barnett 1997a, 1997b). Finally, all of this is best — and possibly only — achieved when learning takes place in ill-structured domains (Spiro *et al.* 1988).

The philosophical roots of the world of work can be traced back to a holistic perspective, which dominated classical Greek philosophy, then became less popular, but re-emerged in the last half of the 20th century (e.g. in Forrester's work on system dynamics 1961). The main problem of a holistic approach is how to deal with complexity. Most authors introduce some notion of "modeling" to attack this problem. For instance, Spector's MFL framework (Model Facilitated Learning 2000) suggests that there must always be a number of phases in learning (cf., Piaget 1970), with a graduated progression from concrete experiences towards more abstract reasoning and hypothetical problem solving. Achtenhagen's (2001) notion of "modeling the model" prescribes a two-step approach to didactic modeling, namely modeling reality and then modeling those models of reality from a didactical perspective. This modeling of the model for didactic purposes allows the designer to determine which elements of the original model can be omitted, and which elements can be made abundant (not in the original, but introduced for supporting the functions of the model).

The World of Knowledge

This world is most easily associated with the traditional field of instructional design, whose foundations were laid by Gagné (1965). In this world, the common answer to the what-to-teach-question lies in taxonomies of learning outcomes, typically referring to particular knowledge elements (e.g. concepts, rules, strategies, etc.). Taxonomies of learning have a long history with the taxonomies of Bloom (1956) and Gagné (1965) still in wide use. Gagné also made clear that specific learning outcomes could often only be determined on the basis of some kind of task analysis, introducing the "learning hierarchy" as a means of task decomposition. This hierarchy holds that a more complex intellectual skill is at the top of the hierarchy with enabling skills at a lower level. Later instructional design models further refined taxonomies of learning (e.g. Merrill's performance-content matrix 1983) and detailed the task-analytical procedures necessary for reaching a highly specific description of "what-to-teach" in terms of particular learning outcomes (e.g. Leshin *et al.* 1992).

In the world of knowledge, the common answer to the how-to-teach question rests on Gagné's idea of "conditions of learning". Theories for the design of instruction (e.g. Merrill's Component Display Theory 1983; Scandura's Structural Learning Theory 1983, and many others) presume that the optimal conditions for learning depend mainly on the goal of the learning process. By analyzing these goals, instructional designers can devise how best to achieve those goals. The theories assume that designers can describe a subject matter domain in terms of learning goals, and can then develop instruction for each of the learning goals — taking the optimal conditions of learning for each goal into account.

In an epistemological sense, the world of knowledge takes an analytical perspective that can be traced back to Descartes' Discourse on Method (1960), which described the process of dividing and subdividing a problem until small, immediately understandable parts were found. But its major strength, namely its analytic approach, is at the same time its major weakness. As argued by Wilson (1998: 146), "the reduction of each phenomenon to its constituent elements, [is] followed by the use of the elements to *reconstitute* [italics added] the holistic properties of the phenomenon". This process of reconstitution works well for a limited set of elements, but for complex learning situations, instructional designers face extremely large sets of highly integrated knowledge elements. They need to synthesize many instructional strategies that are all necessary to reach multiple learning goals. While instructional design models in the world of knowledge are very helpful for analyzing learning goals and apportioning these goals into their constituent elements, they provide far less guidance for synthesizing the large number of instructional strategies that may help to make learning more effective, efficient, and appealing.

The World of Learning

The world of learning is, not surprisingly, primarily rooted in educational and cognitive psychology. The focus is on the description and analysis of learning processes. The starting point for design is not an analysis of the content, but rather a study of the process of learning. Examples can be found in research on reading comprehension, which yielded guidelines for the optimal design of texts (see Hartley 1978); on the acquisition of procedural skills, which yielded guidelines for the design of drill-and-practice computer programs (see Salisbury 1990), or on discovery learning, which yielded guidelines for the design of computer-based educational simulations or discovery worlds (e.g. de Jong & van Joolingen 1998). While the world of knowledge is heavily involved with task and content analysis in order to specify learning outcomes, the world of learning is mainly involved with specifying the instructional conditions that may help to support one particular, pre-defined kind of learning process.

In the world of learning, the "how-to-teach" question is thus typically rephrased as a "how-to-support-learning" question. Whereas in the world of knowledge, instructional strategies often take the form of delivery methods, specifying how to optimally deliver presentations, set up practice and assessment for particular learning outcomes, in the world of learning, instructional strategies deal with methods that support specific learning processes. The focus is on the development of support systems, often called cognitive tools or learning tools, and feedback strategies.

From an epistemological viewpoint, the world of learning takes a synthetic perspective with respect to the designer's activities. The focus is on what people do in the world and on an ontology of action. Activity Theory (Nardi 1996) stresses, for example, that activities quite often involve other persons and various artifacts, and that particular activities require a synthetic process (or "authoring" process) directed at the development of particular kinds of learning supports and facilitation. While the focus of the world of knowledge is typically on "pre-authoring", that is, the analysis of content, tasks, context and target group and the selection of instructional strategies, the world of learning focuses on authoring and authoring tools (i.e. putting the instructional strategies together). The primary role of the real world is to provide a setting in which the curricular goals of the intended education can be applied. Context is for the authors, primarily the organizational context in which the authored system will eventually be applied.

Reconciling the Three Worlds

Summarizing the sections above, there appear to be at least three worlds of instructional design. The world of work takes a holistic viewpoint and stresses real-life or professional task performance and instructional strategies to deal with the complexity of whole-task performance. The world of knowledge stresses the analysis of content and tasks in learning goals and prescribes optimal instructional methods for particular goals. And finally, the world of learning stresses the characteristics of particular learning processes and yields guidelines for the synthesis of instructional systems that support precisely those processes. How can those three worlds be reconciled? Three measures seem to be necessary. First, a common language is needed to discuss the "what-to-teach question" across the different worlds. To answer this question, the world of work now refers to real-life tasks; the world of knowledge to knowledge elements, and the world of learning to cognitive processes. This makes it impossible to reach a common understanding. Van Merriënboer *et al.* (2002) argue that *mental models* may possibly provide the necessary common language to reconcile the three worlds. It falls, however, beyond the scope of this chapter to discuss this issue.

Instead, this chapter will focus on the other two measures, which pertain to the question "how-to-teach"? The second measure is to focus on the commonalities in the three worlds. If there is one such commonality, it is no doubt that all worlds assume that learning only occurs through meaningful — mental — actions on the part of the learners. Thus, any instructional design approach that is consistent with all three worlds is expected to focus on the design of learner activities and make the design of information presentation, or the "transmission of knowledge", subordinate to the design of meaningful practice. The third and final measure is to acknowledge the inherent complexity of learning and the importance of integrated learning goals for reaching transfer of learning. We should not only take an eclectic view on learning and acknowledge that people learn in a countless number of ways, but we should go one step further and also acknowledge that we cannot simply pile up instructional methods to reach integrated learning goals. Complex learning requires the application of an intimately interrelated set of instructional methods, which together sustain different learning processes that often occur simultaneously. This process of complex learning, and the basic components of powerful learning environment for supporting such learning, will be discussed in the next section.

From Complex Learning to Four Blueprint Components

Complex learning is always involved with achieving highly integrated sets of learning goals. Three issues are of utmost importance: (1) coordination; (2) integration; and (3) differentiation. With regard to *coordination*, complex learning has little to do with learning separate skills in isolation, but foremost it is dealing with learning to coordinate the separate skills that constitute real-life task performance. Thus, in complex learning the whole is clearly more than the sum of its parts, because it also includes the ability to coordinate the parts. With regard to *integration*, complex learning stresses that effective performance relies on an integration of skills, knowledge and attitudes — where, for instance, complex knowledge structures are underlying problem solving and reasoning skills and particular attitudes are critical to interpersonal skills or to performing safety procedures. With regard to *differentiation*, complex learning recognizes qualitative differences among the constituent skills that are to be acquired. Some constituent skills are performed in a variable way across problem situations. Experts can effectively perform such *non-recurrent* skills because they have highly complex cognitive schemata available that help them to reason about the domain and to guide their problem solving behavior. Other constituent skills may be performed in a highly consistent way across problem situations. Experts can effectively perform such *recurrent* skills because their cognitive schemata contain rules that directly associate particular characteristics of the problem situation to particular actions.

The classification between non-recurrent and recurrent aspects of complex perform-ance is particularly important because the associated learning processes and instructional methods are fundamentally different from each other. For non-recurrent (novel, effortful) constituent skills the desired exit behavior is guided by cognitive schemata that steer problem-solving behavior (cognitive strategies) and allow for reasoning about the domain (mental models). These schemata enable the *different* use of the *same* knowledge in a new problem situation, because they contain generalized knowledge and/or concrete cases that can serve as analogies. The main learning processes are related to *schema construction*: they include induction or mindful abstraction from concrete experiences and elaboration of new information. For recurrent (routine) constituent skills the desired exit behavior is driven by cognitive rules that link particular characteristics of the problem situation to particular actions. In other words, rules enable the *same* use of the *same* situation-specific knowledge in a new problem situation. The main learning processes are related to *schema automation*: They include restricted encoding or proceduralization of new information in to-be-automated rules and compilation and strengthening of those rules.

To sum up, an environment for complex learning must pay attention to the coordination of all skills that constitute a complex cognitive skill as well as the integration of those skills with subordinate knowledge (e.g. mental models, cognitive strategies) and attitudes, and concurrently promote schema construction for non-recurrent aspects and schema automation for recurrent aspects of the complex skill. By doing so, the training program aims at transfer of learning — the ability to apply what is learned to a wide variety of new real-life situations. Building on those assumptions, the basic idea is that powerful environments for complex learning can always be described in terms of four interrelated components, which are based on four different categories of learning processes. The components are called: (1) learning tasks; (2) supportive information; (3) procedural information; and (4) part-task practice.

Learning Tasks

Learning tasks nicely fit the ideas that are prevalent in the world of work. Learning tasks are concrete, authentic and meaningful real-life experiences that are provided to learners. They allow for the simultaneous practice of — recurrent and non-recurrent — task aspects so that students can learn to coordinate those different aspects. A set of learning tasks is the central component of a powerful learning environment aimed at complex learning. The learning tasks are typically performed in a real or simulated task environment and provide whole-task practice, that is, they ideally confront the learners with *all* constituent skills that make up the whole complex skill.

Learning tasks promote schema construction through *induction*, which is the central learning process for this basic component. That is, the learning tasks stimulate learners to construct cognitive schemata by abstracting away from the concrete experiences that the learning tasks provide. To-be-constructed schemata come in two forms: (1) mental models that allow for reasoning in the domain because they reflect the way in which the learning domain is organized; and (2) cognitive strategies that guide problem solving in the domain because they reflect the way problems may be effectively approached.

Instructional methods that stimulate induction are mainly related to variability and mindful abstraction. To create high-variable practice, learning tasks can be sequenced in a randomized order and can differ from each other in terms of the saliency of defining characteristics, the context in which the task has to be performed, the familiarity of the task, or any other task dimensions that also vary in the real world. This high variability is necessary to promote the development of rich cognitive schemata, which allow for transfer to new problem situations (e.g. Paas & van Merriënboer 1994). Learning tasks may also contain questions that provoke deep processing and so help learners to mindfully abstract away from the concrete experiences, and build general, abstract mental models and cognitive strategies from the given experiences (e.g. Collins & Ferguson 1993).

Supportive Information

Supportive information is presented to learners because it is expected to be helpful to the learning and performance of non-recurrent aspects of learning tasks. It fits nicely within the world of knowledge — and in particular theories of declarative learning. It provides the bridge between what learners already know and what they need to know for fruitfully working on the learning tasks under the motto: *First study for understanding, then practice for application.* Teachers typically call this information "the theory", which is often presented in study books and lectures. Supportive information reflects both mental models and cognitive strategies. Models of how the world is organized may be described in a general sense and are typically illustrated by case studies. Cognitive strategies may be presented as Systematic Approaches to Problem solving (SAPs), describing the successive phases in a problem-solving process and the rules-of-thumb or heuristics that may be helpful to successfully complete each of the phases. They may be illustrated through "modeling", that is, a teacher or expert who is demonstrating the problem-solving process.

Like learning tasks, supportive information is presented in such a way that it promotes schema construction. However, *elaboration* instead of induction is now the central learning process. Elaboration connects newly presented information to already existing schemata, that is, to what learners already know. This allows for structural understanding and ensures that the schemata provide a bridge between what learners already know and what they need to know to perform the learning tasks. This way, schemata are (re-)constructed and embellished with the new information that is relevant to learning and performing the skill.

Instructional methods that aim at elaboration are mainly related to the activation of prior knowledge and the promotion of deep cognitive processing; they help students to establish non-arbitrary relationships between newly presented information elements and their prior knowledge. For instance, inquiry methods ask learners to "discover" the relationships that are illustrated in the materials. They ask learners to analyze particular ideas, to compare and contrast ideas, to make predictions, to give explanations, to re-arrange elements in time and space, and so forth.

Procedural Information

Procedural information is presented to learners because it is necessary for the learning and performance of recurrent aspects of learning tasks. Like supportive information, it nicely fits the world of knowledge, but it is related to theories of procedural learning. It provides learners with the knowledge they need to know in order to perform the recurrent aspect of the learning tasks under the motto: *practice for application and only study when needed.* The step-by-step information concerns "how-to" information as well as the knowledge elements (i.e. facts, concepts or principles) that are prerequisite to learning and taking the steps. It can be in the form of, for example, directions teachers or tutors typically give to their learners during practice or checklists or job aids that can be consulted during practice. The procedural information is specified at the entry level of the learners, that is, at a level that is suitable to present to the lowest-level ability learner.

Procedural information is presented in such a way that it promotes schema automation through *restricted encoding*, that is, embedding the new information in cognitive, highly situation-specific rules that associate particular conditions to particular actions (this process is also called "proceduralization"; Anderson 1996). It is important to present such information precisely when learners need it during practice. This way, the external information is activated in working memory when it is needed, which facilitates the embedding of the information in the rules that are expected to be automated.

Instructional methods that aim at restricted encoding present steps and prerequisite knowledge precisely at the moment the students indicate that they are needed. This is typically called step-by-step instruction. As the need for such knowledge and steps depends on the individual student, it is important for a powerful learning environment to be receptive to signals from students. Furthermore, it may be necessary to demonstrate difficult steps or to exemplify concepts or principles that are prerequisite for performing the steps. Such demonstrations and examples are best given in the context of the learning tasks. This allows learners to place the recurrent skill to which the information pertains in the context of the whole task.

Part-Task Practice

Part-task practice consists of practice items that provide training for a particular recurrent constituent skill. Like procedural information, this component best fits models of procedural learning from the world of knowledge, but research on the acquisition of procedural skills in the world of learning also yields many guidelines for the design of part-task and drill-and-practice training programs. Part-task practice is only relevant if the learning tasks do not provide enough practice for recurrent aspects of a task to reach the desired level of automaticity. Well-known examples of part-task practice are letting children drill on multiplication tables and playing scales on musical instruments. It is critical to start part-task practice within an appropriate "cognitive context" because it has been found to be effective only *after* exposure to learning tasks that concern — a simple version of — the whole complex skill (Carlson *et al.* 1990).

Practice items promote schema automation for recurrent aspects through *compilation* and subsequent strengthening. Schema automation is mainly a function of the amount and quality of practice that is provided to the learners and eventually leads to automated rules that directly control behavior. Compilation chunks rules together that are consistently applied in the same order and strengthening increases the strength of a rule each time it is successfully applied (Anderson 1996).

Instructional methods that stimulate compilation and strengthening are mainly related to repetition. Learners are invited to repeatedly perform the recurrent constituent skill. The saying "practice makes perfect" is actually true for part-task practice. It is important that the whole set of practice items is divergent, meaning that it is representative for all situations that can be treated by the rules. In addition, extensive amounts of overtraining may be necessary to make the skill fully automatic. Relatively short, spaced periods of overtraining yield better results than long, concentrated periods. Therefore, part-task practice is best intertwined with the learning tasks because this provides distributed practice and also enables the learners to relate the recurrent constituent skill to the whole complex skill.

Figure 1 depicts the four blueprint components. The learning tasks are represented as large circles and provide the backbone of the training program. The supportive information is represented in the L-shaped, light gray figure. It describes how the domain is organized and how tasks in this domain can be effectively approached. The procedural information is represented in the black rectangle, with upward arrows that indicate that information units are connected to separate learning tasks. This information is presented precisely when learners need it for their work on recurrent aspects of the learning tasks. Finally, part-task practice is represented by a sequence of small circles, indicating that repetitive practice for one or more selected recurrent task aspects may start after these aspects have been introduced in the learning tasks.

The interrelationships between the three worlds and the four components with their associated learning processes and instructional methods can be summarized as follows. In the world of work, *learning tasks* promote schema construction in the form of mental models and cognitive strategies through induction by abstracting away from the authentic whole-task experiences that the learning tasks provide. Instructional methods are mainly related to variability and mindful abstraction. In the world of knowledge, *supportive information* is related to theories of declarative learning; it promotes the elaboration of already constructed schemata in long-term memory. Instructional methods mainly relate to the activation of prior knowledge and the promotion of deep cognitive processing. *Procedural information* is related to theories of procedural learning and promotes schema automation through restricted encoding. Typically, instruction aims at presenting steps and prerequisite knowledge precisely when they are needed. Finally, *part-task practice* promotes schema automation through compilation and strengthening. Instructional methods mainly aim at repetition of recurrent constituent skills. Thus, the world of learning provides guidelines for instructional methods that sustain the central learning processes for each of the components: induction is the central learning process for learning tasks; elaboration is the central learning process for supportive information; restricted encoding is the central learning process for procedural information, and compilation and strengthening are the central learning processes for part-task practice.

Alignment with Cognitive Architecture

We have now identified the four components and the instructional methods that are needed to attain the associated learning processes. However, for an instructional design

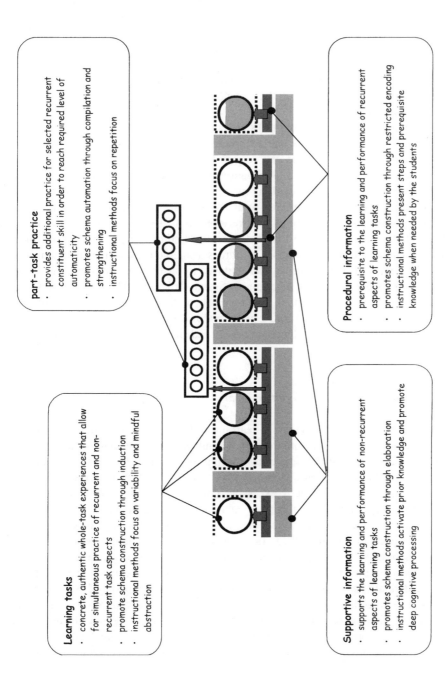

Learning tasks
· concrete, authentic whole-task experiences that allow for simultaneous practice of recurrent and non-recurrent task aspects
· promote schema construction through induction
· instructional methods focus on variability and mindful abstraction

part-task practice
· provides additional practice for selected recurrent constituent skill in order to reach required level of automaticity
· promotes schema automation through compilation and strengthening
· instructional methods focus on repetition

Supportive information
· supports the learning and performance of non-recurrent aspects of learning tasks
· promotes schema construction through elaboration
· instructional methods activate prior knowledge and promote deep cognitive processing

Procedural information
· prerequisite to the learning and performance of recurrent aspects of learning tasks
· promotes schema construction through restricted encoding
· instructional methods present steps and prerequisite knowledge when needed by the students

Figure 1: The four components: (1) learning tasks, (2) supportive information, (3) procedural information, and (4) part-task practice.

to be effective, it needs to be aligned with the human cognitive architecture. According to cognitive load theory (Sweller *et al.* 1998) this architecture consists of a limited-capacity working memory that interacts with an unlimited long-term memory. The limited capacity of working memory creates particular problems in learning, and so needs careful consideration in designing teaching. Cognitive load theory is concerned with the development of innovative instructional methods that efficiently deal with the limitation of working memory and the potential of long-term memory in order to stimulate meaningful learning.

Although authentic whole learning tasks are considered the driving force for learning in powerful learning environments, we acknowledge that their complexity in the form of high element interactivity or *intrinsic cognitive load* in combination with the load caused by the manner in which the information is presented, may hamper learning by the limited processing capacity of working memory. Where that load is unnecessary and so interferes with learning, it is referred to as an *extraneous or ineffective load*, where it is necessary and enhances learning, it is referred to as a *germane or effective load*. Intrinsic, ineffective, and effective load are considered additive in that, taken together, the total load cannot exceed the memory resources available if learning is to occur. It is clear that the control of the cognitive load imposed by instructional designs should be a pre-eminent consideration when determining design structures. The basic idea, which will be elaborated in this section, is that for each of the four components effective instructional control of cognitive load can be realized by applying a delicate mix of instructional techniques that reduces intrinsic and ineffective load and increases effective load.

Scaffold Learners to Decrease Cognitive Load

Whole-task approaches to the design of learning tasks attend to the coordination and integration of constituent skills from the very beginning, and stress that learners quickly develop a holistic vision of the whole task during the training. However, it is clearly impossible to use highly complex learning tasks from the start of a course or training program because this would yield excessive cognitive load for the learners, with negative effects on learning, performance and motivation (Sweller *et al.* 1998). To prevent this, a simple-to-complex sequencing of categories of learning tasks can reduce the intrinsic aspects of cognitive load. Task classes are used to define these simple-to-complex categories of learning tasks. In Figure 1, task classes are represented by the dotted lines around the circles. Learners will typically start working on learning tasks that represent relatively simple versions of whole tasks that experts encounter in the field and progress towards learning tasks that represent more complex versions of the whole tasks as their expertise increases. The final task class represents all tasks, including the most complex ones that professionals encounter in the real world.

At the same time, high variability of learning tasks is used as a technique to increase germane cognitive load. High variability is known to promote meaningful learning by stimulating learners to compare the solutions to the different learning tasks and to abstract more general knowledge for solving a wide range of problems. The learning tasks within the same task class are sequenced in a randomized order so that each next learning task differs from the previous one in terms of the saliency of defining characteristics, the context in which the task has to be performed, the familiarity of the task, or any other task dimension that also varies in the real world. By sequencing learning tasks between task classes from simple to complex and randomly within task classes the cognitive load is optimized because at any time in the training program learners receive learning tasks that are challenging to them but never too demanding on their cognitive capacities.

However, for highly complex tasks the cognitive load associated with the first task class, that is, the simplest version of the whole task may still be too high for novice learners. In this case it is essential to further lower the extraneous cognitive load. Particular types of learning tasks such as worked-out examples, goal-free problems or completion tasks are associated with more learner support and a lower extraneous cognitive load than conventional problem solving. A task class will typically start with learning tasks with a high amount of learner support. As learners acquire more expertise in working on the learning tasks, learner support is gradually decreased until learners are practicing with no support at all. This fading-support principle is visualized in Figure 1 by the dark grey shading of the large circles, which represent learning tasks. One popular way to realize the reduction in extraneous load is by providing the substantial scaffolding of worked examples initially, followed by completion problems and then full problems. Each of these problem forms may provide product support, process support, or both. Product support is provided by giving more or less of the solution to the problem that the learner has to solve in the learning task. Process support is also directed to the problem-solving process itself. Full process support can be provided as a modeling example in which the learner is confronted with an expert who is performing a task and simultaneously explains why the task is performed as it is.

Make High Element Interactivity Information Easily Accessible in Long-term Memory

From a cognitive load perspective the distribution of essential information over a training program and the timing and the format of presentation to students is critical. In many contemporary training programs all information is provided before practice starts and presented in a manner that unnecessarily increases extraneous cognitive load. In this and the next paragraph, we will argue that to prevent this problem within powerful learning environments, supportive and procedural information is identified and presented before practice or just-in-time during practice, respectively (Kester *et al.* 2001).

Experts can effectively perform non-recurrent task aspects because they have cognitive schemata in the form of mental models and cognitive strategies available to reason about the domain and guide their problem solving. To help novice learners construct such mental models and cognitive strategies it is important not to present the information describing the models and strategies to them while they are working on the learning tasks. Since this supportive information typically has a high intrinsic complexity, simultaneously performing the tasks and studying the information would almost certainly cause cognitive overload. Instead, supportive information is best presented before learners start working on the learning tasks. Then, a cognitive schema may be constructed in long-term memory that can subsequently be activated in working memory during task performance. Retrieving this schema during task performance is expected to be less cognitively demanding than activating the externally presented complex information in working memory during task performance. Furthermore, to keep the load resulting from the presentation of supportive information within manageable proportions, the supportive information within a powerful learning environment is connected to task classes and evenly distributed across the whole training program. To increase germane load the information is presented in a format that stimulates learners to elaborate on the material in order to embed it into their existing knowledge structures.

Make Low Element Interactivity Information Directly Available in Working Memory

For novice learners to automate schemata for recurrent task aspects, they need to practice in a learning process known as *knowledge compilation*, where the information that is active in working memory is embedded in highly domain-specific representations, followed by *strengthening*, whereby schemata accumulate strength each time they are successfully applied (Anderson 1996). In combination with the typically low intrinsic complexity of the procedural information prescribing the performance of recurrent task aspects, cognitive load theory indicates that procedural information is best presented when learners need it. At the same time, the theory predicts that just-in-time presentation of procedural information will prevent split attention effects and the associated high extraneous load. Presenting procedural information precisely when it is needed to perform particular actions prevents so-called temporal split attention effects. Information presentation separated in time must be integrated, which results in a higher extraneous cognitive load (Mayer & Sims 1994). Presenting procedural information so that it is fully *integrated* with the task environment prevents spatial split attention effects. Such effects may arise when multiple sources of information must be mentally integrated in order to follow procedural instructions and simultaneously manipulate the task environment. Integrating the multiple sources of information by, for instance, using balloon help or spoken text for procedural information may reduce extraneous cognitive load (Mayer & Moreno 2002).

For our current purpose it is also important to note that procedural information presentation and subsequent knowledge compilation yield an algorithmic description of how to perform recurrent aspects of the learning task. Applying the automated schemata warrants that these aspects are successfully performed. Therefore, procedural information is best connected to the *first* learning task for which the recurrent aspect is relevant. This reflects a perspective that is popular in business training: Practice for application and only study when needed ("just-in-time" learning; Romiszowski 1997). For subsequent learning tasks, procedural information is quickly faded as the learners gain more expertise. This principle of fading is consistent with the idea that when learners have enough expertise, procedural information will become redundant and should thus be removed in order to decrease extraneous cognitive load (Kalyuga *et al.* 1998).

Free Up Processing Resources for Non-recurrent Task Aspects

Learning tasks are designed in such a way that they primarily promote knowledge construction for the performance of the variable aspects of the to be learned complex skill. However, in some cases the cognitive load resulting from performing a consistent skill might be so high that learners do not have enough cognitive resources available and learning of the whole skill is disrupted. In that case, the use of repeated practice for particular parts of the task may be used in order to automate the consistent aspects of the skill is needed. Therefore, in powerful learning environments part-task practice of consistent skills that require high automation should be intermixed with learning tasks. After a consistent skill is introduced in a learning task, repeated short isolated practice sessions are used to automate the performance of the consistent skill and to free up cognitive resources that can be deployed by the learner to cope with the variable aspects of the learning task.

Discussion

This article started from the observation that powerful learning environments are typically defined as environments aimed at complex learning, deep conceptual understanding, and metacognitive skills — but that very little is known about the systematic design of such environments. It was argued that instructional design models for powerful learning environments should at least fulfill three conditions: take an eclectic view on learning and acknowledge that people learn in numerous different ways; distinguish blueprint components and related instructional methods aimed at complex learning, that is, the attainment of integrated sets of learning goals that allow for transfer of learning; and align instructional methods with the human cognitive architecture. These requirements yielded a global framework that may be helpful to the further development of instructional design models and methodologies for powerful learning environments.

It is clear that different models and methodologies may fit the sketched framework. The four-component instructional design model (4C/ID-model; Janssen & van Merriënboer 2002; van Merriënboer 1997; van Merriënboer *et al.* 2002; van Merriënboer & de Croock 2002) is only one example; it focuses on the development of learning environments for complex cognitive skills or professional competencies. Like other modern instructional design models, it assumes that rich learning tasks are the driving force for learning (see Merrill 2002). Furthermore, it can be seen as a "combination model" (Sugrue 2002) because it integrates the different worlds of instructional design, and it is consistent with human cognitive architecture as described by cognitive load theory (van Merriënboer *et al.* 2003). However, there is a clear need for alternative design models that also pay attention to metacognitive skills such as self-regulation, to instructional methods for collaborative learning, and to the explicit use of information and communication technology in the learning environments.

In the last decade, several studies explored the main characteristics of powerful learning environments. This yielded important information on the necessary features of such environments. Now, it becomes important to answer the question how to design and develop powerful learning environments in an efficient and systematic fashion. The main message of this article is that designers acknowledge that students learn in many different ways; attribute a central role to rich learning tasks and treat — supportive and procedural — information as subordinate to those tasks, and design learner activities that seriously take the possibilities and limitations of the human cognitive system into account.

References

Achtenhagen, F. (2001). Criteria for the development of complex teaching-learning environments. *Instructional Science, 29,* 361–380.

Anderson, J. R. (1996). ACT: A simple theory of complex cognition. *American Psychologist, 51,* 355–365.

Barnett, R. (1997a). *Towards a higher education for a new century.* London, U.K.: University of London, Institute of Education.

Barnett, R. (1997b). *Higher education: A critical business.* Buckingham, U.K.: Open University Press.

Bloom, B. S. (1956). *Taxonomy of educational objectives: Cognitive domain.* New York: David McKay.

Brown, J. S., Collins, A., & Duguid, P. (1989). Situated cognition and the culture of learning. *Educational Researcher, 18* (1), 32–42.

Carlson, R. A., Khoo, H., & Elliot, R. G. (1990). Component practice and exposure to a problem-solving context. *Human Factors, 32,* 267–286.

Collins, A. (1988). *Cognitive apprenticeship and instructional technology* (Technical Report No. 6899). Cambridge, MA: BBN Labs Inc.

Collins, A., & Ferguson, W. (1993). Epistemic forms and epistemic games: Structures and strategies to guide inquiry. *Educational Psychologist, 28* (1), 25–42.

De Corte, E. (1990). Towards powerful learning environments for the acquisition of problem-solving skills. *European Journal of Psychology of Education, 5,* 5–19.

De Corte, E. (1994). Toward the integration of computers in powerful learning environments. In: S. Vosniadou, E. De Corte, & H. Mandl (Eds), *Technology-based learning environments: Psychological and educational foundations* (pp. 19–25). Berlin: Springer-Verlag.

De Jong, A. M., & van Joolingen, W. R. (1998). Scientific discovery learning with computer simulations of concept domains. *Review of Educational Research, 68,* 179–202.

Descartes, R. (1960). *Meditations on first philosophy* (translated by L. J. Lafleur). New York: Bobs-Merrill.

Forrester, J. W. (1961). *Industrial dynamics.* Cambridge, MA: MIT Press.

Gagné, R. M. (1965). *The conditions of learning* (1st ed.). New York: Holt, Rinehart, & Winston.

Hartley, J. (1978). *Designing instructional text.* London: Kogan Page.

Janssen, A., & van Merriënboer, J. J. G. (2002). Innovatief onderwijs ontwerpen [Innovative educational design]. Groningen, The Netherlands: Wolters-Noordhoff.

Kalyuga, S., Chandler, P., & Sweller, J. (1998). Levels of expertise and instructional design. *Human Factors, 40,* 1–17.

Kester, L., Kirschner, P. A., van Merriënboer, J. J. G., & Baumer, A. (2001). Just-in-time information presentation and the acquisition of complex cognitive skills. *Computers in Human Behavior, 17,* 373–391.

Leshin, C. B., Pollock, J., & Reigeluth, C. M. (1992). *Instructional design strategies and tactics.* Englewood Cliffs: Educational Technology Publications.

Mayer, R. E., & Moreno, R. (2002). Aids to computer-based multimedia learning. *Learning and Instruction, 12,* 107–119.

Mayer, R. E., & Sims, V. K. (1994). For whom is a picture worth a thousand words? Extensions of a dual-coding theory of multimedia learning. *Journal of Educational Psychology, 86,* 389–401.

Merrill, M. D. (1983). Component display theory. In: C. M. Reigeluth (Ed.), *Instructional-design theories and models: An overview of their current status* (pp. 278–333). Hillsdale NJ: Lawrence Erlbaum Associates.

Merrill, M. D. (2002). First principles of instruction. *Educational Technology, Research and Development, 50* (3), 43–59.

Nardi, B. (Ed.) (1996). *Context and consciousness: Activity theory and human-computer interaction.* Cambridge, MA: MIT Press.

Paas, F., & van Merriënboer, J. J. G. (1994). Variability of worked examples and transfer of geometrical problem solving skills: A cognitive-load approach. *Journal of Educational Psychology, 86,* 122–133.

Piaget, J. (1970). *The science of education and the psychology of the child.* New York: Grossman.

Reigeluth, C. M. (Ed.) (1999). *Instructional-design theories and models: A new paradigm of instructional theory: Volume 2.* Mahwah, NJ: Lawrence Erlbaum Associates.

Romiszowski, A. (1997). Web-based distance learning and teaching: revolutionary invention or reaction to necessity? In: B. Khan (Ed.), *Web-based instruction* (pp. 25–37). Englewood Cliffs, NJ: Educational Technology Publications.

Salisbury, D. F. (1990). Cognitive psychology and its implications for designing drill and practice programs for computers. *Journal of Computer-based Instruction, 17* (1), 23–30.

Scandura, J. M. (1983). Instructional strategies based on the structural learning theory. In: C. M. Reigeluth (Ed.), *Instructional design theories and models* (pp. 213–246). Hillsdale, NJ: Lawrence Erlbaum.

Spector, M. (2001). Philosophical implications for the design of instruction. *Instructional Science, 29,* 381–402.

Spiro, R. J., Coulson, R. L., Feltovich, P. J., & Anderson, D. K. (1988). *Cognitive flexibility theory: Advanced knowledge acquisition in ill-structured domains* (Tech. Rep. No. 441). Champaign, IL: University of Illinois, Center for the Study of Reading.

Sugrue, B. (2002). Performance-based instructional design for e-learning. *Performance Improvement, 41* (7), 45–51.

Sweller, J., van Merriënboer, J. J. G., & Paas, F. (1998). Cognitive architecture and instructional design. *Educational Psychology Review, 10,* 251–296.

Van Merriënboer, J. J. G. (1997). *Training complex cognitive skills: A four-component instructional design model for technical training.* Englewood Cliffs, NJ: Educational Technology Publications.

Van Merriënboer, J. J. G., Clark, R. E., & de Croock, M. B. M. (2002). Blueprints for complex learning: The 4C/ID*-model. *Educational Technology, Research and Development, 50* (2).

Van Merriënboer, J. J. G., & de Croock, M. B. M. (2002). Performance-based ISD: 10 Steps to complex learning. *Performance Improvement, 41* (7), 33–38.

Van Merriënboer, J. J. G., & Kirschner, P. A. (2001). Three worlds of instructional design: State of the art and future directions. *Instructional Science, 29*, 429–441.

Van Merriënboer, J. J. G., Kirschner, P. A., & Kester, L. (2003). Taking the load off a learner's mind: Instructional design for complex learning. *Educational Psychologist, 38*, 5–13.

Van Merriënboer, J. J. G., Seel, N., & Kirschner, P. A. (2002). Mental models as a new foundation for instructional design. *Educational Technology, 42* (2), 60–66.

Von Glasersfeld, E. (1988). *Cognition, construction of knowledge, and teaching* (Eric Document Reproduction Service No. ED 294–754).

Wilson, E. O. (1998). *Consilience: The unity of knowledge*. New York: Alfred A. Knopf.

Chapter 2

Designing Learning Environments that Foster the Productive Use of Acquired Knowledge and Skills

Erik De Corte

Introduction

The importance of being able to apply acquired knowledge and cognitive skills to new learning tasks and problem situations is generally recognized with respect to schooling, but also in non-school educational and instructional settings. This problem of transfer of knowledge and skills has also been on the agenda of research in educational psychology throughout the past century. And, as the available literature shows, the topic has certainly enjoyed an intensified interest over the past ten to fifteen years. Besides numerous research articles, the transfer issue was thoroughly analyzed and critically discussed in at least six volumes: "Acquisition and transfer of knowledge and cognitive skills" (*International Journal of Educational Research*, De Corte 1987); *Transfer of learning: Contemporary research and applications* (Cormier & Hagman 1987); *The transfer of cognitive skill* (Singley & Anderson 1989); *Transfer on trial: Intelligence, cognition and instruction* (Detterman & Sternberg 1993); *Teaching for transfer: Fostering generalization in learning* (McKeough *et al.* 1995); and *Transfer of learning: Cognition, instruction, and reasoning* (Haskell 2001). The topicality of the issue is also illustrated by the lively discussion on transfer a few years ago between Anderson *et al.* (1996, 1997) and Greeno (1997) in the *Educational Researcher*.

Underlying this upsurge in research on transfer is certainly its potential for theory building, on the one hand, but also the significance of transfer of knowledge and skills from a practical perspective (see e.g. McKeachie 1987). This interest comes, of course, traditionally from the side of school education. Indeed, the famous ancient Greek author, Seneca, already wrote: "Non scholae, sed vitae discimus", and this is still echoed today; for instance, Marini & Genereux (1995) argued that transfer of learned knowledge and skills is considered as a fundamental goal of education. But certainly, nowadays, the whole field of industrial and corporate training is also strongly interested in the transfer of learning. This is not at all surprising when one takes into account that the world of business and industry has to invest today enormous amounts of money in in-service training and retraining of personnel. From that perspective acquiring transferable knowledge and skills by workers, employees, and managers is seen as an important component of a "learning economy" resulting in a reduction of money spending.

In this chapter it will first be shown that the issue of transfer has been controversial throughout the twentieth century. It will then be argued that, in view of continued research as well as practical relevance, a reconceptualization of the transfer construct in terms of productive use of knowledge and skills in a variety of situations is desirable. Subsequently, three design experiments will be briefly discussed in which attempts were made to create, implement and evaluate powerful learning environments that facilitate the productive application of acquired knowledge and skills in distinct subject-matter domains (mathematics, reading comprehension, and economics) and at different levels of education (upper primary school and university freshmen).

Transfer: A Controversial Notion

Throughout its long research history, transfer has permanently been a very controversial issue (for a detailed historical overview, see Cox 1997; Mayer & Wittrock 1996; Singley & Anderson 1989). For instance, in the first part of the past century Thorndike's specific transfer theory of identical elements (Thorndike & Woodworth 1901) contrasted with the view of the Gestalt psychologists, like Katona (1940) and Wertheimer (1945), about the transfer of general skills. But also today widely divergent standpoints are argued in the literature, and this is remarkable in that scholars derive these different views more or less from the same set of empirical data. Apparently the data are not compelling, and the conceptual or theoretical lens through which one looks at the available evidence thus becomes a stronger determinant of the conclusion arrived at; moreover, even researchers with a similar or related theoretical background seem to have distinct opinions about the occurrence of transfer.

Some authors coming from different theoretical backgrounds, have taken a very negative position and more or less dismiss the possibility of transfer. For instance, some cognitive psychologists share the view of Detterman (1993): "The lesson learned from studies of transfer is that, if you want people to learn something, teach it to them. Don't teach them something else and expect them to figure out what you really want them to do" (p. 21).

Lave (1988), a proponent of the situated cognition paradigm, also takes a stance against the very idea of transfer, based on the idea that knowledge and skills are context-bound.

While arguing against the occurrence of general transfer, Singley & Anderson (1989) have shown that transfer depends on the degree to which tasks share identical productions, i.e. condition-action pairs of the form "if ... then ...", where the conditions describe some situation and the action specifies something to do when the conditions are fulfilled. As such, Singley and Andersons's research program on transfer has resulted in the presentation of what they call "a modern version of Thorndike's theory of identical elements" (p. 222). In their theory of transfer, Thorndike's identical elements conceived originally as stimulus-response associations are redefined as units of declarative and procedural knowledge. Interestingly, by replacing Thorndike's external behavior elements by purely cognitive operations, Singley and Anderson have, so to say, transposed his associationistic view into a cognitivistic perspective.

The Gestalt psychology view concerning the transfer of general skills is also echoed, from a cognitive psychology standpoint, in a chapter on problem-solving transfer by Mayer & Wittrock (1996). But these authors at the same time extend the notion of transfer by emphasizing the important role of metacognition: "In the metacognitive transfer view, successful transfer occurs when the problem solver is able to recognize the requirements of the new problem, select previously learned specific and general skills that apply to the new problem, and monitor their application in solving the new problem (p. 50)."

This approach is consistent with the general transfer view in the sense that metacognition depends on very general intellectual skills. However, it differs from the general Gestalt view, because metacognition is not conceived as a single monolithic ability, but as a set of high-level skills for self-regulating one's learning, thinking, and problem solving. From a review of the related literature on the teaching of problem solving, Mayer and Wittrock conclude that under appropriate conditions, students can learn to improve their problem-solving transfer.

A similar optimistic perspective derives from several chapters in the book *Teaching for transfer: Fostering generalization in learning* (McKeough *et al.* 1995). For instance, adopting a broad conception of transfer as the understanding and flexible use of resources, Campione *et al.* (1995) conclude from a variety of data collected in the framework of the Fostering Communities of Learning project: "Our view is that there are multiple manifestations of transfer, ranging from the understanding of domain-specific concepts through the deployment of relatively domain-general reading and argumentation strategies" (p. 66).

Finally, while it is often easily taken for granted — referring mostly to Lave's (1988) work cited above — that, according to the situated cognition perspective, knowledge and skills cannot, or can hardly, transfer because they are so strongly embedded in and tied to the context in which they are acquired (see e.g. Anderson *et al.* 1996), a closer look at the literature shows that this is too simple a conclusion. As shown by Law (1994), different adherents of this paradigm have distinct conceptions of situated cognition, leading to different perspectives on transfer. For instance, Greeno *et al.* (1993) have developed an interpretation of transfer within the framework of their situativity theory, which sees learners as acquiring an activity in response to constraints and affordances of the learning situation. Transfer of an activity to a new situation involves a transformation of the initial situation, and an invariant interaction of the learner in the new context. Transfer can occur when the transformed situation contains constraints and affordances similar to those perceived by the learner in the initial context. In line with this situative view, Labato (1996) has defined transfer as the personal construction of similarities across activities; what is crucial in order for transfer to occur is how a new situation is connected with the thinker's conception of previous situations.

From Transfer to the Productive Use of Knowledge and Skills

The continuing diversified and controversial nature of the transfer concept certainly indicates that there is an obvious need for further inquiry aiming at a better and deeper understanding of the processes underlying transfer, and at finding effective research-based and practically applicable ways to facilitate transfer in learners in different educational and training settings.

In our own work we have looked at transfer as part of different research projects, starting from the conception of Mayer & Wittrock (1996) mentioned above namely that, under appropriate conditions, transfer can be achieved. However, taking into account the most recent literature, we still see the need for a reconceptualization of the notion of transfer.

Traditionally, transfer has been narrowly conceived as the transportation of knowledge and skills acquired and stored in one situation to another. Bransford & Schwartz (1999) have called this the *direct application theory of transfer*: can people apply something they have learned directly and independently to a new setting or problem? As argued by these authors, a typical characteristic in this traditional approach to transfer is that the final transfer task takes the form of "sequestered problem solving": while solving the task, subjects do not get opportunities to deploy and show their abilities to learn to approach and solve new problems by invoking help and support from other resources, such as texts or colleagues, or by trying things out, receiving feedback, and getting opportunities to revise. As an alternative to this direct application view, Bransford and Schwartz propose a broader perspective by emphasizing *preparation for future learning (PFL)* as the major aspect of transfer; in this perspective the focus in assessing transfer is on subjects' abilities to learn in new, knowledge-rich contexts, a view that is much more in line with the now prevailing notion of learning as an active and constructive process.

This PFL approach is convergent with a simultaneous redefinition of transfer by Hatano & Greeno (1999). They argue that the view of transfer as direct and independent transportation of acquired elements from one situation to another is in conflict with current perspectives on the contextualized and social nature of knowledge and skills. Taking this into account, they have proposed replacing the term *transfer* by *productivity*, to refer to the generality of learning, i.e. "the extent to which learning in some activity has effects in subsequent activities of different kinds" (p. 647). This interpretation of transfer tallies also well with the broader conception of Campione *et al.* (1995) referred to above.

One can argue whether it is expedient to replace the long-established term *transfer* by a different one, even if the term is not anymore an ideal fit with the current meaning of the concept that emphasizes the broad productive and mediated use of acquired knowledge and skills, as opposed to the direct and sequestered transportation of what has been learned in a previous situation to a new one. For the present discussion we will leave the issue of terminology on the side, and focus on the implications of the reconceptualization of transfer for the design of powerful learning environments that can develop students' preparation for future learning and the productive use of their acquired knowledge and skills. Taking into account that — as mentioned above — this reconceptualization is very much in line with a constructivist and situated perspective on learning, and also recognizing — as shown by Mayer & Wittrock (1996) — the important role of metacognitive self-regulation for successful transfer, the following characteristics of powerful environments for learning in general that have been put forward before (see e.g. De Corte in press), also seem to be appropriate in fostering students' preparation for future learning and their competence in broadly applying their cognitive potential.

First of all, environments that intend to foster the productive use of knowledge and skills should initiate active and constructive learning processes in students. Second, and in line with the previous implication, such environments should enhance students' cognitive and volitional self-regulation. Indeed, there is evidence that learners who have acquired a high degree of self-regulation are better motivated and more competent in using their knowledge productively (see e.g. Campione & Brown 1990; National Research Council 2000). Third, because of the situated and social nature of cognitive tools, promoting its broad and effective application can be enhanced by socio-cultural supports for learning through interaction and collaboration (Hatano & Greeno 1999; Volet 1999). Finally, the situated character also means that productive learning and the preparation for future learning can be fostered by confronting students as much as possible with challenging, realistic problems and situations that have personal meaning for them, and are representative for the kind of tasks they will encounter in the future (De Corte 1996).

Learning Environments that Facilitate the Productive Use of Acquired Knowledge and Skills

Starting from a socio-constructivist perspective on learning from instruction, three recent design experiments of the Leuven Center for Instructional Psychology and Technology have attempted to create and implement learning environments in different domains (mathematics, reading comprehension, and economics) and at distinct levels of education (upper primary school and university freshmen) that facilitate the productive use of acquired skills in different situations. The design of these environments was in accordance with major implications of the new perspective on transfer outlined above.

Design Experiment 1: A Learning Environment for Mathematical Problem Solving

New standards for mathematics in primary school in Flanders stress more than before the importance of mathematical reasoning and problem-solving skills, and the ability to apply them to real-life situations. In this first study we designed, implemented and evaluated a powerful learning environment that can elicit in fifth graders the constructive learning processes required to develop the intended competencies. The learning environment consisted of a series of 20 lessons that were taught by the regular classroom teachers. (For a more detailed report about this study see Verschaffel *et al.* 1999.)

To elicit *active and constructive learning* in pupils, the learning environment in the four participating experimental classes was fundamentally changed in different respects, and as a result embodied major features of instructional settings that can foster productive use of knowledge and skills.

First, the learning environment focused on the acquisition by the pupils of an overall *cognitive self-regulation strategy* for solving mathematical application problems, consisting of five stages, and embedding a set of eight heuristic strategies.

Second, a varied set of carefully designed *realistic (or authentic), complex, and open problems* was used that differs substantially from the traditional textbook tasks.

Third, a variety of *activating and interactive instructional techniques* was applied, especially small-group work and whole-class discussion. Throughout the whole lesson, the teacher's role was to encourage and scaffold pupils to engage in, and to reflect upon, the kinds of cognitive and metacognitive activities involved in the model of skilled problem solving. These instructional supports were gradually faded out as pupils took more responsibility for their own learning and problem-solving processes.

Fourth, an innovative classroom culture was created through the establishment of new socio-mathematical norms about learning and teaching problem solving. Important aspects of this classroom culture were: *stimulating pupils to articulate and reflect upon their solution strategies*, and reconsidering the role of the teacher and the pupils in the mathematics classroom.

The effects of the learning environment were evaluated in an experiment with a pretest-posttest-retention test design with an experimental group and a comparable control group, using a wide variety of data-gathering and analysis techniques. According to the scores on a self-made written word problem pretest and a parallel posttest and retention test, the intervention had — in comparison with the control group — a significant and stable positive effect on the experimental pupils' skill in solving mathematical application problems. In other words, successful initial learning — a necessary condition for transfer (National Research Council 2000) — was achieved. But the results on a standard achievement test that covers, besides word problem solving, also the other aspects of the mathematics curriculum, such as geometry and measurement, showed that in spite of the extra attention in the experimental classes on mathematical problem solving at the expense of those other subject-matter topics, there was no negative influence on the learning outcomes for those other parts of the curriculum. On the contrary, a significant positive transfer effect was observed: the experimental classes performed significantly better than the control classes on this standard achievement test ($p < 0.05$; effect size $= 0.38$). These results thus show that a substantially modified learning environment, combining a set of carefully designed complex and realistic word problems with highly interactive teaching methods and the introduction of new socio-mathematical classroom norms, can significantly boost pupils' self-regulation of their problem-solving activities, but also the productive use of the acquired cognitive skills in subdomains of the mathematics curriculum that were not addressed during the implementation of the powerful learning environment.

Design Experiment 2: A Learning Environment for Strategic Reading Comprehension

New Flemish standards for language learning in primary education put more emphasis than before on the acquisition of skills in communication, expression, comprehension, and text production. And specifically in reading, the learning and teaching of effective cognitive and metacognitive strategies that facilitate text comprehension are stressed.

The major aim of this second study was to design, implement, and evaluate a powerful, but also practicable, learning environment for fostering in fifth graders skilled strategy use when reading a text. As in the previous study, the learning environment, consisting of 24 lessons taught by the regular teachers in four experimental classes, was changed thoroughly to elicit in children *constructive, collaborative, and progressively more self-regulated learning* of reading comprehension strategies. (For a more detailed report see De Corte *et al.* 2001.)

Four specific reading comprehension strategies and one metacognitive strategy were selected as the foci of the powerful learning environment: activating prior knowledge, clarifying difficult words, making a schematic representation of the text, and formulating the main idea of the text. The metacognitive strategy was *regulating one's own reading process*. The four specific reading comprehension strategies were presented to the pupils as a series of steps. When a new strategy was introduced and practised, the previously learned strategy or strategies were also always applied; this combined strategy, used throughout the intervention, aimed at fostering in pupils the integrated application of strategies during text reading. After the four text comprehension strategies were taught, further strategy integration, and especially increasing self-regulation of strategy use by the pupils, was emphasized in the final stage of the implementation of the learning environment. During the last five lessons, pupils had to read texts individually and complete a worksheet using initially, as a guideline, a card on which five steps were listed. The first four steps corresponded to the specific strategies acquired before. The fifth step elicited reflection in pupils by asking them to write down not only what they had learned about the content of the text, but also to describe their activities during text reading (for instance, realizing that the meaning of a difficult word can frequently be found in the text itself). Afterwards, metacognitive self-regulation was fostered by gradually removing the support and guidance of the five-steps card.

Informative texts from half to one page in length were used to facilitate children's acquisition of the intended strategies. This type of text was chosen because, due to their content and structure, informative texts lend themselves very well to the application of those strategies; moreover, pupils are continuously confronted with this kind of texts in school as well as outside it. The *texts* were carefully selected in consultation with the teachers to ensure that they were *meaningful to the children*, and also related to their experiences and interests.

To teach the strategies a variety of *highly interactive instructional methods* were used in each lesson period, namely modeling, whole-class discussion, and small group work. The approach as a whole can be characterized as a variant of Palincsar & Brown's (1984) reciprocal teaching adapted to a normal classroom setting. Strategy modeling by the teacher was not done in small groups, but in front of the whole class. After the modeling phase, whole-class discussion was initiated in the context of actual text reading; although the reading process was still mainly regulated by the teacher, the pupils themselves had to apply and execute the strategies. Whole-class discussion was followed by small-group work. To create the possibility for intensive observation and coaching of the group work by the teacher, the class was divided in two halves. In alternation, one half of the class was further split up in groups of three to four pupils and worked on reading comprehension tasks, while the other half was given an individual assignment from a different subject-matter domain. During small-group work children no longer just executed the strategies, they also took responsibility for regulating and monitoring the reading activity.

As in the previous design experiment, the implementation and the effectiveness of the learning environment were tested using a pretest-posttest-retention test design with four experimental fifth-grade classes and eight comparable control classes. In relation to the pretest, a significant difference in favor of the experimental group was observed on a reading strategy posttest and retained on a parallel retention test with poor readers making somewhat more progress than the better readers. Thus, initial learning, a pre-condition for the potential productive use of strategies in future contexts, was attained. In addition, the results revealed that the experimental pupils were also actually able to apply the reading comprehension strategies acquired in the learning environment successfully in answering questions relating to a text presented outside the context of the reading lessons ($p < 0.0001$). Moreover, this finding was emphasized by the observation mentioned by three of the four experimental teachers that during text reading in different subject-matter domains children referred spontaneously to the strategies they had acquired in the learning environment; this fits nicely with the notion of transfer as preparedness for future learning. In sum, the results of the present study largely parallel the findings of the previous design experiment in a different subject-matter domain; they document the possibility of fostering the acquisition and the productive application of comprehension and self-regulating strategies during text reading in upper primary school children of different ability levels by immersing them in a learning environment based on highly interactive instructional techniques.

Design Experiment 3: A Learning Environment in the Domain of Business Economics

As part of a project aimed at improving metacognitive knowledge and self-regulatory skills in university freshmen in business economy (Masui 2002), we examined the trainability of orienting and self-judging as learning and problem-solving skills, and their effects on academic performance (Masui & De Corte 1999). Orienting is a cognitive self-regulation activity, and involves preparing one's learning and problem-solving process by examining the givens and the characteristics of the learning and problem-solving task, by thinking of possible and desirable goals and cognitive activities, and by taking account of prior knowledge, interest, capacities, and contextual factors. Self-judging is a conative self-regulation activity related to orienting, as orienting activities provide opportunities to assess one's own characteristics and competencies as a learner or problem solver, including prior knowledge and attitudes. This self-judging activity is necessary to provide an accurate appraisal of the efforts needed to accomplish the task at hand successfully.

The learning environment (in the domain of macro-economics) consisted of a series of 10 sessions of 90 minutes each, and a number of exercises and homework aimed at practising and transferring knowledge and skills. The whole intervention was implemented in an experimental group of 47 students spread over a period of seven months. The design of the learning environment was based on an integrated set of instructional principles that are in line with those that underlie the previous two studies, and, thus, also satisfy major implications of the revised perspective on transfer as the productive use of cognitive tools:

- Embed the acquisition of knowledge and skills in the *real study context*;
- Link the activities to the *personal goals* and the learning orientation of the students;
- Sequence learning tasks and teaching methods in such a way that cumulative and *progressively more self-regulated learning* is enhanced;
- Use a *variety of forms of organization and social interaction*, namely modeling, individual assignments, working in pairs, small-group work, and whole-class discussion;
- Take into account informal prior knowledge and individual differences;
- Stimulate articulation of and *reflection* upon learning and problem-solving processes;
- Create ample *opportunities for practice and for the productive use of acquired knowledge and skills* in new domains and problem situations.

Orienting and self-judging relating to the study of macro-economics were explicitly addressed in three of the ten sessions (and the related exercises) of the total intervention. In addition, to foster the skill in self-judging the students received self-judging assignments concerning their examination experiences and their results after the first and second semesters.

The effects of the learning environment were assessed by using a pretest-posttest design with an experimental and two equivalent control groups. Metacognitive knowledge about orienting and self-judging was measured directly using a knowledge test on metacognitive, affective, and conative activities ("What do you have to know at the start of the semester in order to be able to organize and plan your study for a particular course? How can you obtain that information?"). At the end of the intervention we assessed whether students had become more skilled learners, in the sense that they were able to use the trained activities effectively for studying a course which was not involved in the intervention, namely statistics. This preparedness for learning and studying statistics was assessed indirectly by asking students to provide specific orienting information relating to the course (e.g. "How much time do you think to have to invest weekly to the theoretical and practical parts of the statistics course, including the lessons?"), and by giving them a self-judging assignment ("Do you think that the statistics course will be easy or difficult for you? Explain your answer").

The results show that, after immersion in the learning environment, the students of the experimental group had more elaborate and relevant metacognitive knowledge of orienting in a learning or study task as well as of self-judging in comparison to students of the control groups (C1 and C2). But, in addition, the students of the experimental group were significantly better able to use the acquired skills effectively in studying the statistics course that was not involved in the intervention: they could better orient themselves toward the study of that course than both control groups ($p = 0.011$ for C1, and $p = 0.027$ for C2; effect sizes resp. 0.50 and 0.30), and they also gave more evidence of self-judging with regard to statistics ($p = 0.004$ for C1, and $p = 0.003$ for C2; effect sizes resp. 0.59 and 0.45). Moreover, a positive correlation was found between orienting and self-judging behavior and academic performance in statistics. And a linear regression analysis showed that, when studying a new course, being better prepared for orienting and self-judging oneself improves academic performance. Indeed, whereas the entering characteristics measured before the intervention accounted for 41% of the variance in the study results for statistics, the criterion variance explained increased to 51% and 55% after including respectively orienting and self-judging behavior in the regression analysis. In sum, evidence was also found here that by creating the appropriate conditions in a powerful learning environment, students' productive use of acquired knowledge and cognitive and conative skills in new contexts, i.e. the study of a new course, can be fostered.

Conclusion and Discussion

Throughout history, educators have intended to equip their students with cognitive tools that they can use and apply beyond the context in which they were initially learned. However, the scientific study of the notion of transfer dates back only to the beginning of the previous century. And, as documented in the first part of this chapter, the concept has been very controversial throughout that century, conceptually as well as empirically. But by and large there was one common characteristic in the conceptions about transfer, namely the ability to directly transport and apply something that has been learned in one context to a specific new situation. We have shown that this traditional approach to transfer has recently been criticized especially for its narrow view of the criterion for evidence of transfer, and for not being in line with the newer conception of learning as an active, constructive, interactive and contextualized process.

Therefore, transfer has been reconceived in terms of two related constructs, namely preparation for future learning and the productivity of learning outcomes. We endorse this new perspective from which important implications for fostering the productive use of knowledge and skills in educational settings derive. These implications are in line with characteristics of powerful environments for learning in general, and can be summarized as follows: starting as much as possible from tasks and problems that are meaningful and challenging for students, learning environments should initiate socially supported constructive learning processes that enhance students' cognitive and volitional self-regulatory skills.

In three studies that were briefly reviewed, from distinct subject-matter domains and different levels of education, learning environments were designed that are largely in accordance with those implications of the novel approach to transfer. All three of these investigations yield evidence that, by immersing students in such learning environments, it is possible to boost their ability to productively use their knowledge and skills, and thus to prepare them for approaching future tasks and situations more effectively.

However, the evidence provided by these design experiments should not be overrated. Certainly the transfer situations in the two studies at the primary school level were still quite similar to those that were traditionally used in the framework of the direct application theory of transfer, namely the independent and immediate application of something learned in one context to a specific test situation. But this remark does not hold for the investigation with university freshmen, which shows that the students who were immersed in the experimental learning environment could appropriately and productively apply the trained self-regulation skills to the study of a new course. This finding tallies very well with the preparation for future learning perspective. Evidence in line with the broader approach to transfer with regard to younger students has already been reported by other scholars, for instance in the framework of the Fostering Communities of Learning project (Campione *et al.* 1995), and the Jasper project (Cognition and Technology Group at Vanderbilt 1997). However, continued research is necessarily aimed at a deeper understanding of the components of learning environments that facilitate the productive use of acquired tools for learning, thinking, and problem solving, and at unraveling the processes that those learning environments elicit in students.

References

Anderson, R. A., Reder, L. M., & Simon, H. A. (1996). Situated learning and education. *Educational Researcher, 25* (4), 5–11.

Anderson, R. A., Reder, L. M., & Simon, H. A. (1997). Rejoinder: Situative versus cognitive perspectives: Form versus substance. *Educational Researcher, 26* (1), 18–21.

Bransford, J. D., & Schwartz, D. L. (1999). Rethinking transfer: A simple proposal with multiple implications. In: A. Iran-Nejad, & P. D. Pearson (Eds), *Review of research in education* (Vol. 24, pp. 61–100). Washington, D.C.: American Educational Research Association.

Campione, J. C., & Brown, A. L. (1990). Guided learning and transfer: Implications for approaches to assessment. In: N. Frederiksen, R. Glaser, A. Lesgold, & M. G. Shafto (Eds), *Diagnostic monitoring of skill and knowledge acquisition* (pp. 141–172). Hillsdale, NJ: Lawrence Erlbaum Associates

Campione, J. C., Shapiro, A. M., & Brown, A. L. (1995). Forms of transfer in a community of learners: Flexible learning and understanding. In: A. McKeough, J. Lupart, & A. Marini (Eds), *Teaching for transfer: Fostering generalization in learning* (pp. 35–68). Mahwah, NJ: Lawrence Erlbaum Associates.

Cormier, S. M., & Hagman, J. D. (Eds) (1987). *Transfer of learning: Contemporary research and applications*. San Diego: Academic Press.

Cognition and Technology Group at Vanderbilt (1997). *The Jasper project: Lessons in curriculum, instruction, assessment, and professional development.* Mahwah, NJ: Lawrence Erlbaum Associates.

Cox, D. C. (1997). The rediscovery of the active learner in adaptive contexts: A developmental-historical analysis of transfer of training. *Educational Psychologist, 32,* 41–55.

De Corte, E. (Ed.) (1987). Acquisition and transfer of knowledge and cognitive skills. *International Journal of Educational Research, 11,* 601–712.

De Corte, E. (in press). Mainstreams and perspectives in research on learning (mathematics) from instruction. *Applied Psychology: An International Review.*

De Corte, E. (1996). Instructional psychology: Overview. In: E. De Corte, & F. E. Weinert (Eds), *International encyclopedia of developmental and instructional psychology* (pp. 33–43). Oxford, U.K.: Elsevier Science Ltd.

De Corte, E., Verschaffel, L., & Van de Ven, A. (2001). Improving text comprehension strategies in upper primary school children: A design experiment. *British Journal of Educational Psychology, 71,* 531–559.

Detterman, D. K. (1993). The case for prosecution: Transfer as an epiphenomenon. In: D. K. Detterman, & R. J. Sternberg (Eds), *Transfer on trial: Intelligence, cognition, and instruction* (pp. 1–24). Norwood, NJ: Ablex Publishing Corporation.

Detterman, D. K., & Sternberg, R. J. (Eds) (1993). *Transfer on trial: Intelligence, cognition, and instruction.* Norwood, NJ: Ablex Publishing Corporation.

Greeno, J. G. (1997). Response: On claims that answer the wrong questions. *Educational Researcher, 27* (1), 5–17.

Greeno, J. G., Smith, D. R., & Moore, J. L. (1993). Transfer of situated learning. In: D. K. Detterman, & R. J. Sternberg (Eds), *Transfer on trial: Intelligence, cognition, and instruction* (pp. 99–167). Norwood, NJ: Ablex Publishing Corporation.

Haskell, R. E. (2001). *Transfer of learning: Cognition, instruction, and reasoning.* San Diego, CA: Academic Press.

Hatano, G., & Greeno, J. G. (1999). Commentary: Alternative perspectives on transfer and transfer studies. In: E. De Corte (Ed.), On the road to transfer: New perspectives on an enduring issue in educational research and practice. *International Journal of Educational Research, 31,* 645–654.

Katona, G. (1940). *Organizing and memorizing.* New York: Columbia University Press.

Labato, J. E. (1996). *Transfer reconceived: How "sameness" is produced in mathematical activity.* Unpublished doctoral dissertation, University of California, Berkeley, CA.

Lave, J. (1988). *Cognition in practice: Mind, mathematics, and culture in everyday life.* New York: Cambridge University Press.

Law (1994). *Transfer of learning: Situated cognition perspectives* (Research report no. 32). München: Ludwig-Maximilians-Universität, Lehrstuhl für Empirische Pädagogik and Pädagogische Psychologie.

Marini, A., & Genereux, R. (1995). The challenge of teaching for transfer. In: A. McKeough, J. Lupart, & A. Marini (Eds), *Teaching for transfer: Fostering generalization in learning* (pp. 1–20). Mahwah, NJ: Lawrence Erlbaum Associates.

Masui, C. (2002). *Leervaardigheid bevorderen in het hoger onderwijs. Een ontwerponderzoek bij eerstejaarsstudenten* [Enhancing metaknowledge and self-regulation in higher education. A design experiment with university freshmen in business economics, Summary in English]. Leuven: Universitaire Pers Leuven.

Masui, C., & De Corte, E. (1999). Enhancing learning and problem solving skills: Orienting and self-judging, two powerful and trainable learning tools. *Learning and Instruction, 9,* 517–542.

Mayer, R. C., & Wittrock, M. C. (1996). Problem-solving transfer. In: D. C. Berliner & R. C. Calfee (Eds), *Handbook of educational psychology* (pp. 47–62). New York: Macmillan.

McKeachie, W. J. (1987). The new look in instructional psychology: Teaching strategies for learning and thinking. In: E. De Corte, H. Lodewijks, R. Parmentier, & P. Span (Eds), *Learning and instruction. European research in an international context* (Vol. 1, pp. 443–456). Oxford, U.K./Leuven, Belgium: Pergamon Press/Leuven University Press.

McKeough, A., Lupart, J., & Marini, A. (Eds). (1995). *Teaching for transfer: Fostering generalization in learning*. Mahwah, NJ: Lawrence Erlbaum.

National Research Council. Committee on Developments in the Science of Learning and Committee on Learning Research and Educational Practice (2000). *How people learn: Brain, mind, experience, and school*. Washington, D.C.: National Academy Press.

Palincsar, A. S., & Brown, A. L. (1984). Reciprocal teaching of comprehension-fostering and comprehension-monitoring activities. *Cognition and Instruction, 1*, 117–175.

Singley, M. K., & Anderson, J. R. (1989). *The transfer of cognitive skill*. Cambridge, MA: Harvard University Press.

Thorndike, E. L., & Woodworth, R. S. (1901). The influence of improvement in one mental function upon the efficiency of other functions. *Psychological Review, 9*, 374–382.

Verschaffel, L., De Corte, E., Lasure, S., Van Vaerenbergh, G., Bogaerts, H., & Ratinckx, E. (1999). Learning to solve mathematical application problems: A design experiment with fifth graders. *Mathematical Thinking and Learning, 1*, 195–229.

Volet, S. (1999). Learning across cultures: Appropriateness of knowledge transfer. In: E. De Corte (Ed.), On the road to transfer: New perspectives on an enduring issue in educational research and practice. *International Journal of Educational Research, 31*, 625–643.

Wertheimer, M. (1945). *Productive thinking*. New York: Harper & Row.

Chapter 3

Computer-Supported Collaborative Learning: An Approach to Powerful Learning Environments

Erno Lehtinen

Introduction

In the public discourse of the information society, the arguments for the use of ICT in education are typically based on various self-evident benefits of information and communication technology. For example, the possibilities for an interactive relationship between the learner and the system are assumed to be beneficial to learning. Similarly, it seems obvious that the multimedia features of ICT, which open up new possibilities for illustrating learning tasks, facilitate the understanding of the phenomena. The possibility to use ICT in simulating real-life phenomena is one of the features of this new technology that has held out hopes of its educational value. The usefulness of the ICT-based simulation has been self-evident in many special training situations, such as the training of jet plane pilots or nuclear power plant operators, while very fast world-wide access to information sources is currently one of the most promising features of ICT raising enthusiasm among educators. Educators also rely on the Internet as a useful tool for synchronous and asynchronous communication between the teacher and students and among students.

The effects of ICT, however, depend not only on the equipment, but also, above all, on the pedagogical implementation of technology. Thus, the pedagogical approaches used are, in many cases, more important than the technical features of the applied technology. A successful application of ICT in education always means that many systemic changes in the whole activity environment of the classrooms take place (Salomon 1994). ICT has played a noteworthy role in development of new theoretical approaches on learning and instruction. The adaptation of constructivist epistemological principles has particularly encouraged learning scientists to analyze how technology-based environments would provide learners with new opportunities for activities which

Powerful Learning Environments: Unravelling Basic Components and Dimensions
© 2003 Published by Elsevier Science Ltd.
ISBN: 0-08-044275-7

are beneficial for knowledge construction. ICT has played an important role in many attempts to create powerful learning environments for supporting higher order learning and the development of metacognition and self-regulation. One of the desires for the educational use of ICT is that, with the help of information technology, we can develop environments that present complex problem situations while, at the same time, providing students with a rich variety of tools, which effectively support their attempts to control the complex relationships of learning tasks (Lehtinen 2002; Lesgold *et al.* 1992; Steinkuehler *et al.* 2002).

During the early years of computer-aided instruction (CAI), the leading idea about the power of this new technology was based on the so-called solo-learner model, and the opportunities to individualize learning processes. This was supposed to be the crucial feature of computers. The desire to find methods for individualizing teaching, according to the precise current level of knowledge and skills of individual students, was a strong desire in the pedagogy of the 20th century. This was especially true for CAI-programs based on the ideas of programmed instruction, but the emphasis of individualistic models was also typical of many learning environments designed according to constructivist principles (Crook 1994). It was particularly the omission of social interaction in computer-based learning environments which worried many educators in the eighties (Hawkins *et al.* 1982; Turkle 1984).

During the last ten to fifteen years, the situation has changed dramatically. Most of the recent research on the use of information and communication technology in education is more or less explicitly considering technology's possibilities to facilitate social interaction between teacher and students, and among students. Collaboration and communication is certainly a main idea in network-based learning environments, but social interaction has also been increasingly taken into consideration in the design and implementation of systems running in separate workstations (Crook 1994; Lehtinen *et al.* 1999).

Most of the recent research on the use of information and communication technology in education more or less explicitly considers technology's possibilities to facilitate social interaction between teacher and students and among students (Koschmann 1996; Koschmann *et al.* 2002; Kumpulainen & Wray 2002; Lehtinen *et al.* 1999). Crook (1994) has widely analyzed how computers can facilitate collaborative learning in schools. He makes a distinction between interacting *around* and *through* computers. The first perspective stresses the use of computers as tools to facilitate face-to-face communication between student pairs or in a small group. According to Crook (1994) technology may, in these situations, serve to support collaboration by providing students with something he calls points of shared reference. He claims that a traditional classroom situation is too thinly resourced for successful collaboration. There are not enough anchor points available at which action and attention can be co-ordinated. The capabilities of computers can be used as mediating tools that help students to focus their attention on mutually shared objects (Järvelä *et al.* 1999).

Many of the current studies, however, focus on collaboration through the computer, or computer-supported collaborative learning (CSCL), facilitated by different network-based collaboration tools. When Koschmann (1996) edited his first CSCL book, the majority of the chapters still described experiments based on collaboration around computer. In the CSCL 2 book edited five years later, almost all chapters describe "collaboration through computer" experiments (Koschmann *et al.* 2002). During the last few years there has been an explosive increase in the use of computer networks in education and training. Although all "e-Learning" or virtual learning environments do not include any systematic collaboration, the ideas of CSCL are increasingly applied in different practical methods of network-supported learning. Technical applications used in CSCL typically include possibilities for sharing documents and a variety of specific tools for network mediated communication. The communication tools can be based on synchronic media like chat, voice mail, one-line visualization tools, and video-conferencing or they can support asynchronous communication (Lehtinen *et al.* 1999).

On the Theoretical Rationale of CSCL

Many different theoretical approaches have been used in developing the collaborative use of ICT in learning environments. In recent years, several researchers have tried to classify the distinct approaches in the theories and models of learning. These classifications can be used in presenting the theoretical ideas, which have had an influence on the development of CSCL. For example Sfard (1998) has made a division between two main metaphors of learning: the acquisition metaphor and the participation metaphor. The first metaphor describes learning in terms of the acquisition of something in an individual mind, and knowledge in terms of property and possession. The second approach deals with learning as becoming a participant, and with knowledge as an aspect of practice, discourse and activity (Sfard 1998).

Hakkarainen and his colleagues (Hakkarainen *et al.* 2002) have proposed that a third metaphor, knowledge creation, should be added to the metaphors presented by Sfard. This metaphor would include emerging theoretical approaches that refer to models of how new knowledge and skills are created in cultural practices. Prototypes of these theories are the theory of knowledge creations in organizations by Nonaka & Takeuchi (1995), the activity theory-based model of expansive learning by Engeström (1987) and the knowledge building idea of Bereiter (2002; but see also Chapter 4).

When presenting the theoretical rationale for their technology-based collaborative learning environment, "Fifth Dimension", Kaptelin & Cole (2002) argued that there are two distinct, but not necessarily mutually exclusive ways to see the role of social interaction in learning. The first defines learning as an individual process that can be facilitated or inhibited by various forms of social interaction. The features of social situation and the interactions taking place between the learner and his or her collaborators are seen as a "set of external modifiers" (Kaptelin & Cole 2002: 303). The second view assumes that individual learning, and interaction and activity in a social system are only two different aspect of the same phenomenon. In the literature this approach is typically called Vygotskian, based on his notion of the two-step development of new abilities. At first they emerge on a social level between people, later to be internalized by the individual. However, the basic idea of the fundamentally social nature of knowledge and abilities has been developed in many different theoretical schools, not only in the Vygotskian tradition (Valsiner & van der Veer 2000).

Co-operative Learning and Technology-Based Learning Environments

In many studies on the possibilities for making use of information technology in facilitating social interaction in learning environments, the authors have relied on the traditional ideal of co-operative learning. In these theories the focus is on the learning processes taking place in individual learners, although various models of co-operation in peer groups may have facilitated learning processes. Co-operative or group learning refers to instructional methods in which students are encouraged or required to work together on learning tasks.

Slavin (1995) has presented different theoretical perspectives aimed at explaining the achievement effects of co-operative learning. In the following review, the first two perspectives (motivational and social) are mentioned as theories of co-operative learning, while the two other perspectives (developmental and cognitive elaboration) will be discussed as approaches belonging to the collaborative learning camp. The first two could be seen as typical theories of traditional co-operative learning that have been developed as didactical methods in more or less traditional classroom situations.

The *motivational perspective* focuses primarily on the reward or goal structures under which students operate. From a motivational perspective, co-operative incentive structures create a situation in which the only way group members can attain their own personal goals is if all the members of the group are successful. The *social cohesion perspective* is related to the motivational viewpoint. According to this approach, effects of co-operative learning on achievement are mediated by the cohesiveness of the group. This perspective also emphasizes primarily motivational rather than cognitive explanations for the instructional effectiveness of co-operative learning. There is, however, an important difference. Motivational theory stresses social rewards: students help others in their group learn because it is in their own interests to do so. Social cohesion theorists, in contrast, emphasize the idea that students help their group members learn because they care about the group. The social cohesion perspective emphasizes teambuilding activities in preparation for co-operative learning, as well as group self-evaluation, instead of external incentives and individual accountability. A well-known application of this theory is Aronson's (Aronson *et al.* 1978) "Jigsaw" method, where students concentrate on different topics in thematic groups and subsequently share their expertise in groups where students from all thematic groups come together. The theoretical idea in the Jigsaw method is to create interdependence between the group members in a way that would increase social cohesion. Johnson & Johnson (1992) have proposed a similar method, and the ideas have also been applied in the so-called Fostering Community of Learners model (FCL) developed by Brown & Campione (1996). Computer and network environments have proved to be very helpful in organizing applications of Jigsaw-based methods in teaching-learning situations (Pata *et al.* 2002).

From Co-operation to Collaboration

Co-operative learning models in their original forms have not satisfied the researchers developing new technology supported environments, mainly because they have very little to say about the quality of communication and how it is related in the knowledge construction processes. Many authors agree that it is meaningful to make a distinction between co-operation and collaboration (Dillenbourg *et al.* 1996; Roschelle & Teasley 1995). The distinction is based on different ideas of the role and participation of individual members in the activity. Co-operative work is accomplished by the division of labor among the participants where each person is responsible for a portion of the problem solving, whereas collaboration involves the mutual engagement of participants in a co-ordinated effort to solve the problem together (Roschelle & Teasley 1995).

Both major traditions of developmental psychology, the Vygotskyan and the Piagetian, have substantially contributed to the theory of collaborative learning. Although Vygotsky (e.g. 1934/1994) did not believe in the general usefulness of spontaneous collaboration among children of the same age, his theoretical ideas have been widely used in later theories of collaborative learning. Particularly Vygotsky's (1978) idea of the "zone of proximal development" has been useful for understanding mechanisms in collaborative learning. According to this view, collaborative activity among children promotes growth if children have developmental differences. More advanced peers are likely to be operating within one another's proximal zones of development, modeling in the collaborative group behaviors more elaborated than those that the less advanced children could perform alone.

Piaget (1926) held that social-arbitrary knowledge — language, values, rules, morality, and symbol systems — can only be learned in interactions with others. Peer interaction is also important in logical-mathematical thought in disequilibrating the child's egocentric conceptualizations and in the provision of feedback to the child about the validity of logical constructions. On the basis of Piaget's theory many researchers have conducted systematic empirical investigation of how social interaction affects individual cognitive development (cf. Doise & Mugny 1984). These researchers borrowed from the Piagetian perspective its structural framework and the major concepts, which were used to account for development. Especially the concepts of socio-cognitive conflict and the coordination of points of view (centrations) have offered a basis for further development of a theory about the role of social interaction in cognitive development (see Dillenbourg *et al.* 1996).

Cognitive research on peer interaction indicates that cognitive conflicts emerging in social interaction facilitate cognitive performances (Mugny & Doise 1978; Piaget 1980); subject pairs tend to perform better than subjects working alone. Moreover, collaboration fosters the learning process of both less and more advanced students. Doise & Mugny (1984) argued that the learning process is more progressive when children with different cognitive strategies work together and engage in conflictual interaction. This argument has also been used in supporting the use of computer-mediated collaboration in learning environments. The conversation, multiple perspectives, and arguments that arise in groups, or in networks of learners, may explain why collaborative groups facilitate greater cognitive development than the same individuals would achieve when working alone.

Making Thinking Visible

In a collaborative situation, individuals have to explain their ideas and conceptions to others, and through this externalization process they also have to construct a better mental model about the issue or concept in question. These can be subsequently elaborated further by collaborators. Explaining problems to oneself fosters cognitive achievements. Hatano & Inagaki (1992) have argued that deep conceptual understanding is fostered through explaining a problem to other learners. In order to explain one's view to one's peers, an individual student has cognitively to commit him or herself to some ideas, to explicate beliefs, and also to organize and reorganize existing knowledge (Hatano & Inagaki 1992).

The cognitive value of externalization in social interaction is based on a process of making internal processes of thought 'visible' (Collins & Brown 1988; Collins *et al.* 1991; Lehtinen & Rui 1996; Lesgold 1998). From a cognitive point of view, it is particularly important to transform internal and hidden processes into a public form in which they can be examined and imitated. The well known Reciprocal Teaching model, developed by Palincsar & Brown (1984), can also be considered as an example of a model in which externalization of an individual's mental processes is essential for the advancement of metacognitive skills. According to this approach, students are taught to formulate questions about a text for one another. Students have to process the material themselves and learn how to focus on the essential elements of the reading passages before they are able to do comprehension modeling. Many empirical studies have provided evidence about the effects of reciprocal teaching (Järvelä 1996).

Computer environments can be used as tools to make the thinking processes visible in many different ways. The written communication within a learning platform makes the conversation history visible, and so can have a strong effect on the collaborative processes. Many applications, however, go further and try to externalize and make visible, for example, steps and qualitatively different contributions in the inquiry process (Hewitt 2002; Scardamalia & Bereiter 1994), decision-making paths (e.g. Lehtinen & Rui 1996), and argumentation structures (Suthers *et al.* 1997). Pea (1994) argued that, through computer-supported collaborative transformative communication, a type of learning facilitating new ways of thinking and inquiring in education could be fostered. It seems that for the purposes of transformative communication, written communication combined with face-to-face communication is more effective than face-to-face communication alone, because it requires more extensive thinking processes (Woodruff & Brett 1993).

Learning Through Distributed and Shared Activities

Traditionally, cognitive theories have examined learning as an individual and mental process. As a consequence, cognitive theories have focused on analyzing how an individual agent processes mental representations. Scientific thinking has traditionally been seen as a characteristic of an individual mind. However, in explaining human intelligent activity, both cognitive theory and the current philosophy of science increasingly emphasize the socially distributed (or shared) nature of cognition (cf.

Hakkarainen *et al.* 2002; Hutchins 1995; Pea 1993; Perkins 1993; Resnick *et al.* 1997). Distributed cognition refers to a process in which cognitive resources are shared socially in order to extend individual cognitive resources or to accomplish something that an individual agent could not achieve alone. Human cognitive achievements are based on a process in which an agent's cognitive processes and the objects and constraints of the world reciprocally affect each other.

Miyake (1986) and Hutchins (1995) have argued that social interaction, combined with the tools of technological culture provide new cognitive resources for human cognitive accomplishment. According to Miyake's analysis, understanding is iterative in nature, i.e. it emerges through a series of attempts to explain and understand the processes and mechanisms being investigated. In a shared problem-solving process, agents who have partial but different information about the problem in question all appear to improve their understanding through social interaction.

Miyake (1986) and Hutchins (1995) argued that the cognitive value of social interaction appears to be based on the fact that human beings cannot keep more that one complex hypothesis activated at a time. By using cognitive tools (Resnick *et al.* 1997), multiple forms of representation, and other artifacts, learners are able to reduce the cognitive processing load and take on more complicated problems than would otherwise be possible (Pea 1993; Salomon *et al.* 1991). The complexity of problems or learning tasks has been a major cause for the development of many CSCL applications. In many technology-based collaborative learning environments, the complexity of the content area has been consciously considered. Instead of teaching sequences of isolated content units, these environments present the students with complex problems while they are studying the sub-elements of problems. The features of the technology and the intended collaboration with the help of the technology is meant to facilitate students in managing the requirements of the complex tasks (Feltovich *et al.* 1996; Lehtinen 2002; Lehtinen & Rui 1996).

Locating the Learning in Social and Cultural System

In many recent studies on CSCL, the conceptual frameworks are based on a theoretical assumption that learning is entirely located in a social and cultural system. In this framework learning is seen as "the process of change in social relations in which the learner is imperatively situated" (Suzuki & Kato 2002). This theoretical approach relays on the widely used notion of "legitimate peripheral participation" developed by Lave & Wenger (1991). The emerging way to conceptualize the process of learning distances it from an individual learner and locates it in the changes taking place in the "community of practice" (Wenger 1998). That is, learning is described in terms of participation in the practices of a community. This approach has been elaborated further especially in the working life context (see Wenger 1998; Wenger *et al.* 2002), and it has been used as the theoretical basis in many CSCL experiments (e.g. Suzuki & Kato 2002; several papers in Stahl 2002). In many cases, the practical consequences of these approaches for the design of learning environments have remained unclear. The original idea of the communities of practice and peripheral participation is based on observations in traditional and stable communities, in which some kind of apprenticeship type learning has been the dominating form for the socialization of young generations into the community. In modern educational situations, however, we deal with rapidly changing situations and it is difficult to see how traditional ideas about apprenticeship could be a sufficient basis for powerful learning environments in the future.

The rapidly changing environment is taken seriously in new forms of activity theory (Engeström 1987, 1999). Activity theory indicates that, in many cases, individuals, groups and organizations face new challenges and possibilities that cannot yet be conceptualized, and that interplay between practical exploration and theoretical contemplation produces innovation. Activity theory is a dynamic and systemic approach based on the analysis of the contradictions between different aspects of the activity situation, including subject, object and instruments, as well as rules, community, and the division of labor. In the research and development of CSCL, the activity theory framework can be used as a tool to implement new teaching-learning approaches in educational organizations and for analyzing the processes of computer-supported collaboration in general (see Halloran *et al.* 2002). In developing current forms of the activity theory approach, the main aim has been to create a solid tool to deal with organizational change. This is an important presupposition for all educational innovations, but the theoretical framework for developing concrete models and tools for computer-supported collaborative learning needs more specific concepts referring to the collaborative and individual processes taking place in these learning environments.

One of the most widely used concepts in the CSCL literature is the notion of knowledge building, a concept originally introduced by Scardamalia & Bereiter (1989, but also see Chapter 4). With this concept they aimed at emphasizing the process of producing externally visibly "knowledge objects", such as scientific concepts and theories. Hakkarainen and his collaborators have developed a so-called "progressive inquiry" model of computer-supported learning, in which they present a detailed description of the steps or elements of a research like process in a school environment (Hakkarainen *et al.* 2002). This model is based partly on Bereiter's knowledge building approach, but is elaborated further by using the dynamic and pragmatic conceptions of inquiry emphasized in the philosophy of science. The progressive inquiry model includes the following subtasks: (a) creating the context; (b) setting up research questions; (c) constructing working theories; (d) critical evaluation; (e) searching deepening knowledge; (f) generating subordinate questions; and (g) constructing new working theories. These steps can be fulfilled in a flexible order and repeated several times. During all these phases the ideas should be shared among the peer group by using a suitable network-based platform supporting collaboration (Hakkarainen *et al.* 2002).

Interpersonal Links, Social Grounding and Shared Regulation in CSCL

The ability to understand other participants' thinking and their interpretative framework is particularly important in CSCL environments. Very often developers of learning environments presuppose that any social interaction between learners is helpful to learning. This belief is, however, not so self-evident in technologically rich classrooms, and problems of mutual understanding come to a head in various network-based virtual environments. The teaching-learning process is a complex social situation containing multiple actors, each with his or her own intentions and interpretations that influence one another's knowledge, opinions and values. For such a process to be successful, the players must participate in the construction of joint cognitive products, which requires shared understanding based on a common focus and shared presuppositions. (Järvelä *et al.* 1999)

In our own work, we have made use of the analysis of the strength of the ties between the collaborators. The distinction between weak and strong ties has proved to be helpful in analyzing the communication and collaboration in organizations and networks (Hakkarainen *et al.* 2002; see also Granovetter 1973; Hansen 1999). Table 1 presents a summary of characteristics of knowledge exchange associated with weak and strong ties.

Strong ties typically exist between people who have a long history of joint collaboration history. The bi-directionality of strong ties is important for assimilating non-codified knowledge because the recipient is not likely to acquire the knowledge completely during the first interaction, but needs multiple opportunities to assimilate it. Problems of assimilation can be overcome only through creating strong links between the actors in question.

So-called e-Learning and virtual distance-learning approaches have paid only little attention to the strength of the ties between the participants. The basic weakness of virtual learning — as commonly considered — is that there is too much talk about

Table 1: Nature of knowledge exchange and the strength of ties.

Characteristic of knowledge exchange	The strength of ties	
	Strong	**Weak**
Information flow	Redundant and reciprocal	Non-redundant and often asymmetric
The nature of knowledge exchanged	Usually complex	Simple or well-defined
Form of knowledge	Often non-codified or tacit	Often codified and transferable
Relation to knowledge environment	Context-bound, i.e. a part of a larger knowledge structure	Often context-free and independently understandable
Type of communication	"Thick", including chunks, expert terms, and scripts	"Thin" and widely understandable
Management of network connections	Usually takes up a lot of resources	Not so much resources needed

information and knowledge delivery, and little or no discussion about the role of social communities in learning and knowledge creation (Brown & Duguid 1999). Mere network-based contact between the learners can hardly create truly strong ties among the participants. Effective methods supporting social grounding (Dillenbourg & Traum 1999; Mäkitalo et al. 2002) could, however, move the participants of a virtual learning environment from weak links towards moderate ties, indicating interpersonal relations, which will already include some common experience, perspective taking and mutual understanding.

The problem of mutual understanding has been an important topic in developing CSCL applications (Järvelä et al. 1999) and has been studied from many different perspectives based on traditional theoretical ideas, including for example the notions of social formation of self (Mead 1934), social perspective taking in which individuals' points of view are related and co-ordinated with one another (Selman 1980), or mutual commitment in the use of language (Nystrand 1986). Dillenbourg and his collaborator (Baker et al. 1999; Dillenbourg & Traum 1999) have stressed the problem of shared understanding in technology-based environments by introducing the concept of social grounding in the CSCL research. Dillenbourg & Traum (1999) define social grounding as a mechanism by which two participants in a discussion try to elaborate the mutual belief that their partner has understood what they meant, to a level or criterion sufficient for the purpose of the activity.

Thousands of studies have shown that self-regulation and metacognition are important preconditions for high level learning. The research on learning related regulative processes has almost exclusively focused on individuals' behavior and learning (Vauras et al. in press). In the Vygotskian tradition, however, the development of these processes is described as a social process of guided participation between an adult and a child in which the learner internalizes and transfers the "other-regulation" to self-regulation (Rogoff 1990; Wertsch 1978). In this asymmetric interaction, it is the adult (or more advanced partner) who regulates and monitors the process. In peer interaction, however, the situation is more equal and it is not so clear who is the agent in the regulation of the process.

In a well-developed peer collaboration, there is a special kind of reciprocity and interdependence between the participants, and even the thinking processes seem to be transactive in nature (King 1998). This kind of (face-to-face) discussion is based on jointly shared, but unconscious, meta-communicative rules or contracts, which makes it possible for the collaborator to construct and maintain a shared conception of the problem (see Roschelle & Teasley 1995). When the joint problem-solving faces difficult obstacles, or when the communication takes place in a virtual environment, more conscious regulation is needed. In the literature, there are few attempts systematically to focus on the shared regulation and metacognition in technology-based collaborative learning environments (Vauras et al. 2002).

Empirical Evidence of the Effects of CSCL

According to Salomon (1995), the possibility of intellectual partnerships with both peers and advanced information technology has changed the criteria for what is counted to be the effects of technology. Instead of only concentrating on the amount and quality of learning outcomes, we need to distinguish between two kinds of effects: "effects with a tool and/or collaborating peers, and effects of these". Salomon used the term "effects with" to describe the changes that take place while one is engaged in intellectual partnership with peers or with a computer tool including for example the changed quality of problem-solving in a team. By "effects of" he means those more lasting changes that take place when computer-enhanced collaboration teaches students to ask more exact and explicit questions, even when not using that system.

A traditional approach to deal with the impact of effectiveness of new instructional methods is to compare the achievements of students in traditional and experimental environments. Thousands of experimental studies on the educational impact of ICT have been carried out since the first attempts to assess the educational use of information technology in the early 1970s. These results have been summarized in dozens of review articles and meta-analyses. Our overviews of these reviews, covering more than 1000 original experiments, have allowed some general conclusions to be drawn (Lehtinen *et al.* 2001).

In summary, the reviews and meta-analyses of the experiments showed that ICT students learned more, and faster, than students in control groups, and also showed improved motivation and social interaction.

In their review, Whelan & Plass (2002) summarized the results of more than 300 articles on network-based learning published from 1993 to 2001. Their main conclusion was that there are very few real experimental studies comparing learning outcomes between network-based and traditional educational situations. In our own review (Lehtinen *et al.* 1999), we also found in most of the studies on CSCL that the authors described the tools they used, the working processes, and students' attitudes, but there was very seldom any rigorous experimental evidence about the effects of these learning environments.

In older studies, the experimental comparisons of achievement effects were more frequent. For example, Rysavy & Sales (1991) published a review in which they summarized the results of 13 studies on cooperative computer-based instruction (published between 1982 and 1988). In six studies, the computer-based co-operative condition resulted in better learning results than in the control conditions, whereas in four studies there were no significant differences. In the study of Hooper & Hannafin (1988), the achievement measures were also related to different ability groupings. According to their results, the achievement of low ability students was higher in heterogeneous groups than in homogenous groups.

In their review, Lehtinen *et al.* (1999) summarized results from over 50 empirical studies on CSCL. They found some experimental evidence that collaboration, facilitated with information and communication technology, had improved student learning. For example, the well-known CSCL environments like CSILE and Belvedere have proved to be helpful for higher order social interaction and, subsequently, for better learning in terms of deep understanding (Scardamalia *et al.* 1994; Suthers 1998). Many of the successful studies were, however, short-term experiments using very small experimental groups. This conclusion was also reached in another recent meta-analysis (Cavanaugh 2001) which summarized the effects of technology-based distance education in 19 empirical studies which included CSCL features. In addition, Cavanaugh found that studies in which interactive technology was used as a supplementary method, linked to face-to-face teaching, resulted in positive achievement effects. These results support the above-mentioned theoretical assumptions about the importance of strong ties and social grounding for high level learning.

In the proceedings of the last three conferences on Computer Supported Collaborative Learning (Dillenbourg *et al.* 2001; Hoadley & Roshelle 1999; Stahl 2002), there were only a few papers aimed at presenting experimental evidence about the effects of CSCL on academic achievement. This may indicate that the CSCL research community agrees, at least partly, with Koschmann (1996) who argued that CSCL represent, not only a new way to use technology in education, but a completely new paradigm which also differs from the older educational technology paradigms in terms of the research methods adopted. According to this paradigm, CSCL research is not focused on instructional efficacy, rather it is studying instruction as enacted practice. This methodological position resembles the "effect with" approach described by Salomon (1995).

The CSCL research has been rich in different innovative research approaches that focus on the communicative and social processes in the environments. In addition to the classical psychological and education approaches, CSCL research has adopted methods from anthropology, linguistics, sociology and communication studies. Ethnographical methods and discourse analysis are very much emphasized in recent studies in order to capture the social level processes without reducing them to individual level behaviors or mental processes (see Lipponen 2002). The studies based on discourse analysis of collaborative processes in different technology-based environments open a rich view into the interaction sequences at a collective level and into social knowledge-building processes (Koschmann *et al.* 2002). It is, however, very difficult to extract any generalized main findings from this rich qualitative data.

Many studies focused on discourse processes in CSCL environments report increased activity of collaboration and improved quality of students' communication when a CSCL environment is implemented in the classroom (e.g. Hewitt 2002). Other studies, on the other hand, have shown that the activity and the quality of students' contributions during the collaboration, when the same applications are used, can vary strongly in different classrooms (e.g. Hakkarainen *et al.* 2002). Studies on the quality of students' argumentation strategies in network-based environments have shown controversial results. Although there are promising results in some studies (e.g. Murphy *et al.* 1998), most of the research studies refer to difficulties in reaching high level argumentation in virtual environments without systematic training or scaffolding (Marttunen & Laurinen 2001; Nussbaum *et al.* 2002).

Besides these qualitative methodological approaches, some researchers have tried to describe the social level phenomena of collaborative learning processes by using social network analysis methods (Cho *et al.* 2002; Nurmela *et al.* 1999) and other quantitative analyses describing the relations between communicative acts (e.g. Beck *et al.* 2002). These methods have proved to be useful for describing large amounts of information about the interaction processes in a compact and illustrative way. The results of social network studies clearly demonstrate the unequal participation in CSCL processes, and the differentiated roles, of different participants. Because of the opportunities to present the network analysis data in a various visual representations, these methods can also be used as tools to give feedback for teachers and students during the collaborative learning processes.

Conclusions

In the early years of CSCL research, authors such as Salomon (1995) and Koschmann (1996) proposed that research on collaborative use of technical tools in learning environments cannot be characterized as a gradual extension of the tradition of learning environment research but rather by a deeper change of the theoretical and methodological thinking.

The contributions of CSCL researchers during last ten years have clearly confirmed this assumption. Computer Supported Collaborative research has been very rich both in terms of theory development and methodological approaches. The theoretical work done in this tradition can have a remarkable influence for the development of powerful learning environments in the future. There is however no unified theory underlying the different applications; rather, the field is divided into many parallel and partly conflicting theoretical schools. A fundamental aspect of scientific activity is the attempt to find or create coherent conceptual systems that highlight and label a group of phenomena in the world to be instances in a distinct conceptual category. The borderlines of the categories are often problematic and subject to continuous debate between different theoretical schools. This is true especially in the social sciences, where the content of many frequently used concepts is continuously changing. The concept of learning is an example of the kind of phenomena which is difficult to define in an exact way, which is one of the reasons for the weak accumulation of knowledge in the field of learning and instruction.

There are two seemingly contradictory problems in the current traditions of learning research. Because of the overemphasized boundaries between theoretical schools, we have not been able maximally to make use of the cumulated results of learning research and because of insufficient analyses of the fundamental ontological differences in different theories, many attempts to combine them have led to unfruitful, eclectic models. In the field of CSCL research, it is hardly possible to create a single coherent theory that could adequately describe all the varying forms of learning. On the contrary, it seems necessary to create a co-ordinated combination of different theoretical approaches of collaborative learning that take into consideration the specific features of the learning tasks, while at the same time locating them in their specific historical, cultural, organizational, and physical contexts.

Reviews of experiments on network-based collaborative learning show some positive learning effects when CSCL systems have been applied in classroom learning in face-to-face learning situations. Experiences in pure virtual environments seem to be more problematic. Most of the studies are, however, rather limited in terms of the duration of the experiment, the number of participants, and the proportion of the curriculum covered. During the last few years, empirical studies on CSCL have moved away from the traditional experimental model of dealing with the effectiveness of the environment.

Instead, the research community has produced hundreds of very detailed qualitative analyses of collaborative processes by using content analysis, ethnographic approaches and discourse analysis, as well as social network analysis. Due to the theoretical work and the qualitative analysis of the collaborative processes in different technology enriched environments, the developers of learning environments have obtained detailed information about possible, and typical, processes of collaboration mediated with different artefacts. The approaches used in developing CSCL tools and models, as well as the CSCL research from the last few years, provide us with novel ideas and empirically proofed information base, which can be used in developing powerful learning environments for different educational purposes. This information is, however, useful only if the learning environment developer is able to reinterpret it in the cultural context in question, and situate it within the frames of the actual activity systems.

References

Aronson, E., Blaney, N., Srephan, C., Sikes, J., & Snapp, M. (1978). *The jigsaw classroom*. Beverly Hill, CA: Sage.

Baker, M., Hansen, T., Joiner, R., & Traum, D. (1999). The role of grounding in collaborative learning tasks. In: P. Dillenbourg (Ed.), *Collaborative learning. Cognitive and computational approaches* (Advances in Learning and Instruction Series) (pp. 31–63). Amsterdam: Pergamon.

Beck, R. J., Brown, R. S., Marshall, S. K., & Schwarz, J. (2002). Reflective communicator roles in preservice teacher team email discussions. In: G. Stahl (Ed.), *Computer support for collaborative learning: Foundations for a CSCL community* (pp. 275–280). Hillsdale, NJ: Erlbaum.

Bereiter, C. (2002). *Education and mind in the knowledge age*. Hillsdale, NJ: Erlbaum.

Brown, A. L., & Campione, J. C. (1996). Psychological theory and the design of innovative learning environments: On procedures, principles, and systems. In: L. Schauble, & R. Glaser (Eds), *Innovations in learning. New environments for education* (pp. 289–325). Mahwah, NJ: Erlbaum.

Brown, J. S., & Duguid, P. (1999). *The social life of information*. Harvard, MA: Harvard Business School Press.

Cavanaugh, C. (2001). The effectiveness of interactive distance education technologies in K-12 learning: A meta-analysis. *International Journal of Educational Telecommunications, 7* (1), 73–88.

Cho, H., Stefanone, M., & Gay, G. (2002). Social information sharing in a CSCL Community. In: G. Stahl (Ed.), *Computer support for collaborative learning: Foundations for a CSCL community* (pp. 43–50). Hillsdale, NJ: Erlbaum.

Collins, A., Brown, J. S., & Holum, A. (1991). Cognitive apprenticeship: Making thinking visible. *American Educator, 6* (11), 38–46.

Collins, A., & Brown, J. S. (1988). Computer as a tool for learning through reflection. In: H. Mandl & A. Lesgold (Eds), *Learning issues for intelligent tutoring systems* (pp. 1–18). New York: Springer.

Crook, C. (1994). *Computers and the collaborative experience of learning*. London: Routledge.

Dillenbourg, P., Baker, M., Blaye, A., & O'Malley, C. (1996). The evolution of research on collaborative learning. In: H. Spada, & P. Reimann (Eds), *Learning in humans and machines*. New York: Pergamon.

Dillenbourg, P., Eurelings, A., & Hakkarainen, K. (2001). *European perspectives on computer-supported collaborative learning: Proceedings of the First European Conference of Computer-Supported Collaborative Learning*. Maastricht, The Netherlands, March 22–24, 2001.

Dillenbourg, P., & Traum, D. (1999). Does a shared screen make a shared solution? In: C. Hoadley, & J. Roschelle (Eds), *Computer support for collaborative learning* (pp. 127–135). Palo Alto, CA: Stanford University

Doise, W., & Mugny, W. (1984). *The social development of the intellect*. Oxford: Pergamon Press.

Engeström, Y. (1987). *Learning by expanding*. Helsinki: Orienta-Konsultit.

Engeström, Y. (1999). Activity theory and individual and social transformation. In: Y. Engeström, R. Miettinen, & R.-L. Punamäki (Eds), *Perspectives on activity theory* (pp. 19–38). Cambridge: Cambridge University Press.

Feltovich, P. J., Spiro, R. J., Coulson, L., & Feltovich, J. (1996). Collaboration within and among minds: Mastering complexity, individually and in groups. In: T. Koschmann (Ed.), *CSCL: Theory and practice of an emerging paradigm* (pp. 25–44). Mahwah, NJ: Erlbaum.

Granovetter, M. S. (1973). The strength of weak ties. *American Journal of Sociology, 78*, 1360–1380.

Hakkarainen, K., Lipponen, L., & Järvelä, S. (2002). Epistemology of inquiry and computer-supported collaborative learning. In: T. Koschmann, R. Hall, & N. Miyake (Eds), *CSCL 2: Carrying forward the conversation* (pp. 129–156). Mahwah, NJ: Erlbaum.

Hakkarainen, K., Palonen, T., Paavola, S., & Lehtinen, E. (2002). *Networked expertise: Professional and educational perspective*. Manuscript submitted for publication.

Halloran, J., Rogers, Y., & Scaife, M. (2002). Taking the 'no' out of Lotus Notes: Activity theory, groupware and student groupwork. In: G. Stahl (Ed.), *Computer support for collaborative learning: Foundations for a CSCL community* (pp. 169–178). Hillsdale, NJ: Erlbaum.

Hansen, M. T. (1999). The search-transfer problem: The role of weak ties in sharing knowledge across organization subunits. *Administrative Science Quarterly, 44* (1), 82–102.

Hatano, G., & Inagaki, K. (1991). Sharing cognition through collective comprehension activity. In: L. B. Resnick, J. M. Levine, & S. D. Teasley (Eds), *Perspectives on socially shared cognition* (pp. 331–348). Washington, D.C.: American Psychological Association.

Hatano, G., & Inagaki, K. (1992). Desituating cognition through the construction of conceptual knowledge. In: P. Light, & G. Butterworth (Eds), *Context and cognition. Ways of knowing and learning* (pp. 115–133). New York: Harvester.

Hawkins, J., Sheingold, K., Gearhart, M., & Berger, C. (1982). Microcomputers in schools: Impact on the social life of elementary classrooms. *Journal of Applied Developmental Psychology, 3*, 361–373.

Hewitt, J. (2002). From a focus on tasks to a focus on understanding: The cultural transformation of a Toronto classroom. In: T. Koschmann, R. Hall, & N. Miyake (Eds), *CSCL 2: Carrying forward the conversation* (pp. 11–41). Mahwah, NJ: Erlbaum.

Hoadley, C., & Roschelle, J. (Eds) (1999). *Proceedings of the computer support for collaborative learning (CSCL) 1999 Conference*. Mahwah, NJ: Erlbaum.

Hooper, S., & Hannafin, M. J. (1988). Cooperative CBI: The effects of heterogeneous versus homogeneous grouping on the learning of progressively complex concepts. *Journal of Educational Computing Research, 4*, 413–424.

Hutchins, E. (1995). *Cognition in the wild*. Cambridge, MA: The MIT Press.

Johnson, D. W., & Johnson, R. T. (1992). Positive interdependence: Key to effective cooperation. In: R. Hertz-Lazarowitz, & N. Miller (Eds), *Interacting in cooperative groups. The theoretical anatomy of group learning* (pp. 145–173). New York: Cambridge University Press.

Järvelä, S. (1996). New models of teacher-student interaction: A critical review. *European Journal of Psychology of Education*, 6, 246–268.

Järvelä, S., Bonk, C. J., Lehtinen, E., & Lehti, S. (1999). A theoretical analysis of social interactions in computer-based learning environments: Evidence for reciprocal understandings. *Journal of Educational Computing Research*, *21*, 359–384.

Kaptelin, V., & Cole, M. (2002). Individual and collective activities in educational computer game playing. In: T. Kosmann, R. Hall, & N. Miyake (Eds), *CSCL 2: Carrying forward the conversation* (pp. 303–316). Mahwah, NJ: Erlbaum.

King, A. (1998). Transactive peer tutoring: Distributing cognition and metacognition. *Educational Psychology Review*, *10*, 54–74.

Koschmann, T. (1996). Paradigm shifts and instructional technology: An introduction. In: T. Koschmann (Ed.), *CSCL: Theory and practice of an emerging paradigm* (pp. 1–23). Mahwah, NJ: Erlbaum.

Koschmann, T., Hall, R., & Miyake, N. (2002). *CSCL 2: Carrying forward the conversation*. Mahwah, NJ: Erlbaum.

Kumpulainen, K., & Wray, D. (2002). *Classroom interaction and social learning*. London: Routledge.

Lave, J., & Wenger, E. (1991). *Situated learning: Legitimate peripheral participation*. Cambridge: Cambridge University Press.

Lehtinen, E. (2002). Developing models for distributed problem based learning: Theoretical and methodological reflection. *Distance Education*, *23* (1), 109–117.

Lehtinen, E., Hakkarainen, K., Lipponen, L., Rahikainen, M., & Muukkonen, H. (1999). *Computer supported collaborative learning: A review* (The J.H.G.I. Giesbers Reports on Education, No. 10). The Netherlands: University of Nijmegen.

Lehtinen, E., & Rui, E. (1996). Computer supported complex learning: An environment for learning experimental method and statistical inference. *Machine Mediated Learning*, *5* (3&4), 149–175.

Lehtinen, E., Sinko, M., & Hakkarainen, K. (2001). ICT in Finnish education: How to scale up best practices. *International Journal of Educational Policy, Research and Practice*, *2* (1), 77–89.

Lesgold, A. (1998). Multiple representations and their implications for learning. In: M. V. Someren, P. Reimann, H. P. A. Boshuizen, & T. de Jong (Eds), *Learning with multiple representations* (pp. 307–319). Amsterdam: Pergamon.

Lesgold, A., Lajoie, S. P., Brunzo, M., & Eggan, G. (1992). A coached practice environment for an electronics troubleshooting job. In: J. Larkin, & R. Chabay (Eds), *Computer assisted instruction and intelligent tutoring systems: Shared goals and complementary approaches* (pp. 201–238). Hillsdale, NJ: Erlbaum Associates.

Lipponen, L. (2002). Exploring foundations for computer-supported collaborative learning. In: G. Stahl (Ed.), *Computer support for collaborative learning: Foundations for a CSCL community* (pp. 72–81). Hillsdale, NJ: Erlbaum.

Marttunen, M., & Laurinen, L. (2001). Learning of argumentation skills in networked and face-to-face environments. *Instructional Science*, *29*, 127–153.

Mead, G. H. (1934). *Mind, self, and society*. Chicago: University Chicago Press.

Miyake, N. (1986). Constructive interaction and the iterative process of understanding. *Cognitive Science*, *10*, 151–177.

Mugny, G., & Doise, W. (1978). Socio-cognitive conflict and structure of individual and collective performances. *European Journal of Social Psychology*, *8*, 181–192.

Murphy, K. L., Drabier, R., & Luepps, M. (1998). A constructivist look at interaction and collaboration via computer conferencing. *International Journal of Educational Telecommunications, 4,* 237–261.

Mäkitalo, K., Häkkinen, P., Salo, P., & Järvelä, S. (2002). Building and maintaining the common ground in web-based interaction. In: G. Stahl (Ed.), *Computer support for collaborative learning: Foundations for a CSCL community* (pp. 571–572). Hillsdale, NJ: Erlbaum.

Nurmela, K., Lehtinen, E., & Palonen, T. (1999). Evaluating CSCL log files by social network analysis. In: C. Hoadley, & J. Roschelle (Eds), *Computer support for collaborative learning* (pp. 434–444). Palo Alto, CA: Stanford University.

Nonaka, I., & Takeuchi, H. (1995). *The knowledge-creating company: How Japanese companies create the dynamics of innovation.* New York: Oxford University Press.

Nussbaum, E. M., Hartley, K., Sinatra, G. M., Ralph, E., Reynolds, R. E., & Bendixen, L. D. (2002, April). *Enhancing the quality of on-line discussions.* Paper presented at the annual meeting of the American Educational Research Association, New Orleans, LA.

Nystrand, M. (1986). *The structure of written communication: Studies of reciprocity between writers and readers.* London: Academic Press.

Palincsar, A. S., & Brown, A. L. (1984). Reciprocal teaching of comprehension fostering and comprehension monitoring activities. *Cognition and Instruction, 1* (2), 117–175.

Pata, K., Sarapuu, T., & Lehtinen, E. (2002). *Scaffolding environmental decision-making role-play in a synchronous environment.* Manuscript submitted for publication.

Pea, R. D. (1993). Practices of distributed intelligence and designs for education. In: G. Salomon (Ed.), *Distributed cognitions. Psychological and educational considerations* (pp. 47–87). Cambridge: Cambridge University Press.

Pea, R. D. (1994). Seeing what we build together: Distributed multimedia learning environments for transformative communications. *Journal of the Learning Sciences, 3,* 283–298.

Perkins, D. N. (1993). Person-plus: A distributed view of thinking and learning. In: G. Salomon (Ed.), *Distributed cognitions. Psychological and educational considerations* (pp. 88–110). Cambridge: Cambridge University Press.

Piaget, J. (1926). *The child's conception of the world.* Paris: Alcan.

Piaget, J. (1980). *The constructivist approach.* Geneva: Foundation Archives Jean Piaget.

Resnick, L. B., Säljö, R., Pontecorvo, C., & Burge, B. (1997). *Discourse, tools, and reasoning.* Berlin: Springer.

Rogoff, B. (1990). *Apprenticeships in thinking: Cognitive development in social context.* New York: Oxford University Press.

Roschelle, J., & Teasley, S. (1995). The construction of shared knowledge in collaborative problem solving. In: C. O'Malley (Ed.), *Computer-supported collaborative learning* (pp. 69–97). New York: Springer.

Rysavy, S. D. M., & Sales, G. C. (1991). Cooperative learning in computer based instruction. *Educational Technology, Research & Development, 39* (2), 70–79.

Salomon. G. (1994). Differences in patterns: Studying computer enhanced learning environments. In: S. Vosniadou, E. De Corte, & H. Mandl (Eds), *Technology-based learning environments: Psychological and educational foundations* (pp. 79–85) (NATO ASI Series F: Computer and System Science, Vol. 137). Berlin: Springer.

Salomon, G. (1995). *What does the design of effective CSCL require and how do we study its effects?* Proceedings of the CSCL '95 Conference. http://www-cscl95.indiana.edu/cscl95/outlook/62_Salomon.html

Salomon, G., Perkins, D. N., & Globerson, T. (1991). Partners in cognition: Extending human intelligence with intelligent technologies. *Educational Researcher, 1991,* 2–9.

Scardamalia, M., & Bereiter, C. (1989, October). *Schools as knowledge-building communities.* Paper presented at the Workshop on Development and Learning Environments, University of Tel Aviv, Tel Aviv, Israel.

Scardamalia, M., & Bereiter, C. (1994). Computer support for knowledge-building communities. *The Journal of the Learning Sciences, 3*, 265–283.

Scardamalia, M., Bereiter, K., & Lamon, M. (1994). The CSILE project: Trying to bring the classroom into world 3. In: K. McGilly (Ed.), *Classroom lessons: Integrating cognitive theory and classroom practise* (pp. 201–228). Cambridge, MA: Bradford Books/MIT Press.

Selman, R. L. (1980). *The growth of interpersonal understanding.* New York: Academic Press.

Sfard, A. (1998). On two metaphors for learning and the dangers of choosing just one. *Educational Researcher, 27* (2), 4–13.

Slavin, R. E. (1995). *Cooperative learning: Theory research and practice.* Boston: Ally & Bacon.

Stahl, G. (2002). *Computer support for collaborative learning. Foundations for a CSCL Community. Proceedings of the CSCL 2002.* Hillsdale, NJ: Erlbaum.

Steinkuehler, C. A., Derry, S. J., Hmelo-Silver, C. E., & DelMarcelle, M. (2002). Cracking the resource nut with distributed problem-based learning in secondary teacher education. *Distance Education, 23* (1), 23–39.

Suthers, D. D. (1998). *Computer aided education and training initiative.* Technical Report (12 January 1998).

Suthers, D., Erdosne Toth, E., & Weiner, A. (1997). An integrated approach to implementing collaborative inquiry in the classroom. In: R. Hall, N. Miyake, & N. Enyedy (Ed.), *Computer support for collaborative Learning '97. Proceedings of The Second International Conference on Computer Support for Collaborative Learning. December 10–14, 1997.* Toronto, Ontario, Canada.

Suzuki, H., & Hiroshi, K. (1997). Identity formation/transformation as the process of collaborative learning through AlgoArena. In: R. Hall, N. Miyake, & N. Enyedy (Eds), *Computer support for collaborative learning '97. Proceedings of The Second International Conference on Computer Support for Collaborative Learning. December 10–14, 1997.* Toronto, Ontario, Canada.

Suzuki, H., & Kato, H. (2002). Identity formation/transformation as process of collaborative learning of programming using AlgoArena. In: T. Kosmann, R. Hall, & N. Miyake (Eds), *CSCL 2: Carrying forward the conversation* (pp. 275–296). Mahwah, NJ: Erlbaum.

Turkle, S. (1984). *The second self.* New York: Simon & Schuster.

Valsiner, J., & van der Veer, R. (2000). *The social mind.* Cambridge: Cambridge University Press.

Vauras, M., Iiskala, T., Kajamies, A., Kinnunen, R., & Lehtinen, E. (in press). Shared regulation and motivation of collaborating peers: A case analysis. *Psychologia, an International Journal of Psychology in the Orient.*

Vygotsky, L. (1934/1994). The development of academic concepts in school aged children. In: R. van der Veer, & J. Valsiner (Eds), *The Vygotsky reader* (pp. 355–370). Oxford: Blackwell. (Originally published in Russian)

Vygotsky, L. S. (1978). *Mind in society: The development of higher psychological processes.* Cambridge, MA: Harvard University Press.

Wenger, W. (1998). *Communities of practice: Learning, meaning, and identity.* Cambridge: Cambridge University Press.

Wenger, E., McDermott, R., & Snyder, W. M. (2002). *A guide to managing knowledge: Cultivating communities of practice.* Boston, MA: Harvard Business School Press.

Whelan, R., & Plass, J. (2002). Is e-Learning effective? A review of literature from 1993–2001. *AACE, 2002* (1), 1026–1028.

Wertsch, J. V. (1978). Adult-child interaction and the roots of metacognition. *The Quarterly Newsletter of the Institute for Comparative Human Development*, 2 (1), 15–18.

Woodruff, E., & Brett, C. (1993). Fostering scholarly collaboration in young children through the development of electronic commenting. *Research in Education, 50*, 83–95.

Chapter 4

Learning to Work Creatively With Knowledge

Carl Bereiter and Marlene Scardamalia

Introduction

It is easy to produce a list of "soft skills" needed for work in the Knowledge Age. More than 140,000 Web pages contain the phrase, and a sampling among the first 4,000 indicates most of them advertise training — communication skills training, thinking skills training, human-relations skills training, and so on. Without presuming to evaluate these multitudinous efforts, we think a fair generalization is that they are relatively short-term interventions that do not so much develop new skills as sharpen or repurpose old ones. The ability to write a coherent paragraph, to utter a cogent statement, to make sense of numerical data, to mathematize and solve a quantitative problem, to read people's intentions and moderate personal goals in the interests of team success — these and many other soft or semi-soft skills take years to develop. People look to the schools to do the long-term work. The soft skills are all very difficult to teach and their transferability to new situations must always be questioned. Curriculum standards and guidelines, in echoing the business world's list of soft skills, tend to treat them as if effective means of teaching them were readily at hand. Even learning scientists often lend support to this unwarranted and facile optimism, claiming their approaches teach a range of 21st century skills, similar to those in the curriculum guidelines and in the 140,000 Web pages.

We take it that the actual belief among most learning scientists is that only in the basic academic skill areas of reading, writing, and elementary mathematics do we know how to teach cognitive skills with fair confidence that they will transfer to a wide range of situations. Yet we must respect the demands of society for the schools to turn out people who, in addition to being proficient in these basic skills, will be prepared to learn new things, collaborate in the solution of novel problems, and produce innovations in areas that presently may not even exist. In the absence of tested methods, how do we do this? The time-honored and still the only promising way is *immersion*. If you do not have an effective way of *teaching* a foreign language, then place the students in an environment where that is the dominant language and trust that their natural adaptive abilities will lead them to master the language. By the same reasoning, if we want students to acquire the skills needed to function in knowledge-based, innovation-driven organizations, we should place them in an environment where those skills are required in order for them to be part of what is going on. That, as we understand it, is the main reason the focus of this conference book is on powerful learning *environments* rather than on powerful instructional *methods*. For a range of very important objectives we have no effective instructional means and therefore must rely on environmental immersion.

Belief Mode and Design Mode

Both schooling and knowledge work are about knowledge, and so it would seem that they ought to have a great deal in common. However, there is a strong intuition, implicit in the various pronouncements about education for the 21st century, that present-day schools deal with knowledge in quite different ways from the ways it is dealt with in the working world. We suggest that the difference is a difference between two modes that characterize our dealing with knowledge in all kinds of contexts; the problem is that schooling almost exclusively emphasizes one of these modes, whereas knowledge work in the real world mainly emphasizes the other. These two modes we call the *belief mode* and the *design mode*.

When in belief mode, we are concerned with what we and other people believe or ought to believe. Our response to ideas in this mode is to agree or disagree, to present arguments and evidence for or against, to express and try to resolve doubts. When in design mode, we are concerned with the usefulness, adequacy, improvability, and developmental potential of ideas. Switching back and forth between modes is common. The main work of a planning committee, for instance, is in design mode, but the planners may frequently pause to consider such belief mode issues as the reliability of certain data or the soundness of a certain assumption. However, it is possible for discourse to go on indefinitely within belief mode, never venturing into design. This is characteristic of much academic discourse (in fact, that is what we imply when we say a question is "purely academic").

Good educational programs generally do a good job of equipping students to think in the belief mode. They teach them to turn a critical eye on beliefs, to use evidence and logic, to resist propaganda, and they provide them with the background knowledge needed to evaluate truth claims. Bad educational programs also equip students to function in the belief mode, except that they do it badly. They turn out students who are unquestioning of authority or too fond of their own opinions (or both), who have little sense of how to apply evidence, and who lack sufficient knowledge to form intelligent judgments in most areas. Good or bad, however, educational programs in all their familiar variations operate almost exclusively in the belief mode *as far as ideas are concerned*.

Activity in the design mode is not absent from schools. It is to be found in crafts, dramatic productions, creative writing, and the increasingly ubiquitous "project". In many of these the focus is on creating artifacts, but the artifacts are not *conceptual* artifacts (cf. Bereiter 2002). They may embody ideas, reflect ideas, use ideas, but the artifacts are not themselves ideas. They are not theories, proofs, problem formulations, interpretations, or things of that sort. When ideas are presented for consideration, they are almost always presented in belief mode. The focus is on whether the idea is true or warranted. If experiments are conducted, their purpose is to validate, to provide an empirical basis for accepting the idea. Questions that would be asked in design mode — questions that would be asked in a real-world knowledge-based organization — are questions like the following:

What is this idea good for?
What does it do and fail to do?
How could it be improved?

If, in the school context, someone has an idea about a fund-raising event, those design mode questions will be raised. But if the idea under consideration is a theoretical idea — an idea like static force, natural selection, oxidation, or capital — it is treated quite differently. Students learn to treat such ideas as fixed entities, to be accepted or rejected and sometimes to be applied. They do not learn to treat them as improvable objects and to carry out the kind of design work with ideas that leads a knowledge-based society forward.

The essence of the design mode is idea improvement. This is obvious when the design is about physical machines, tools, or other artifacts. No one even thinks of designing the ultimate computer or refrigerator. One only thinks of improvement — advancing the state of the art. There is no ultimate computer or refrigerator, because with each advance new possibilities arise for further advances. But the same is true of the ideas that emerge in science, history, and other disciplines. Modern practitioners of those disciplines do not look for final answers but for continual idea improvement. Again, each advance in the state of the art opens up possibilities for further advance. Somehow, if the schools are to enculturate students into the Knowledge Age, they must introduce this dynamic of continual idea improvement. They must bring the design mode into the heart of the educational program instead of relegating it to extracurricular or peripheral activities.

Contemporary Efforts to Bring the Design Mode into the Academic Curriculum

In the remainder of this chapter we examine four constructivist educational approaches, considered as environments for initiating students into practices that characterize knowledge work in the design mode. Customarily, these approaches are considered from the standpoint of activity structures, and from this standpoint they appear as procedural variations on a common constructivist theme. Considered as environments, however, we find deeper differences that amount to quite different kinds of experience in working with knowledge. Our conclusion is that each of the approaches offers a different and significant way of bringing design-mode activity into the academic curriculum, but that one of them, Knowledge Building, offers the possibility of integrating all the approaches into an overarching learning environment that provides fuller and more authentic immersion in the actual life of a knowledge society.

The four approaches are Learning by Design, as developed at Georgia Tech; Project-Based Science, as developed at the University of Michigan; Problem-Based Learning, as developed at Southern Illinois University; and Knowledge Building, as developed at the Ontario Institute for Studies in Education/University of Toronto. We attach institutional names to these movements, not because they are unique to those institutions but because the conceptual labels are easily appropriated and sometimes used indiscriminately. A Web search on any of these labels will bring up a number of examples that are inconsistent with the defining characteristics of the exemplary approaches. Henceforth we will capitalize the labels when we refer to the exemplary versions and will use lower case when we refer to the broader range of activities that use the same labels.

Although the four approaches have been used in various subjects, their common ground is science education, and so we will focus our comparisons in that area. They have all demonstrated effectiveness in teaching science content. Our purpose here, however, is to consider them as potential environments within which students may experience working with ideas in design mode.

As a framework for this examination of design-mode approaches to science learning, we propose a continuum that runs from context-limited to context-general work with ideas. In the adult world, much creative work with ideas is of a context-specific nature. Materials engineers working for a floor covering manufacturer, who may be developing a new bonding agent for floor tiles, have a very limited context within which ideas are created, evaluated, and improved. It will be only a lucky accident if their inventions prove to have application elsewhere. The manager of a health care organization, who is trying to design a more productive way for the professional staff to interact, is working with ideas that are applicable within the context of a particular organization. In this case, however, there is more likelihood that ideas proving fruitful in one organization will have some generalization to other, related contexts, and so this instance of knowledge work would occupy a more intermediate position on the continuum. At the extreme context-general end of the continuum we have what is commonly known as "basic research" — efforts to develop theories of universal application.

School activities can similarly be ordered according to this continuum. As preparation for adult life, it is desirable for students to have experience in design-mode work with ideas across the whole continuum. However, it is in the nature of general education that its main concern is with knowledge of high generalizability. We want students to understand the nature of photosynthesis and how this differs from animal nutrition; we will have failed if all they have learned is how to sprout beans in a pan of dirt. Therefore it is significant that most of the approaches we shall examine appear to emphasize activities toward the context-limited end of the continuum. By default, that leaves the context-general end to be dealt with in belief mode. An important conclusion we shall urge is that this need not be the case — that students can engage in creative design work with fundamental ideas of wide generality.

Learning by Design™

In Learning by Design, as described by Holbrook & Kolodner (2000: 221),

> Science learning is achieved through addressing a major design challenge (such as building a self-powered car that can go a certain distance over a certain terrain) . . . . To address a challenge, class members develop designs, build prototypes, gather performance data and use other resources to provide justification for refining their designs, and they iteratively investigate, redesign, test, and analyze the results of their ideas. They articulate their understanding of science concepts, first in terms of the concrete artifact which they have designed, then in transfer to similar artifacts or situations, and finally to abstract principles of science.

Design projects with this general intent are now fairly common, planning a trip to Mars being the most frequently encountered example in North American schools. However, in the approach taken by the Georgia Tech group, the students are challenged to design something that they can actually build and test — unlike those planning a Mars landing module. Moreover, the design challenges are planned so that faulty science will lead to performance failure.

The bridge between context-specific engineering problems and context-general science is a narrow one, however. The researchers found that teachers want to teach the science first and then introduce the design problems, whereas the intent is that the design problems should motivate inquiry into the underlying science. Kolodner (2002) offered the following example of scientific inquiry motivated by product design. The design task was to maximize the distance traveled by a toy car driven by air expelled from a balloon through a straw. The inquiry pursued by the students was to determine how variations in the length and diameter of the straw affected performance. It is not clear how this context-limited inquiry could bring students into contact with underlying scientific ideas — such as Newton's Third Law.

There are cases in which a design problem leads to engagement with deep scientific principles. They are cases in which the design must simulate or intervene in a natural process. Examples are designing an artificial organ (one of the early ventures in Learning by Design used this as a problem), designing a specific antibiotic, and building a rainmaking machine. By their nature, design problems of these kinds lie beyond the scope of what students could actually build and test. Consequently, activity methods in general, and Learning by Design is no exception, depend on rather forced connections between the activity and basic ideas. The result, whether the ideas are taught first or afterward or in the course of the design project, is that the ideas are dealt with in the belief mode, in parallel with but not intrinsic to activity in the design mode.

Learning by Design has obvious relevance to creative knowledge work. Engineering and design play leading roles in modern life and students should gain experience in doing them, learn intelligent ways of going about them, see the relevance to them of different kinds of knowledge and skill. We only argue that one should not expect

Learning by Design to provide direct engagement in the creation and improvement of underlying theoretical ideas.

Project-Based Science

As defined by Marx *et al.* (1997: 341),

> Project-based science focuses on student-designed inquiry that is organized by investigations to answer driving questions, includes collaboration among learners and others, the use of new technology, and the creation of authentic artifacts that represent student understanding.

Unfortunately, much of what is currently promoted and practiced under the label of "project-based learning" does not fit this definition but instead represents the traditional "project" or research report dressed up in modern technology. The crucial difference is in the phrase "investigations to answer driving questions". The traditional project is defined by a topic, not a question — much less a "driving" question. This traditional approach is exemplified in a widely circulated video produced a few years ago by a computer company to demonstrate the great new things that digital media will make possible. It showed an elementary school pupil preparing a report on volcanoes, collecting material from the Web to use in a presentation. Then it showed the student at the front of the room giving his presentation, which ended with a view of a volcano erupting, shown on a screen that extended across the width of the classroom and accompanied by a roaring sound that had classmates gasping in awe. Great educational experience if you are going to be a television producer. But great science education? No, probably a shade worse than what would come from a conventional report, where ideas would count for a little more and their absence could not so easily be hidden behind media glitz.

Examples of "driving questions" related to volcanoes are:

What causes volcanoes?
What is the risk that a volcano will erupt near here?
Are volcanoes related to earthquakes?
Why do new volcanic islands keep coming up in Hawaii?

Such questions could give rise to Project-Based Science as envisaged by the Michigan researchers. Ideally, such a Project-Based Science unit will include simulations with computers or physical models, so that students are not limited to authoritative sources for answers to the question. If directed toward sufficiently deep questions, Project Based Science can indeed engage students in creative work with important ideas.

Therein lies a shortcoming of Project Based Science, however. How does one get students engaged with sufficiently deep questions? The four driving questions listed above are in a roughly increasing order of depth. The first two questions are the ones most likely to occur spontaneously to students, and the first question, "What causes volcanoes?", is a good starting point for inquiry. The last two questions are likely to arise only after students have made progress in understanding and become acquainted with the formation and location of volcanic islands. For the teacher to pose these questions at the outset would not be a good idea, because the students would not be in a position to recognize their significance. They are questions that should emerge as a consequence of progress in work with ideas. It is characteristic of successful work with ideas in design mode that the questions or problems evolve as well as the answers and solutions and that there is a creative interplay between them. Project-based methods tend to curtail this iterative process.

The curtailment is in large part caused by another stipulation. The original question "drives" a process that is directed toward the production of a concrete artifact — a report, a performance, a model, a letter to the city council, or whatever. This provides closure for the project but, unfortunately, it also gives closure to the advancement of knowledge. In some instances, pursuit of the "driving question" gets completely derailed as students' attention focuses on producing the "authentic artifact" (e.g. Yarnall & Kafai 1995). Even in the more successful instances, however, the project structure discourages the progressive reformulation of questions and problems, for to do so sets back design and production of the "authentic artifact".

Problem-Based Learning

Problem-Based Learning is often treated as synonymous with project-based learning, Although the two have more in common than a shared acronym, Problem-Based Learning grows out of a different tradition with a different focus. Originating in a medical school, Problem-Based Learning was designed to teach medical knowledge and skills by engaging students in solving problems similar to those they could expect to encounter in practice — that is, problems of diagnosis and treatment involving simulated cases. Students are expected to determine among themselves what information they need to solve the problem, dig out and share the information, and work together toward a satisfactory solution, with guidance but little direct help from the instructor. As typically employed in medical schools, problem-based work is run according to a tight schedule and fixed procedures, with only limited opportunity for iterative idea improvement; but these are not essential features of the approach and are not mentioned among the minimum requirements for Problem-Based Learning at the Problem-Based Learning Initiative's website (http://www.pbli.org/pbl/generic_pbl.htm). Unlike Project-Based Science, Problem-Based Learning is not focused on a tangible end product. The end product is a problem solution — a purely conceptual artifact. Thus, iterative idea improvement is, at least in principle, something that Problem-Based Learning could promote. In medical education, the goal is to turn out doctors who can solve diagnostic problems instead of relying on rote procedures and typical cases. A similar goal can motivate its application to education in general.

When applied to school learning, however, Problem-Based Learning immediately runs into a problem with one of its main principles. Whereas in medical education it is possible to select cases that engage students with problems very similar to those they will encounter in later work, this is not a realistic possibility in general education. The closest schooling can come to solvable problems that all students will likely encounter in later life are home management and personal finance problems, but these are usually of little interest to children and adolescents. There is one major exception, however. Schooling can engage students in solving the kinds of problems they will encounter in later education. Given that most students in wealthy nations do pursue education beyond secondary school and that more would probably do so if they were better prepared, Problem-Based Learning that succeeded in equipping students to deal creatively with future educational challenges would deserve a central place in any school curriculum.

To serve this purpose, however, Problem-Based Learning must depart even farther from its medical school roots. Case-based problems are inherently context-limited. A case acquires general significance when it is considered in the context of a more fundamental inquiry. Deep inquiry may start with an intriguing case: In an example provided by Hunt & Minstrell (1994), inquiry starts with the problem of what happens to an object on a spring balance as the air is evacuated from around it. But attention quickly shifts to the students' explanatory ideas and to the testing and revision of these ideas through experiments that broaden the inquiry to general concerns about gravity, the difference between weight and mass, and weight of the atmosphere. In this shift from context-limited to context-general, the nature of the problem itself undergoes transformation, and this is something that Problem-Based Learning has not been designed to address.

Knowledge Building

"Knowledge Building" may be defined simply as "creative work with ideas that really matter to the people doing the work" (Scardamalia & Bereiter in press). It is not confined to education but applies to creative knowledge work of all kinds. Whether they are scientists working on an explanation of cell aging or first-graders working on an explanation of leaves changing color in the fall, knowledge builders engage in similar processes with a similar goal. That goal is to advance the frontiers of knowledge as they perceive them. "As they perceive them" is an important qualification when Knowledge Building is undertaken in educational contexts. Identifying frontiers and judging what constitutes an advance are essential parts of Knowledge Building, which students need to learn to carry out themselves, not depend on a teacher or a textbook to do for them.

As a constructivist approach, Knowledge Building shares many characteristics with the other constructivist approaches discussed earlier. There are, however, important differences in strategy. The following are some of the more salient ones that have evolved through a decade and a half of work by teachers and researchers. A fuller account is presented in Scardamalia (2002).

- *A focus on idea improvement.* Idea improvement is a primary and sustaining goal. Students are encouraged to put forth their own ideas early. From then on their task is to work together on improving those ideas, and to use the full range of available strategies and resources to improve them.
- *Problems versus questions.* Although problems are often expressed as questions, we have found that pursuing solutions to problems rather than answers to questions best encourages knowledge building. Answers have a certain finality to them, whereas

problem solutions are generally continually improvable. Whereas comparing answers to questions puts students into the belief mode, solutions to problems, including solutions to knowledge problems, can be carried out in design mode — judging what different solutions do and do not accomplish, what new problems a solution raises and what problems need to be solved in order to progress in solving the main problem. Knowledge Building pedagogy differs from Problem-Based Learning in that the preferred problems are ones of considerable generality.

- *Knowledge of value to the community.* In Knowledge Building, conceptual artifacts themselves — developed ideas — are an important product, used by community members — primarily as tools that enable further knowledge advances. Thus, the progressive character of modern sciences and disciplines is also characteristic of knowledge building pedagogy. This does not mean that the students are expected to produce an original theory of gravitation to stand alongside Newton's. Rather, what they produce would likely be consistent with Newton but enriched by insights that made gravitational theory come alive for them and made it something they could apply to new problems of understanding. Considerable original scientific thought on the part of the students will have gone into such a product. (Centuries elapsed between Newton and Einstein, yet creative scientific work was being done throughout that period; so we should not expect students to do better than that in a school term.)
- *Emergent goals and products.* Students in Knowledge Building classrooms typically produce tangible or visible products — reports, multimedia presentations, playlets, demonstrations — but these are not predetermined and made the ultimate objective of a "project". They may emerge at any point in the iterative knowledge building process. They may take various forms and serve various purposes, from highlighting a problem to disseminating results. It is important to note, however, that in many instances there is no tangible product other than the computer record of the online work that was done in achieving the knowledge advances (Bereiter *et al.* 1997).
- *Constructive use of authoritative sources.* When functioning in belief mode, contemporary educators have a good deal of trouble deciding how to treat authoritative sources such as textbooks and encyclopedias. Should the material be treated as truth, as a current best guess, as personal opinion, or as what some authoritative group has agreed to treat as true? Each way has its drawbacks, and so the choice tends to be made on ideological grounds. In a Knowledge Building design mode, however, all ideas are treated as improvable; ideas that have been the result of extensive work and development are treated with respect and judged according to what they can contribute to the group's current problem-solving effort. This does not eliminate problems of truth or validity, but it puts them in a context where they can be dealt with along with other difficulties. One does not expect to achieve perfect understanding any more than one expects to produce the perfect computer; one only expects to improve on the present state of things.

To educators acclimatized to approaches like those previously discussed, Knowledge Building may sound arid and abstract, suitable perhaps for a graduate seminar but not for the schoolroom. However, Knowledge Building research has accumulated compelling demonstrations that school-age children, even the youngest, find joy in working with ideas.[1] Their ideas are as real to them as physical objects, and their interest intensified as they watch their ideas take new forms and engage others. Furthermore, the hands-on activities that enliven modern classrooms are present in Knowledge Building classrooms as well. What distinguishes them is that they are enlisted in the creation and improvement of theories and "big" ideas. Students in a Knowledge Building classroom may build and test paper airplanes, but they are not, as one project-based version of this activity has it, trying to isolate the variables that affect how far a paper plane will fly. Instead, the students are trying to understand the physics of lift — what keeps airplanes aloft. Control of variables will come into play, as they create and improve their ideas, but the focus is on theoretical ideas, not variable-testing. By the time they are finished they may also understand water skiing and hydroplaning, how propellers work, and may have investigated whether Bernouli's principle applies under water.

All four of the approaches discussed here — along with virtually all serious approaches to education in the schools — aim to bring about understanding of the big ideas that make a knowledge society possible in the first place. Knowledge Building additionally aims at the fullest possible immersion in the work by which such ideas are created and improved.

Comparisons and Possibilities of Synthesis

The differences among the four approaches are often minimized, lumping them together as constructivist. Kolodner (2002), for instance, explicitly identifies Learning Science by Design as a variety of Project-Based Science, as defined by the Michigan group. From a Knowledge Building perspective we see an important distinction. Learning Science by Design, according to the description set out by Kolodner, lacks the main defining characteristic of Project-Based Science: It is not "organized by investigations to answer driving questions" but instead is organized around efforts to meet challenges in design of physical devices. In terms of the continuum that runs from context-limited to context-general, Learning by Design lies farthest toward the context-limited end. It is explicitly focused on building concrete things that actually work. Ideas enter the process insofar as they are relevant to producing a device that fulfills its intended function (Kolodner 2002). Project-Based Science, in contrast, is explicitly concerned with finding answers to significant questions; this presumably places it farther along the continuum in the context-general direction. However, to the extent that projects settle into explanations limited to a particular context (a survey of local water quality is a popular example) they lean in the context-limited direction. In Problem-Based Learning, the products are problem solutions, but the problems themselves are context-limited insofar as they focus on particular cases — diagnosing the illness of a particular real or simulated patient, devising a plan of action for a particular situation, explaining a particular observed phenomenon. Of the four approaches, only Knowledge Building

---

[1] References to this research, including many online documents, are available at www.ikit.org

explicitly supports design-mode work at the context-general end of the continuum — that is, design work directly aimed at creating and improving broadly significant theories, problem formulations, interpretations, and the like.

Considered as learning environments, each of the approaches offers a distinct kind of experience in working with ideas in design mode. An obvious strategy is to ensure that the curriculum engages students, at various times, in each of the four approaches. This has several drawbacks, however. In real life, creative knowledge work does not stay focused at one point on the context-limited to context-general continuum but moves back and forth according to needs and opportunities. Even the most nuts-and-bolts engineering projects can profit from a consideration of basic ideas and their implications, and it is rare for theoretical inquiry to be carried on in the absence of hands-on experimentation, model building, and the like. A curriculum that has students doing Learning by Design one month and Problem-Based Learning on an unrelated topic the next month does not provide the necessary flexibility in the pursuit of long-term goals.

A more serious drawback to an eclectic or mixed approach is that it does not provide for socializing students into a Knowledge Age culture, such as exists in leading university centers of research and innovation-oriented companies. A powerful learning environment, after all, should be something that students are *in* rather than just something that structures their activity for a certain period of time. It should, to a certain extent, foster a *way of life* that manifests itself throughout the school day and beyond. Accordingly, an environment for developing Knowledge Age soft skills ought to be one in which creative work with ideas is, as Peter Drucker (1985: 151) put it, "part and parcel of the ordinary, the norm, if not routine".

Of the four approaches, Knowledge Building is the least bound to particular activity structures and is explicitly defined as an approach to knowledge that "is not confined to particular occasions or subjects but pervades mental life — in and out of school" (Scardamalia 2002: 81). Thus, it provides a comprehensive framework for incorporating other approaches, while at the same time preserving a coherent emphasis. Within a knowledge building framework, design of physical devices, experiments, information-gathering and problem-solving efforts would all be marshaled to the basic knowledge building objective — to advance the frontiers of knowledge as these are perceived by the students. Toy building, contrived projects, and problems whose main purpose is to develop skills would give way to constructions and inquiries designed by the students to advance their ideas and to make worthwhile contributions to the "state of the art" as it exists in the classroom.

A comprehensive knowledge-building environment would provide a means of initiating students into a knowledge-creating culture — to make them feel a part of humankind's long-term effort to understand their world and gain some control over their destiny. Knowledge would not be seen as something handed down to them from dead White males. Rather, they would look on those dead White males — and other intellectual forbears of different race and gender — as fellow workers whose work they are carrying forward. The Knowledge Society, as it is taking shape today, seems headed toward a very sharp separation between those who are in it and those who, whether they live a continent apart or on the same street, are on the outside looking in. A knowledge building environment should provide all students an opportunity to be on the inside looking out.

Technology for Knowledge Building

All of the approaches we have been discussing feature collaboration, and all make some use of ICT (information and communication technology) to support the collaboration. However, only in Knowledge Building is a software environment the principal environment in which the collaborative work goes on. In Learning by Design, the principal environment is the physical workbench where something is being built; the software environment is an adjunct for sharing ideas and information and developing plans. In Project-Based Science, the principal environment is that in which data are being collected. It could be a stream where water samples are gathered; it could be a laboratory where experiments are run. The principal software is that used in data collection and analysis, but with a discussion environment serving again as an adjunct. In Problem-Based Learning, the principal environment is the tutorial room. ICT figures primarily as a means for information gathering and for communication among participants between tutorial sessions. In Knowledge Building, however, a software environment — Knowledge Forum® or a derivative of it — is the principal environment in which work with ideas goes on. It is where ideas are set forth, discussed, revised, organized, combined, and so on. If, as in Project-Based Science, real-world or experimental data are collected, they are put to use by being brought into the work in Knowledge Forum. Other learning technologies, such as simulations and video recordings, are integrated as closely as possible into the Knowledge Forum work, preferably by running inside Knowledge Forum notes.

Discussion is, of course, central to collaborative work with ideas, but if a software environment is to serve as a workspace for knowledge building it must provide for more than the usual concatenation of discussion threads. If you have ever tried to do serious collaborative work in a conventional discussion, chat, or bulletin board environment you will have experienced how frustrating it is. It is all one thing after another, with no way to bring about integration and coherence. The essence of creative (as distinct from argumentative) work with ideas is making connections. But current designs of collaborative learning environments do not take account of this. Instead, they represent variations on what is essentially a message-passing model. This model may be fine for the opinion-stating and question-answer dialogue that prevails in public online forums, but it is grossly inadequate for what we have called "progressive discourse" — discourse that gets somewhere, advances on a problem, produces a conceptual artifact.

A Knowledge Building environment needs multiple ways of representing and organizing ideas and flexible ways to link them. It should provide not only for subordination (which threaded discourse typically provides) but also for superordination — a new idea subsuming or integrating previously recorded ideas. An elementary requirement for idea improvement is that it should be possible to revise a previous formulation — something that message-based systems generally forbid. The technology needs to do more than that, especially if it is to be used for educational purposes (cf.

Scardamalia 2002), but our purpose here is not to lay out design specifications or to describe Knowledge Forum in detail. Instead, it is to argue that technology intended to develop skills for the knowledge age needs to be designed on the basis of some articulated conception of what it means to create and work with knowledge.

Conclusion

Alfred North Whitehead (1929: 83) said that education must equip students with the ideas and the capacities that would enable them "to appreciate the current thought of their epoch". In our epoch, which is coming to be known as the Knowledge Age, it is impossible to appreciate the "current thought" and to take part in it unless one thinks of ideas as serving purposes and as being continually improvable so as to serve those purposes better. The traditional concerns with truth and warranted belief are not abandoned, but they are subordinated to the mission of advancing the frontiers of understanding and efficacy on all fronts. A powerful learning environment for the present age, accordingly, is an environment that immerses students in the effort to advance the frontiers of knowledge as they perceive them.

In a series of reports from classrooms organized around this Knowledge Building effort, we and our co-workers have provided evidence that students at all ages can in fact do creative work with knowledge, while at the same time performing well according to the usual criteria of school achievement (e.g. Bereiter *et al.* 1997; Hewitt 2002; Oshima 1977; Scardamalia 2002; Scardamalia *et al.* 1994). The creative work students do is not just creative work with concrete artifacts and media, although they do that, too. It is creative work with ideas that are at the heart of the sciences, scholarly disciplines, and knowledge-creating enterprises.

To extend Whitehead's statement, we may say that you cannot appreciate the current thought of this epoch unless you are an active participant in advancing it, because continual advancement of knowledge in all spheres is what constitutes the current thought of the Knowledge Age. The schools, even those most attuned to the new informational media and to the ideas of constructivism and active learning, have by this standard not yet entered the Knowledge Age. In order for them to enter, we need a radical innovation in educational experience that brings ideas and idea improvement to the center.

References

Bereiter, C. (2002). *Education and mind in the knowledge age*. Mahwah, NJ: Lawrence Erlbaum Associates.

Bereiter, C., Scardamalia, M., Cassells, C., & Hewitt, J. (1997). Postmodernism, knowledge building, and elementary science. *Elementary School Journal, 97*, 329–340.

Drucker, P. (1985). *Innovation and entrepreneurship: Practice and principles*. New York: Harper and Row.

Hewitt, J. (2002). From a focus on tasks to a focus on understanding: The cultural transformation of a Toronto classroom. In: T. Koschmann, R. Hall, & N. Miyake (Eds), *Computer supported cooperative learning: Vol. 2. Carrying forward the conversation* (pp. 11–41). Mahwah, NJ: Lawrence Erlbaum Associates.

Holbrook, J., & Kolodner, J. L. (2000). Scaffolding the development of an inquiry-based (science) classroom. In: B. Fishman, & S. O'Connor-Divelbiss (Eds), *Fourth International Conference of the Learning Sciences* (pp. 221–227). Mahwah, NJ: Lawrence Erlbaum Associates.

Hunt, E., & Minstrell, J. (1994). A cognitive approach to the teaching of physics. In: K. McGilley (Ed.), *Classroom lessons: Integrating cognitive theory and classroom practice* (pp. 51–74). Cambridge, MA: MIT Press.

Kolodner, J. L. (2002). Learning by Design™: Interations of design challenges for better learning of science skills. *Cognitive Studies, 9*, 338–350.

Kolodner, J. L., Crismond, D., Gray, J., Holbrook, J., & Puntambekar, S. (1998). Learning by Design from theory to practice. *Proceedings Third International Conference of the Learning Sciences '98*, 16–22.

Marx, R. W., Blumenfeld, P. C., Krajcik, J. S., & Soloway, E. (1997). Enacting project-based science. *Elementary School Journal, 97*, 341–358.

Oshima, J. (1997). Students' construction of scientific explanations in a collaborative hyper-media learning environment. In: R. Hall, N. Miyake, & N. Enyedy (Eds), *Computer support for collaborative learning '97, Proceedings of The Second International Conference on Computer Support for Collaborative Learning. December 10–14, 1997*. Toronto, Ontario, Canada.

Scardamalia, M. (2002). Collective cognitive responsibility for the advancement of knowledge. In: B. Smith (Ed.), *Liberal education in a knowledge society* (pp. 76–98). Chicago: Open Court.

Scardamalia, M., & Bereiter, C. (in press). Knowledge building. In: *Encyclopedia of Education* (2nd ed.). New York: Macmillan.

Scardamalia, M., Bereiter, C., & Lamon, M. (1994). The CSILE project: Trying to bring the classroom into World 3. In: K. McGilley (Ed.), *Classroom lessons: Integrating cognitive theory and classroom practice* (pp. 201–228). Cambridge, MA: MIT Press.

Smith Lea, N., & Scardamalia, M. (1997). Progressive curriculum and knowledge building uses of networked multimedia resources. *Paper presented at the Annual Meeting of the American Educational Association, Chicago, March 24, 1997 Session 5.13*. Available at http://csile.oise.utoronto.ca/abstracts/aera_pcn_kb_uses/

Whitehead, A. N. (1929). *The aims of education*. New York: Macmillan.

Yarnall, L., & Kafai, Y. (1996, April). *Issues in project-based science activities: Children's constructions of ocean software games. Paper presented at the annual meeting of the American Educational Research Association.*
Available at http://www.gse.ucla.edu/kafai/Paper_Kafai%2FYarnall.html

Part II

Identifying and Measuring Components and Dimensions of Powerful Learning Environments: Experiences and Reflections

Chapter 5

Measuring Behavioral Change Processes During an Ongoing Innovation Program: Scope and Limits

Monique Boekaerts and Alexander Minnaert

Introduction

Since 1995, our research group has been engaged in a large-scale innovation program in vocational schools in the Netherlands. The aim of this project is to change the behavior of students, teachers, and school managers in an attempt to improve students' self-regulatory skills. During the course of the innovation program, we enjoyed many successes, but we also encountered many setbacks. We discovered the hard way that it is rather complicated to initiate and sustain the target innovation strategy. In this chapter, we will not give an overview of the studies conducted in connection to the innovation (interested readers are referred to Boekaerts 1997; Boekaerts & Minnaert 2003; Minnaert & Boekaerts 2002; Rozendaal 2002; Rozendaal *et al.* 2003; Van Grinsven 2003; Van Velzen 2002; Witteman 1997). Instead, the focus of this chapter will be on the experiences and reflections concerning the identification and measurement of major components and dimensions of powerful learning environments in secondary vocational education.

Hence, we begin with a brief description of the conceptualization and implementation of the Interactive Learning group System (ILS) innovation program, followed by some methodological concerns that may have compromised the credibility of our intervention studies and its conclusions, and by some misconceptions we had about the nature of the outcome variables. After that we will critically decompose the power of the program to unfold the major components of the ILS learning environment. Finally, we will formulate some recommendations within the context of evaluating novel learning environments.

Initiating the Interactive Learning Group System

Finding a Way to Change Teachers' Beliefs and Their Way of Doing Things

Due to the widespread attention that had been given to school reforms in the Netherlands prior to the start of our innovation program, most Dutch teachers were already aware that classroom practice had to change sooner or later. But the wide array of reform ideas proposed by various Dutch researchers and educators had obscured their view of the necessary and sufficient skills that they would need to acquire in order to translate the new educational philosophy (i.e. instruction set up according to the principles of social constructivism) into everyday practice. This confusion made some teachers hesitant and others reluctant to initiate the behavioral change process. We were convinced that teachers need to know that someone has hold of the compass in order to steer the behavioral change process in their school in the intended direction, before they embark on a major innovation program like ILS. Teachers also expect that somebody will be monitoring changing classroom practice in their school and coordinating the emerging results in such a way that improvements and side effects become visible at an early stage. This guarantees that the course of the ship can be changed, if necessary.

Anyone who has tried to change the behavior of professional groups knows that the groups that are hardest to change are those who have least control over their behavior. The challenge for our research team was to find ways of also reaching those teachers and their students who are poor at adopting to change. Those are precisely the ones who have a weak sense of control over their teaching, who have the least personal and social resources, and who lack the high self-esteem and self-worth it takes to translate knowledge about the new forms of instruction into sound teaching behavior. We realized that to reach the teachers most in need of our help it was the system, and not merely the teachers, that needed to change. In order to persuade teachers that they have to change their behavior, they must first be convinced that they are valued for what they are, and are not blamed for failing to fit into the new educational structures. In the second place they should be told that all classrooms, and not only theirs, have to change in order to make learning more successful. Apart from changing teachers' beliefs about good practice, on-the-job training should be offered so that the new skills can be practiced and teachers can judge for themselves whether or not these skills fit into their frame of reference and their way of doing things. Anything less is not sufficient to initiate and maintain the behavioral change process. In short, we realized at the start of the innovation program that we were making an attempt to initiate and sustain a multifarious behavioral change process in diverse groups of participants, including teachers, students, consultants, and school managers. To change classroom practice, a strong partnership (see De Corte 2000) must be built between those in charge of the compass (researchers, school managers facilitating the innovation, consultants monitoring the process of change, and the principal coordinating teachers), and the teachers and students on the work floor who are involved in the process of change. As such, innovations should be planned and well managed. Therefore, it is important to ensure the undivided support of the school managers (see West 1990). In line with these recommendations, we first established formal relationships with four ROCs and ensured that the board of directors endorsed the objectives of the innovation program. These ROCs are large regional educational centers that overarch all vocational and trade schools within a region.[1]

Identifying the Major Components of the Instructional Intervention

Our innovation program has its roots in the educational movement that focused on the description of essential instructional principles for the design of powerful learning environments. We wanted to promote self-regulated learning in vocational school students. In order to build a strong partnership, the members of this partnership should accept a common definition of what is meant by "equipping students with self-regulatory skills". If the different partners of the partnership have different views of the objectives of the program, efforts at partnership quickly dissolve. In our program this essential first step was not overlooked in the rush to move ahead. We identified features that are involved in the design of a powerful learning environment and discussed within the partnership whether these features would promote self-regulation in a vocational school. These features were synthesized from three separate research lines, namely: (1) studies that examined the effect of teaching according to the principles of social constructivism (see Cobb 1994, 1996); (2) studies on cooperative learning (Slavin 1996); and (3) self-report studies with Vermunt's (1998) learning style instrument to register students' level of processing (deep-level vs. surface-level processing) and type of regulation (self-regulation vs. external regulation). On the basis of these three sources, supplemented by examples of good practice in vocational schools and research into the barriers of self-regulation, we identified the major components and dimensions of the ILS learning environment. We referred to these components as "*the ILS instruction principles*". We also identified a small range of targets that could be measured reliably to get a good view of the aspects of the students' changing self-regulation. These were: increased deep-level processing, decreased surface-level processing, increased self-regulation and decreased external regulation. We hypothesized that the ILS instruction principles have a positive effect on all the target outcomes. In order to demonstrate this relationship, three things were important. First, teachers should understand and endorse the ILS instruction principles. Second, they should be willing to acquire the ILS instruction strategy based on these principles and apply it consistently. Third, we needed a reliable instrument to measure students' changing learning and regulation styles in order to register baseline data and compare these data to data collected six months later.

It was decided to keep the number of classes small in the beginning. We therefore selected, in each of the four participating ROCs, only those teachers who were motivated to change their own and their students' behavior. Right from the beginning,

---

[1] The largest ROC in the Netherlands groups together about 45,000 students and their teachers and the smallest ROC has about 14,000 students and their teachers.

we distinguished between short-term and long-term objectives of the innovation program and convinced all members of the partnership that the range of targets should be kept small in the first stage of the program. We anticipated that the first stage would last four to five years. We worked with groups of volunteers in each participating school for two reasons. First, these teachers were already convinced that classroom practice should be changed, and they were eager to learn how they could bring their teaching practice in line with the principles of social constructivism. Second, these teachers were willing to share their experiences while the behavioral change process was unfolding. This information would allow us to test the ILS instruction strategy and re-design it "en-route" taking into account perceived constraints and affordances. Furthermore, we wanted these pioneering teachers to be the future on-the-job trainers. They would be able to sustain the momentum in their school when the teacher consultants were no longer available. The major components of the innovation program as they were formulated at the beginning of the program can be seen in Table 1.

We provided on-the-job training to all participating teachers. This training program was organized and supervised by TSM, jointly with our research staff. It started as soon as the board of directors of each participating ROC agreed to join the partnership, implying that they were prepared to pay the cost of the initial stage of the innovation program in one of their departments (later, extra funding was obtained from the Dutch Ministry of Education to continue the program and extend it to other departments) and endorsed the following objectives of the innovation program.

(1) To familiarize the partnership members with the ILS instruction principles, specifying what the new complementary roles of teachers and students entail.
(2) To familiarize the pioneering teachers with the new teacher roles:
    • decrease knowledge transmission to a quarter of a lesson unit;
    • write productive assignments for group work on the blackboard;
    • help students activate prior knowledge;
    • divide their class into ILS groups (i.e. a group composed of four students on the basis of a variety in learning styles);
    • familiarize students with learning with and from each other;
    • increase coaching behavior.
(3) To familiarize the pioneering students with the new learner roles. At the end of the program the students will:
    • be more active in class;
    • enjoy learning from and with each other in ILS groups;
    • have increased deep-level processing and reduced surface-level processing;
    • have increased self-regulation and decreased external regulation.
(4) To increase social interaction between:
    • students in the context of the classroom;
    • teachers in the context of their department;
    • coordinating teachers and school managers in the context of the innovation program.

Recursive Bootstrapping

It is generally assumed that innovation is not a linear process. Rather, it is conceived as a cyclical process with innovative attempts followed by periods of implementation, adaptation, and stabilization (Van de Ven *et al.* 1999). In Figure 1, the theoretical model of the cyclical intervention process is depicted as well as the actual cyclical process realized in different ROCs. As this figure shows, adaptation continued long after the first innovation attempts and the implementation process did not begin at the same point in time in the various ROCs.

Table 1: Major components of the Interactive Learning group System (ILS) intervention program.

(1) The innovation program puts the emphasis on three interconnected behavioral change processes that occur simultaneously, namely behavioral change in teachers, students, and school managers.
(2) It is a group program. Participating schools should act as a team; teachers should learn to work as teams; students should work in interactive learning groups (ILS).
(3) The program calls for self-regulation in all participants.
(4) The innovation program replaces standard teaching practice in the subject-matter areas of the participating teachers (new complementary roles of teacher/student).
(5) The program is offered at the beginning of a school year to all participating teachers who are supervised by TSM[2] and receive on-the-job training.
(6) The main features of the program are
   • that teachers teach according to a set of instruction principles
   • that they organize their classroom in interactive learning groups (ILS)
   • that they use Selector[3] to determine group composition.
(7) It is the intention to provide further on-the-job training to the pioneering ILS teachers so that they can replace the teacher consultants in their school.

Winne & Perry (2000) described the first stage of an innovation project as "recursive bootstrapping". This recursive bootstrapping process was the object of our first intervention study. As can be seen in Figure 1, some of our intervention studies began quite early in the intervention trajectory and continued throughout the implementation process. This meant that the bootstrapping process (adaptation and re-formulation of the target ILS instruction strategy, as well as validation of the measurement instruments)

[2] TSM refers to Teaching and School Management Consultants. It is an organization that was founded at the start of the innovation program to coach teachers and schools.
[3] Selector is a digital instrument used to measure the students' learning style before the start of the program and it is also used as a criterion for group composition (see Witteman 1997).

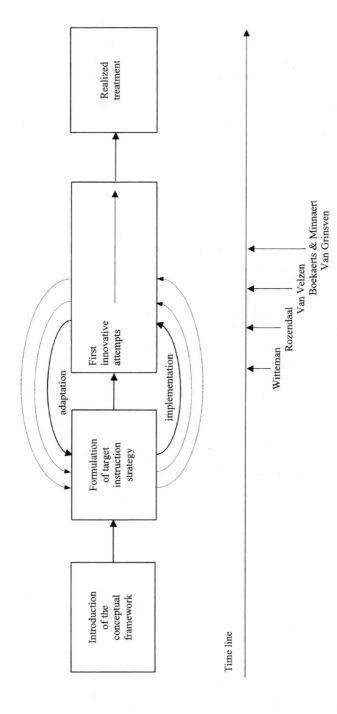

Figure 1: Theoretical model of the cyclical intervention process (boxes and connecting full lines), the actual cyclical process in the participating ROCs (boxes, full lines, and dotted lines), and the mentioned intervention studies (on the time line).

was still going on in some of the schools that participated in the innovation while stabilization was already taking place in other schools. As mentioned previously, we focused on a small set of targets, namely the students' learning strategies and the type of regulation they used. The Inventory of Learning styles (Vermunt 1998) was used to measure the students' preferential ways of processing information at the start of the intervention program and again six months later (see Witteman 1997). Eleven classes from three of the four ROCs were divided over the intervention and non-intervention groups. The teachers, who had received training in the use of the ILS instruction strategy, taught the students in the intervention groups. The students in the non-intervention group were taught according to the principles of direct teaching (normal classroom practice). It was hypothesized that the ILS instruction principles have a positive effect on the target changes in learning and regulation styles. More specifically, we hypothesized that students, who are well prepared by their teachers to work on productive group assignments in ILS groups, interact with the content of the lesson. In turn, this active engagement in the ILS group improves deep-level processing and self-regulation, as measured six months later. The results of the first intervention study showed that students in the intervention group reported increased use of deep-level processing compared to the non-intervention group. The expected decrease in surface-level processing, as well as the increase in self-regulation and decrease in external regulation did not materialize. This meant that the implied relationships between the ILS instruction principles and the targeted outcomes only hold for one specific educational outcome, namely deep-level processing. An alternative explanation is that the combined ILS instruction principles do not have a direct relationship with all the targeted educational outcomes, but that this effect is mediated by other variables.

Encouraged by the first empirical success of our innovation program and by the enthusiastic reports from members of the partnership, we standardized the ILS instruction strategy. A sequence of seven steps was specified and trained, namely: (1) prepare productive group assignments at home and write them on the blackboard as soon as you enter the classroom; (2) activate relevant prior knowledge; (3) prepare the students for the group assignments by providing the necessary resources; (4) leave three quarters of the scheduled time for coaching and feedback; (5) invite students to work in ILS groups on the assignments; (6) coach their behavior; and (7) give them feedback on the learning process as well as on the outcomes of the group learning activity. Teachers were urged to adopt the full set of ILS principles and apply the ILS instruction strategy consistently. At that stage in the innovation trajectory we had also had time to examine the psychometric properties of the Inventory of Learning Styles questionnaire that had been used to measure the students' learning and regulation strategies. A digital version had been constructed, called the Selector. This instrument was introduced in all the participating schools and most departments registered students' learning and regulation style at the beginning of each school year. This information was used to assign students to the ILS groups, namely group composition was such that at least one student with a deep-level processing style and one who scored high on self-regulation were included. Such group composition ensured that the students who were low on deep-level processing and/or on self-regulation had a model in their own group.

Intended Change in Learning Conditions Versus Realized Change in Learning Conditions

We set up a second intervention study, because we wanted to replicate Witteman's results in an independent sample. More specifically, we wanted to confirm the finding that there is a connection between the combined ILS principles and one of the target educational outcomes, namely deep-level processing. In addition we wanted to explore further the relationship between the combined ILS principles and the three other target educational outcomes. Accordingly, classes were selected from four ROCs that participated in the innovation program. Participants in this two-year longitudinal study were first year students in secondary vocational education and their teachers. Initially, 17 classes formed the intervention group and the non-intervention group consisted of 8 classes. In the latter classes students were still being taught according to the principles of direct teaching.

During this study, we discovered that the local conditions in the ROCs had affected the implementation process. To a certain extent this had been anticipated. Clearly, local conditions, such as the perceived support from school managers, the facilities given to ILS teachers, and the collegial climate in a department have an effect on the ILS teachers' motivation. For example, teachers of one ROC acted as an engine for change. Spurred by reward and the support of the managing directors, these teachers took the lead and ran well ahead of the music.

Our basic assumption was that all ILS teachers' behavior would mirror the target instruction strategy that they had acquired and practiced in the on-the-job training program. However, this assumption was often violated. The teachers involved in the innovation program took note of the conceptual model and the target ILS instruction strategy, but adapted the strategy to suit their own principles of best practice. We came across many examples of incorrect implementation and there were numerous reasons as to why the unintended learning conditions arose. These included incomplete understanding of the conceptual framework and the target instruction strategy, conflicting beliefs about "best practice", limited capacities, and limited resources (e.g. not enough time, support, material). Teachers easily lapsed back into their daily routine when task demands increased (e.g. before an exam period) and they liked to adapt the target ILS instruction strategy to the local conditions. Also, teacher mobility was quite high in the participating vocational schools. Some teachers entered our program with a lot of experience in relation to a different instruction strategy, namely, problem-based learning and this created rival groups within and between departments. All these reasons for changing the target ILS instruction strategy, either deliberately or unintentionally, produced specific changes in the treatment. This implied that there was doubt about whether observed changes in student behavior could be attributed to the target ILS instruction strategy (intended changes in learning conditions). Hence, we could not be sure that the students who took part in our intervention studies had been exposed to the same treatment.

Toward the end of the second intervention study, we discovered that 74% of our teachers had used the most essential feature of the training program, namely having students work in ILS groups of four students working on productive group assignments at least half of the time. Only 51% had used the available Selector data (i.e. the results obtained with a digital instrument to assess the students' learning style) for group composition. Group size was changed by 40% of the teachers (three or five students instead of four in a group), whilst 58% of the teachers changed group composition during the year. Some 42% of the teachers adhered consistently to the target ILS instruction strategy and 45% used a *popular curtailed version* of the ILS instruction strategy. The questions that were raised at that point in time were: What can be done when one discovers that the teachers in the intervention group did not consistently expose their students to the intended treatment? What can be done when teachers in the non-intervention group have gradually adopted some of the principles that should have been reserved for the intervention group? We did not have ready answers to these important questions, but raised them nonetheless because we wanted to be sure that the concepts measured at the individual level and the aggregate level measured the same thing. We fully realized that inconsistencies in the actual treatment endangered the validity of the intervention study. In order to draw attention to the dangers that lurk behind such inconsistencies, we will digress slightly in the next paragraph and examine the credibility and ecological fallacy of intervention studies.

A major issue with regard to research on intervention studies is the "credibility" of the research findings and the associated conclusions. In a substantive discussion of this issue, Levin & O'Donnell (1999) describe credibility as the trustworthiness of the educational intervention study and argue convincingly that inconsistencies in the educational intervention or treatment jeopardize the credibility of the research evidence. As such, credibility is intertwined with internal validity. One of the basic questions in all intervention studies, whether school based or laboratory based, is: Can one attribute the educational outcomes to the educational intervention? In this respect, Levin & O'Donnell (1999) identified four criteria that should be met in intervention studies:

> . . . evidence linking an instructional intervention to a specified educational outcome is scientifically convincing if: (1) the evidence is based on a Comparison that is appropriate (e.g. comparing the intervention with an appropriate alternative or non-intervention condition); (2) the outcome is produced by the intervention Again and again (i.e. it has been "replicated", initially across participants in a single study and ultimately through independently conducted studies); (3) there is a direct Relationship (i.e. a connection or correspondence) between the intervention and the outcome; and (4) all other reasonable competing explanations for the outcome can be Eliminated (typically, through randomization and methodological care) (p. 190).

Three issues were at stake in our second intervention study, namely: (1) Did we include an appropriate comparison group? (2) How stable was the treatment in the respective intervention groups? and (3) What happened in the non-intervention groups? Concerning the appropriateness of the so-called "experimental" and "control" group(s) within a pretest/posttest design, Levin and O'Donnell noted that establishing a "control group" means different things to different educational researchers. To some it means the absence of any instruction, to others it means learning in a different educational system or teaching according to different instructional principles, compared to the experimental group(s). It is important to realize in this respect that one always needs to aggregate different units in order to compare the results obtained in the intervention group with those obtained in the appropriate control group. At such a point, one needs to ask: How sure are we that all the characteristics of the treatment have been appropriately realized in all the participating classes that made up the intervention group? In other words, were the treatment conditions invariant? In a classical experiment, subjects are the units of analysis and these units ought to be randomly assigned to the systematically manipulated and controlled conditions (see Campbell & Stanley 1966; Judd & Kenny 1981; Kazdin 1999). In an intervention study, however, classrooms, educational units, project teams, or schools are the units of analysis and these units ought to be randomized. If classrooms have not been assigned randomly to interventions, the intervention effects are confounded with selection biases. Levin & O'Donnell (1999) noted that appropriate randomization and control are often conspicuously absent in instructional design experiments that are characterized by authentic research contexts and by the unfolding modifications made "en-route" by the designer and/or teachers.

Given the credibility criteria formulated by Levin & O'Donnell (1999), we must conclude that the internal validity of our second intervention study is poor. The intervention prescriptions (i.e. the steps in the target instruction strategy) were not consistently applied. Accordingly, our intervention study lacks appropriate randomization and control in the sense that the intended randomization of classrooms to treatments was confounded and the major instructional principles have been altered "en-route". Therefore, our intervention study did not meet the four criteria specified by Levin & O'Donnell (i.e. comparison, replication, relationship, and elimination) in a credible way. Does that mean that our study was useless? It certainly does not. The added value of our study is the identification of stable outcomes across independently conducted interventions. Our study provides insight into the why's, what's, and how's of the ILS learning environment and helps us to identify and measure the major components and dimensions of powerful learning environments. As such, this study should be seen as part of the first stage of "an innovation project", namely "recursive bootstrapping".

Misconceptions About the Nature of the Outcomes Variables

At the start of the innovation project, we had some clear ideas about the nature of self-regulated learning. These ideas were based on the literature on cognitive strategy use, learning style, and metacognition. In fact, we followed the lead of Entwistle (1992) and Vermunt (1992) who assumed that deep-level processing and surface-level processing are the opposite ends of one cognitive strategy dimension and hence are negatively correlated. In other words, we took for granted that deep-level processing (DLP) was superior to surface-level processing (SLP) and that students who relied more on DLP would score lower on SLP, and vice versa. This message was communicated to the participating teachers and, in turn, to the students in their respective classes. In line with the research of Pintrich & De Groot (1990) and Corno & Rohrkemper (1985) we also believed that the value that students attach to tasks within a domain, as well as their subjective competence and anxiety affect their cognitive strategy use and their regulation strategies. Hence, we made an empirical distinction between the target educational outcome variables per se and the internal conditions that students create in the learning situation (e.g. motivation, anxiety). In view of the fact that the teachers had communicated to their students that deep-level processing is superior to surface-level processing, we expected that student motivation would be positively associated with deep-level processing and negatively with surface-level processing. On a related note, we expected that anxiety would be positively associated with surface-level processing and negatively with deep-level processing. In a recent study, Rozendaal *et al.* (2003) found that the anxiety hypothesis was confirmed but that motivation was positively associated with both SLP and DLP. Surprisingly, a modest positive correlation was found between SLP and DLP (0.12), suggesting that these two processing strategies are not the opposite ends of a continuum. This finding encouraged us to examine whether some students have a dual processing system, using DLP and SLP when appropriate. We identified those students in our sample that had indicated that they were predominantly surface-level processors (high on SLP and low on DLP), those who were predominantly deep-level processors (high on DLP and low on SLP), and those who seemed to be familiar with both processing modes (high on SLP/DLP). We found that 50% of our sample ($N = 310$) had the potential to process information either in a deep- or surface-level processing mode; 10% were predominantly surface-level processors, and 20% were predominantly deep-level processors. After constructing a measurement model for the estimation of the relations between motivation, anxiety, and processing modes, we calculated the relations between processing modes and the students' affective internal states (motivation and anxiety), separately for the three different types of information processors. We found that motivation was associated with the dominant processing mode. In the group of deep-level processors, a positive association was noted between motivation and the use of DLP (0.23) and no association between motivation and SLP (0.05). In contrast, there was a positive association (0.53) between motivation and SLP and no association between motivation and DLP (0.00), in the group of surface-level processors. Interestingly, dual processors had a positive association between motivation and both SLP (0.31) and DLP (0.43).

The patterns of correlations between anxiety and the two processing modes were also quite interesting, indicating that low anxiety was positively associated with the use of DLP in deep-level processors (0.20) and dual processors (0.18). No association was found in surface-level processors (0.02). Notably, low anxiety was negatively associated with SLP in students who predominantly used the deep-level processing mode (–0.35). The relationship between low anxiety and SLP was not significantly different from zero in surface-level processors (–0.11) and dual processors (–0.09). These results suggest that when motivated, students tend to use their dominant information-processing mode. Students who have a dual processing system use both processing modes. Furthermore, when students have to work in a threatening learning environment (high anxiety) they seem to make less use of the deep-level processing mode. Before the start of the innovation project we had no in-depth knowledge about how students' motivation and anxiety were related to their processing mode. Our studies in vocational school allowed us to unmask a number of misconceptions about students' processing modes that seriously endanger our communication with teachers. We discovered that deep-level processing and surface-level processing are not the opposite ends of a cognitive strategy continuum. Remarkably, more than 70% of the students in our sample (vocational schools) regularly used DLP and 50% of the students have access to both processing modes. It is plausible that their preferential or dominant use of one of these modes is domain and/or context dependent.

Decomposing the Power of the ILS Instruction Strategy

An additional point that we like to discuss is the power of the intervention strategy. Should we attribute the change noted in educational outcomes to the joint effect of the intervention strategy, or to one of the more specific components of the ILS instruction strategy? Decomposing the power of the intervention is necessary to disentangle the unique effects of the intervention characteristics involved. In the context of the ILS innovation project one may ask: What really mattered? Was it the fact that teachers planned the productive group assignments prior to coming to class and communicated them to the students at the start of each lesson unit? Was it the ILS collaborative learning setting and the amount of time allowed for active engagement in the task? Was it the coaching behavior of the teachers or the teachers' adherence to the target instruction strategy? Or, was it a combination of these characteristics? We had no fine-grained knowledge about how these different characteristics contributed to the students' selection of deep-level vs. surface-level processing strategies. In order to generate testable hypotheses, we used the data from our second intervention study and examined the effect of the different ILS instruction principles on the target educational outcomes. Contrasting comparison groups were determined post facto. We reasoned that, provided the different principles of the ILS instruction strategy are clearly specified in the empirical model, the teachers' adherence to these principles could be used as a criterion to differentiate between the different independent units of analyses (classes). By means of cluster analytical techniques (maximizing the between-group variance and minimizing the within-group variability) teachers who adhered to the same set of ILS instruction principles fell into one group, and teachers who differed considerably on these features formed one or more contrasting groups (see Rozendaal 2002).

Using the approach of contrasting groups, the gap between the intended and realized treatments can be narrowed substantially, because the actual differences between the groups can be maximized, not the presumed or intended differences. This approach stems from clinical and medical research (see e.g. Lange *et al.* 1995), and has not often been used within an educational research setting (see e.g. De Jong 1988; Seifert 1995). Due to the fact that we had serious doubts that the students in the intervention group of our second intervention study had been exposed to the intended treatment (see discussion above), we decided to form contrasting groups within the ROCs that participated in the innovation program, following the method outlined above. It has become evident during the initial stages of the intervention program that most teachers preferred a curtailed version of the ILS instruction strategy. They used five of the seven instruction principles, leaving coaching and feedback out of the instructional sequence. We used the teachers' adherence to the curtailed version of the instruction principles as input data and this yielded three significantly different treatment clusters, indicative of the variability in the realization of the major components of the ILS instruction strategy. Rozendaal (2002) described these clusters as follows: (1) classrooms working frequently according to the seven core principles of the ILS instruction strategy (see Section 2.3); (2) classrooms working occasionally; and (3) classrooms working infrequently according to these core principles. Out of all the classes (i.e. 14) that had initially been assigned to the intervention group in our second intervention study, only five classes (i.e. 36% of the treatment clusters) had been exposed to the intended treatment. An additional 21% of the classes realized teaching according to these principles only from time to time, leaving 43% of the "intervention" classes exposed to an infrequent use of the ILS instruction principles.

It would take us too far to discuss the results of this study in detail. Suffice it here to say that the treatment received in the three contrasting clusters yielded substantially different effects on strategy use over time. We observed the expected behavioral changes only in the treatment cluster that had enjoyed *frequent* exposure to the core ILS instruction principles, providing preliminary evidence that the curtailed version of the ILS instruction strategy is an ingredient in the ILS learning environment. Students who reported using DLP at the start of the intervention program showed increased DLP six months later (0.35), as well as increased motivation (0.26) and decreased anxiety (−0.20). Students who had indicated that they used SLP at the beginning of the intervention project still used SLP six months later (0.61). They also showed an increase in DLP (0.25), but their motivation decreased (−0.28). These findings suggest that the ILS instruction conditions affected student motivation differentially. The students who already used DLP at the beginning of the project profited most from the ILS conditions. The ILS instruction principles seemed to be a favorable backdrop against which they could further develop their strategy use, allowing them at the same time to develop their motivation strategies (i.e. interest and persistence) and coping strategies (dealing with performance and test anxiety). The ILS learning conditions may have been perceived by the students, who predominantly relied on SLP at the beginning of the project, as unfavorable for learning. These students were forced to replace their preferential strategy use (SLP) with strategies that somebody else deemed important (DLP). Such persuasion promotes compliant behavior rather than intrinsic motivation and adequate coping strategies (see Boekaerts 2002).

It is important to realize that these are only hypotheses generated during the intervention study and not inferences drawn from the data. We feel that the use of contrasting groups, as an alternative way to explore the data that had originally been collected to assess the effect of the intervention study, provided insight into the components and dimensions of powerful learning environments. It seems then that the curtailed version of the ILS-instruction strategy, namely providing students with productive group assignments and inviting them to learn from and with each other, after activating their prior knowledge and providing relevant resources, works well for deep-level processors. Surface-level processors may be tempted to use more DLP but they have not changed their preferential SLP processing style yet. We speculate that they still consider DLP alien to their learning process. It is highly likely that the ILS instruction strategy has induced increased performance and test anxiety in some students and decreased anxiety in other students. The point being made is that motivation and affective variables may have mediated the effect that the ILS instruction principles had on the educational outcome variables. These variables refer to the internal state that students create on the basis of activated information in the actual learning situations, thus forming the context, or conditions for learning. Recent research on the effect of context on learning and achievement (for a review, see Volet & Järvelä 2001) has amply demonstrated that motivation variables create a mindset that impacts on cognitive strategy use. In order to link the ILS instruction strategies unequivocally to increases or decreases in the use of the two processing modes and to examine the mediating effect of the motivation variables, it is essential that we set up "randomized classroom trial studies" that meet the standards of internal and external validity that have been specified in the literature (see Judd & Kenny 1981; Kazdin 1999; Levin & O'Donnell 1999). Such intervention studies are critical to establishing the link between the initial development and limited testing of the intervention and the prescription and implementation stage. Note that the use of contrasting groups has also its shortcomings. Indeed, this approach may lack external validity due to uncontrollable cohort or sample fluctuations and due to the absence of fine-grained, theoretically sound, a priori criteria to split groups into subgroups. Moreover, skewed distributions of group sizes over the different features, as well as improper use of analysis of variance (violation of basic assumptions, e.g. homogeneity of variances) may endanger the validity of such studies.

Discussion and Recommendations

Taken together, the findings about the effectiveness of the ILS instruction principles for developing self-regulated learning are still inconclusive. We do not have solid evidence to link the ILS learning environment causally to the development of deep-level processing or self-regulation. There are two main reasons why the results of our intervention studies are still inconclusive. Firstly, the teachers in the non-intervention groups were influenced by the new ideas. They gradually adopted several principles of the target instruction strategy. Apart from the fact that it is unethical to prevent teachers from improving their teaching, it is impossible to control teachers' thinking and their actual practice. Therefore it is of paramount importance that safeguards are built into the monitoring procedure in order to be sensitive to potential threats to internal validity. Secondly, it has proven quite difficult to convince the teachers in the intervention group that they had to adhere to the complete set of ILS instruction principles during the intervention period. This highlights the need for better communication between teachers and researchers. We have to find a way to convince educators and teachers that it is essential that rigorous research be set up in which the intervention principles proposed by Levin & O'Donnell (1999) are fully realized. We also have to convince teachers and teacher consultants that they cannot prescribe the instruction principles on the basis of the current inconclusive research evidence.

Does that mean that we remain empty handed and that we cannot help teachers to design more powerful learning environments? The answer to this question is no. What we can do is to make a clear distinction between research-based intervention studies and best practice-based school improvement projects. In research-based intervention studies we must convince researchers that they have to navigate the cyclical innovation process, deciding when the recursive bootstrapping process is over and the stabilization process begins. Following Levin & O'Donnell (1999), we view classroom-based studies and design experiments as preliminary studies. These researchers acknowledged the importance of these studies within the different stages of instructional research inquiry (see our discussion on recursive bootstrapping). Our message to intervention researchers is that they have to go beyond understanding a phenomenon and accumulate classroom-based, scientifically credible evidence using the four criteria specified by Levin & O'Donnell (comparison, replication, relationship, and elimination). In the school improvement projects we can give teachers and educators insight into the processes that underlie students' choice of processing modes and regulation strategies. By providing this insight, they are better equipped to observe the changing psychological needs of their students and adapt their instruction strategy to the local conditions. For example, we can inform teachers that we had naive conceptions about the students' information-processing mode and the way that motivation and anxiety affect their choice of processing modes. Our exploratory research allowed us to generate some testable hypotheses about possible side effects of teaching according to the ILS instruction principles. We can alert teachers that teaching according to the ILS instruction principles may create a different backdrop for students who predominantly use SLP or DLP, or who have access to both processing modes. We can also inform them that students' perception of the ILS learning environment affects their motivation and their coping with anxiety in differential ways. These are testable hypotheses that we are currently investigating in our intervention studies.

We would like to conclude this chapter with a few recommendations for researchers who are, like us, struggling with the complexity of classroom-based interventions and the evaluation of powerful learning environments. Firstly, teachers who participate in large-scale innovation projects expect that the interventions are tailor-made to their characteristic needs. If a proposed treatment is not tailor-made to their needs, they will adapt it "en route" thus causing many problems for the collection of solid and credible research evidence. Many researchers give teachers and educators the impression that they are presenting them with a set of open-ended design principles. This invites teachers to replace some principles and drop others. In order to ensure teacher adherence to a target instruction strategy, their involvement in the design of this strategy is required. Hence, partnerships should be set up for planning and implementing powerful learning environments in the classroom (see also De Corte 2000). Secondly, the instruction principles that are tested in the intervention studies should be clearly formulated and limited to a small set of core principles. More often than not, researchers include too many instruction principles in the target instruction strategy. At this juncture we would like to refer to the famous principle formulated by Miller half a century ago (Miller 1956). It still applies: The chunks of information that a person can simultaneously process in short-term memory is seven plus or minus two. The fact that

45% of our teachers spontaneously reduced the number of instruction steps to a manageable set, i.e. a set that they could easily remember, name and use is a case in point.

We realize that these recommendations are rather general, yet we have observed that they are not always applied in practice. Designing and evaluating novel learning environments has become increasingly popular, but persuading school managers, teachers and teacher consultants to implement instruction strategies in the appropriate way, to monitor the realization of these principles "en route", and to find appropriate comparison groups to draw valid conclusions about their effectiveness has proved to be a challenging, but stimulating task for researchers involved in the design of powerful learning environments.

References

Boekaerts, M. (1997). Self-regulated learning: A new concept embraced by researchers, policy makers, educators, teachers, and students. *Learning and Instruction, 7*, 161–186.

Boekaerts, M. (2002). Bringing about change in the classroom: Strengths and weaknesses of the self-regulated learning approach. *Learning and Instruction, 12*, 589–604.

Boekaerts, M., & Minnaert, A. (2003). Assessment of students' feelings of autonomy, competence, and social relatedness: A new approach to measuring the quality of the learning process through self-assessment. In: M. S. R. Segers, F. J. R. C. Dochy, & E. C. Cascallar (Eds), *Optimising new modes of assessment: In search of quality and standards* (pp. 225–246). Dordrecht, The Netherlands: Kluwer Academic Publishers.

Campbell, D. T., & Stanley, J. C. (1966). *Experimental and quasi-experimental designs for research*. Chicago: Rand-McNally.

Cobb, P. (1994). Where is the mind? Constructivist and socio-cultural perspectives on mathematical development. *Educational Researcher, 23* (7), 13–20.

Cobb, P. (1996). Where is the mind? A coordination of socio-cultural and cognitive constructivist perspectives. In: C. T. Fosnot (Ed.), *Constructivism: Theory, perspectives, and practice* (pp. 34–52). New York: Plenum.

Corno, L., & Rohrkemper, M. (1985). The intrinsic motivation to learn in classrooms. In: C. Ames & R. Ames (Eds), *Research on motivation in education: The classroom milieu* (pp. 53–90). New York: Academic Press.

De Corte, E. (2000). Marrying theory building and the improvement of school practice: A permanent challenge for instructional psychology. *Learning and Instruction, 10*, 249–266.

De Jong, P. (1988). An application of the prototype scale construction strategy to the assessment of student motivation. *Journal of Personality, 56*, 487–508.

Entwistle, N. (1992). *The impact of teaching on learning outcomes in higher education — A literature review*. Edinburgh: University of Edinburgh, Centre for Research on Learning and Instruction.

Judd, C. M., & Kenny, D. A. (1981). *Estimating the effects of social interventions*. Cambridge: Cambridge University Press.

Kazdin, A. E. (1999). Overview of research design issues in clinical psychology. In: P. C. Kendall, J. N. Butcher, & G. N. Holmbeck (Eds), *Handbook of research methods in clinical psychology* (pp. 3–30). New York: John Wiley & Sons.

Lange, A., Dehghani, B., & Beurs, E. de (1995). Validation of the Dutch adaptation of the Buss-Durkee Hostility Inventory. *Behavioral Research Therapy, 33*, 229–233.

Levin, J. R., & O'Donnell, A. M. (1999). What to do about educational research's credibility gaps? *Issues in Education, 5,* 177–229.

Miller, G. A. (1956). The magical number seven plus or minus two. *Psychological Review, 63,* 81–87.

Minnaert, A., & Boekaerts, M. (2002, January). *Monitoring students' quality of working in groups: Towards a multi-perspective and reflective assessment procedure.* Paper presented at the 15th Annual International Congress for School Effectiveness and Improvement (ICSEI) in Copenhagen, Denmark.

Pintrich, P. R., & De Groot, E. V. (1990). Motivational and self-regulated learning components of classroom academic performance. *Journal of Educational Psychology, 82,* 33–40.

Rozendaal, J. S. (2002). *Motivation and information processing in innovative secondary vocational education.* Doctoral dissertation, Leiden University.

Rozendaal, J. S., Minnaert, A., & Boekaerts, M. (2003). Motivation and self-regulated learning in secondary vocational education: Information processing type and gender differences. *Learning and Individual Differences, 13,* 273–289.

Seifert, T. (1995). Characteristics of ego- and task-oriented students: A comparison of two methodologies. *British Journal of Educational Psychology, 65,* 125–138.

Slavin, R. E. (1996). Research on co-operative learning and achievement: What we know, what we need to know. *Contemporary Educational Psychology, 21,* 43–69.

Van de Ven, A. H., Polley, D., Garud, R., & Venkaraman, S. (1999). *The innovation journey.* New York: Oxford University Press.

Van Grinsven, C. C. M. (2003). *Leeromgevingen in het Middelbaar Beroeps Onderwijs en hun effect op motivatie en strategiegebruik* [Learning environments in Secondary Vocational education and their effect on motivation and strategy use]. Doctoral dissertation, Leiden University.

Van Velzen, J. H. (2002). *Instruction and self-regulated learning: Promoting students' (self-) reflective thinking.* Doctoral dissertation, Leiden University.

Vermunt, J. D. (1992). *Leerstijlen en sturen van leerprocessen in het hoger onderwijs – Naar procesgerichte instructie in zelfstandig denken* [Learning styles and regulation of learning in higher education – Towards process-oriented instruction in autonomous thinking]. Amsterdam: Swets & Zeitlinger.

Vermunt, J. D. (1998). The regulation of constructive learning processes. *British Journal of Educational Psychology, 68,* 149–171.

Volet, S., & Järvelä, S. (Eds) (2001). *Motivation in learning contexts: Theoretical advances and methodological implications.* Amsterdam/New York: Pergamon.

West, M. A. (1990). The social psychology of innovation in groups. In: M. A. West, & J. L. Farr (Eds), *Innovation and creativity at work: Psychological and organizational strategies* (pp. 309–333). Chichester: John Wiley.

Winne, P. H., & Perry, N. E. (2000). Measuring self-regulated learning. In: M. Boekaerts, P. Pintrich, & M. Zeidner (Eds), *Handbook of self-regulation* (pp. 531–566). San Diego, CA: Academic Press.

Witteman, H. P. J. (1997). *Styles of learning and regulation in an interactive learning group system.* The Netherlands: Nijgh & Van Ditmar Universitair.

Chapter 6

Investigating Ways of Enhancing University Teaching-Learning Environments: Measuring Students' Approaches to Studying and Perceptions of Teaching

Noel Entwistle, Velda McCune and Jenny Hounsell

Introduction

This chapter describes the early stages of a research project into "Enhancing teaching-learning environments in undergraduate courses" (the ETL project — see http://www.ed.ac.uk/etl). The project is part of a major Teaching and Learning Research Programme (TLRP) established by the U.K. Economic and Social Research Council (ESRC) that is intended to carry out collaborative research with practitioners to bridge the gap between researchers and "end-users". Within the ETL project, the intention is to work with colleagues in university departments to discuss ways in which findings from research can help to create more powerful learning environments for students. We take the term "powerful learning environment" to refer not to any predetermined set of characteristics. Rather it describes designs of the curriculum, and arrangements for teaching and learning, that are found to maximise the overall engagement of students in their studying and the quality of the learning outcomes achieved, for particular students in specific settings. While research findings can be used to suggest generic features to act as guidelines for setting up teaching-learning environments, in higher education the marked differences across subject areas and university contexts (including contrasting student intakes) suggest systematic differences in the nature of powerful learning environments. Those differences represent the main focus of our investigation.

The ETL project is now nearing the end of the second of its four years' duration and involves two forms of collaboration. The research team is drawn from three universities — Edinburgh (which is the lead institution), Coventry and Durham, and we will be collaborating with some 15 departments, drawn from five subject areas — electronic engineering, cell and molecular biology, economics, history, and media and communication studies — chosen to ensure contrasts in subject matter and approaches to teaching and learning. The departments have been selected to represent all the main institutional types in British higher education. During the first year, reviews of the literature were carried out, along with the development of data gathering instruments. We began pilot work with several departments during the second year, and this chapter focuses on that work, paying particular attention to our attempts to describe teaching-learning environments and students' perceptions of them. The research design involves working with departmental partners, first to collect base-line data about the existing situation within a particular course unit. We then negotiate with them a collaborative initiative designed to enhance the teaching-learning environments in ways indicated by the base-line evidence and by previous research findings and theoretical frameworks. The data involve descriptions of the teaching-learning environment drawn from documents and staff interviews, questionnaire measures of students' orientations, approaches to studying and perceptions of the environment, and group interviews with students about their experiences. The effects of this "tailor-made intervention" will then be assessed, using the same data gathering procedures as before.

This chapter is concerned with measuring major components and dimensions of teaching-learning environments in higher education. After looking briefly at some of the main concepts used in *student learning research* (Biggs 1999), it reports the development of student questionnaires designed to measure approaches to studying and perceptions of the teaching-learning environment. The development of the environment questionnaire necessitated a thorough review of the literature to establish what represented high quality or powerful teaching-learning environments within higher education. Our preliminary analyses indicate some main factors within students' perceptions of the environments they have experienced, and indicate the relationships between these and their reported approaches to studying.

Previous Research on Student Learning

What is understood to be high-quality student learning will obviously differ both within and between the subject areas involved in the project, and a more complete description of what colleagues and students in these areas are seeking to achieve will emerge as the research progresses. We will gradually be developing an understanding of what are seen as high-quality learning outcomes in these subject areas and what kinds of learning help students to achieve these outcomes. In this chapter, we will focus on the more generic literature that has informed the development of the questionnaires we are using. One key theme within this work is the considerable body of research begun in the mid-1970s by Marton and his co-workers (Marton & Säljö 1976, 1997).

The key concept emerging from the initial work was the approach to learning with its categories of deep and surface, to which was subsequently added an approach to studying described variously as strategic (Entwistle & Ramsden 1983) or achieving (Biggs 1987). The strength of this conceptualisation has been to focus attention not only on differences in the ways in which students go about their academic work, but also on how differing types of teaching and assessment affect those approaches. A number of studies have linked the deep and strategic approaches to positive learning outcomes in higher education, although the findings do vary, probably due to differences in the extent to which understanding is explicitly rewarded in the assessment procedures (Entwistle & Tait 1990; Marton 1976; Marton & Säljö 1976, 1997; Provost & Bond 1997; Tait *et al.* 1998; Trigwell & Prosser 1991; Van Rossum & Schenk 1984).

There is now a set of concepts which describe aspects of students' learning affecting the approaches to learning and studying they choose to adopt. While there would not be general agreement about which concepts to include, several probably would attract broad support. Students' prior educational experiences are reflected in their conceptions of learning (Marton & Säljö 1997; Säljö 1979) or epistemological beliefs (Hofer & Pintrich 1997; Perry 1970), and also in their reasons for studying and learning orientations (Beaty *et al.* 1997). A deep approach seems to be encouraged by more sophisticated conceptions and epistemological beliefs and by intrinsic learning orientations (Entwistle 2000; Morgan & Beaty 1997; Van Rossum & Schenk 1984; Vermunt 1996, 1998).

This body of research offers a clear and relatively straightforward conceptual framework for thinking about students' learning in higher education. But how complete is it and how firm is its evidential basis? Many of the interview studies are based on small samples in specific subject areas, while inventory studies assume that students can accurately, and will honestly, describe how they study. In striving for simplicity and parsimony, the conceptual bases of the most popular inventories have left out some important aspects of studying (Entwistle & McCune, in press). Not only does more emphasis need to be put on concepts such as self-regulation (Schunk & Zimmerman 1998) and emotion (Volet 2001), but also on ideas coming from social psychology and sociology stressing learner identity (Mentowski 2000), collaboration in learning, and "communities of practice" (Wenger 1998). In our current project, we have managed to incorporate some of these additional aspects into our inventory on approaches to studying, but others were outside our particular concerns and have been omitted.

The very popularity of the student learning conceptualisations has been criticised as creating a hegemony that effectively excludes alternative theoretical approaches to teaching and learning (Webb 1997); but their strength lies in the description of a recognisable reality in accessible and parsimonious terms.

Development of a Learning and Studying Questionnaire (LSQ)

As already indicated, two questionnaires have been developed within the project. The first of these (LSQ) has been designed to indicate students' general learning orientations and approaches to studying as they embark on the target module. The second (Experiences of Teaching and Learning Questionnaire, ETLQ) focuses on the ways students have actually studied that module and on their perceptions of the teaching-learning environment they experienced during it. In this way, it should be possible to detect any differences in approach (general to specific) and relate these to aspects of the environment. However, the much stronger test will be to see whether any detectable changes are found during the following year, in relation to the particular changes in teaching and learning that are to be introduced through the "collaborative initiatives".

The LSQ consists of four sections. The first section contains ten items covering learning orientations, defined as "all those attitudes and aims which express the student's individual relationship with a course of study and the university" (Beaty *et al.* 1997: 76). The categories, derived from interviews with students, reflect four main functions of higher education — academic, vocational, personal and social — and two distinctive kinds of interest in the courses being taken — extrinsic and intrinsic. Two additional items cover, firstly, "independence" — the idea that higher education will develop self-confidence and the self as a person (France & Beaty 1998) and, secondly, "lack of purpose", which represents a negation of the defined orientations. Factor analyses of this group of items for different sub-samples suggest a clear single factor covering all four aspects of intrinsic interest (academic, vocational, personal and social) to which "independence" is also related, but the extrinsic items and "lack of purpose", although showing some commonality, do not hold together consistently.

The second section contains nine items covering the reasons for taking a particular course unit. These items were selected to parallel the more general intrinsic and extrinsic learning orientations, and factor analyses confirmed the existence of two groupings, described as extrinsic and intrinsic reasons. The final (fourth) section is a single item asking students to rate on a nine-point scale how well they have been doing on the course so far, and based, where possible, on the actual grades obtained.

The third, and longest, section of the questionnaire is a 36-item *Approaches to Learning and Studying Inventory (ALSI)* developed from earlier inventories — initially, the *Approaches to Studying Inventory (ASI)* (Entwistle & Ramsden 1983) and, most recently, the *Approaches and Study Strategies Inventory for Students (ASSIST)* (Tait *et al.* 1998). The continued development of this inventory has been described elsewhere (Entwistle & McCune, in press), culminating in the version designed for the current project. As before, the wording of each item has been carefully chosen to make it colloquial, and pilot studies were used to reduce the length of the new inventory to 36 items and to establish the scale structure. (A report of these analyses can be found on the project web site at http://www.ed.ac.uk/etl.) The resulting *Approaches to Learning and Studying Inventory (ALSI)* contains five scales. *Deep approach* is defined explicitly by a combination of intention and process, with items covering "intention to understand" together with the associated thinking processes of "relating ideas" and "use of evidence" that parallel Pask's holist and serialist strategies (Pask 1976). Additional items have been included to cover aspects of constructivist thinking (Phillips 2000), and these link closely with the earlier items describing "relating ideas". An additional scale — *monitoring studying* — was created by combining items describing "monitoring understanding", "monitoring generic skills" and "monitoring study effectiveness". This scale is empirically related to deep approach, but is conceptually distinct, describing metacognitive aspects of learning and studying. The *surface approach* covers four aspects — "unreflective studying", "unthinking acceptance", "memorising without understanding" (Meyer 2000), and "fragmented knowledge" (Meyer 1991). The final main factor in the *RASI* was described as a "strategic approach" (Tait *et al.* 1998), but since then successive changes have gradually lost the more obvious strategic elements in this domain, and it is now more concerned with organised study and directed effort. The original factor is now covered by two scales, one indicating *organised studying* (including time management), and the other *effort management* (including concentration).

Descriptions of the Teaching-Learning Environment

The term *teaching-learning environment* was used in the project title to cover a broad range of potential influences on student learning, both within and beyond particular course units. Our discussions identified an extensive and varied set of concepts that had been used to describe this overarching notion. The resulting concept map is too large to present here; at the broadest level it described the social, cultural and political contexts within which higher education operates. It then covered institutional and departmental contexts, as well as disciplinary and professional contexts. Narrowing down even further, as shown in Figure 1, it indicated aspects of course design and organisation, teaching and assessing course content, staff-student relationships, and of the student cohort on a particular course.

The concepts shown in Figure 1 are those most directly related to the experiences of students, and likely to have a noticeable impact on learning and studying; the effects of the specific institutional and disciplinary contexts are indicated simply by the box at the centre of the diagram. This map helped to fix the meaning of the term "teaching-learning environment" as we are using it, but our project is attempting to find ways of "enhancing" the environments currently provided to students, in ways which encourage greater engagement with the subject matter and higher quality learning. In other words, we are seeking to create powerful learning environments with a specific focus. We have thus had to identify not just descriptive concepts, but also the particular aspects of teaching-learning environments that seem most likely to affect student engagement with studying and the quality of learning achieved.

Early work on the influences of the contexts within which learning takes place showed that a deep approach was related to what students perceive as "good teaching" and "freedom in learning" (choice in what and how to learn), while a heavy work load was linked to a surface approach (Entwistle & Ramsden 1983; Entwistle 1998a). It has subsequently been established that multiple-choice questions and short-answer tests tend to induce surface approaches, while more open forms of assessment (certain types of essay, authentic problems and project reports) seem to encourage deep approaches (see, for example, Scouller 1998). But it is students' *perceptions* of the teaching and assessment procedures, rather than the methods themselves, that show the strongest relationships with the learning of the individual student (Entwistle 1998a, 1998b; Ramsden 1997).

The effects of different forms of teaching and assessment led researchers to investigate differences in the ways in which university teachers describe their teaching and carry it out. From interview research came a set of concepts paralleling the work on student learning. Staff apparently differ in both their conceptions of teaching and their approaches to teaching, based on a series of overlapping categories that distinguish a

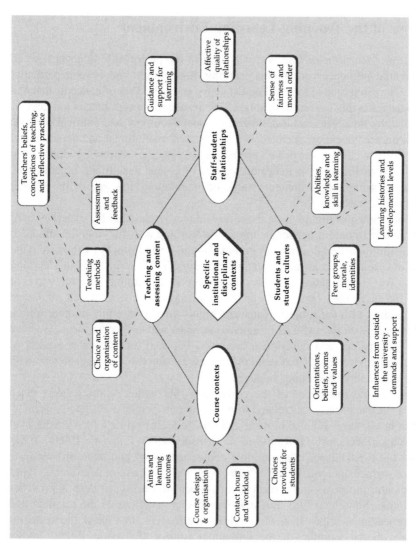

Figure 1: Conceptual map of the "inner" teaching-learning environment.

teacher-focus linked to *information transmission* from a *student-focus* with an emphasis on *encouraging conceptual change* (Prosser & Trigwell 1999).

University teachers' conceptions of teaching presumably have their origins in their prior experience and beliefs, and these conceptions seem to influence decisions about how to design courses and how to teach and assess them (Prosser & Trigwell 1999). Within this conceptual framework, a sophisticated, integrated conception of teaching with a focus on the conceptual development of the student, will lead to teaching and assessment methods that emphasise and support the students' understanding, and so encourage a deep approach to studying (Entwistle & Walker 2002). There is now clear evidence that the approaches to teaching actually adopted, and the ways in which students perceive them, do affect the approaches to studying that students adopt (Trigwell *et al.* 1999). However, the extent to which conceptions directly, or consciously, translate into equivalent action is much less certain (Eley 2002). The research can also create a misleading impression that strong and direct links have been established between teaching and learning; the findings indicate patterns of general relationships, but obscures the many additional factors involved. The experienced reality still involves a complex and dynamic interplay of attitudes, emotions, and pressures among the people involved, and a variety of influences from the social and academic environments provided for the students.

The student learning research has, nevertheless, clarified thinking about the relationship between teaching and learning in important ways. For example, it has led to a recognition of the importance of *constructive alignment* (Biggs 1999) within any "constructivist" teaching-learning environment. Each element among the teaching, learning and assessment activities experienced by students has to be designed to induce or support an active, deep approach in the students. In the ETL project, we shall be considering, more broadly, how the environments of the units we are studying might be better aligned to achieve the kinds of high-quality learning sought by staff in those contexts. We shall also be drawing on other curriculum frameworks, such as *Teaching for Understanding*, that suggest how to develop a curriculum systematically so as to help students focus their efforts on developing their understanding (Wiske 1998).

Ideas drawn from cognitive apprenticeship (Collins *et al.* 1989) suggest additional ways in which teachers can use the environment to foster high-quality thinking. And De Corte (1995, 2000) has used this model to develop specially designed learning materials that teachers use in carefully controlled ways to create powerful learning environments. These involve:

- provision of authentic, open problems and learning materials presented in a variety of formats and designed to make connections with students' previous knowledge and interests;
- teaching methods which arouse interest, activate prior knowledge, clarify meanings, and model appropriate learning strategies and reflective processes;
- specific learning strategies specified in detail, with these props removed by degrees to encourage subsequent self-regulation of studying; and
- students monitoring their own strategies and discussing them with other students, to produce a classroom culture that encourages reflection on process.

Although De Corte and his co-workers have worked mainly in school settings, reviews of the literature related to higher education, and derived from several theoretical bases, produced a virtually identical set of suggestions for practice (Tynjälä 1997; Vermetten 1999).

Other research has looked at the amount of support that students need, and in particular at the balance between external regulation and self-regulation of studying (Vermunt 1998). Students coming straight from school expect to be given considerable support by their teachers, but often do not receive it, even during their first year at university. Vermunt & Verloop (1999) suggest that teachers need to create "constructive friction" by gradually reducing the amount of support they provide, challenging students to develop their own ways of learning for themselves. However, "destructive friction" may occur if too little support is provided, leaving the students unable to bridge the gap to the type of learning required at university.

Studies by Perry (1970) and Taylor (1986) have also suggested the importance of challenging students' existing ideas or beliefs as a way of provoking development. And Säljö (1982) found that the conceptions of learning of some of the students in his research were changed by their realisation that the learning currently required of them differed from what they had used previously. Snyder (1971) noted that students' sense of their progress in relation to tasks in higher education can have a powerful effect on their sense of their worth as students, suggesting that challenges must be made sensitively, particularly with inexperienced students.

Gaining access to the discourse of a discipline seems to be a gradual and difficult process. Hounsell (1987) argues that it often requires profound changes in students' thinking and thus cannot just be "made" to happen. He suggests this process will be best facilitated through dialogue that takes the students' perspective into account in exploring and developing these ideas, arguing that simple information-giving is unlikely to be sufficient. Anderson (1997) found that students only gradually gain access to the practices of a discipline over the course of years of tutorials in which tutors gradually challenge and shape their students' understanding within a supportive climate permeated by a sense of fairness and moral order. The extent to which this process could be facilitated by more explicit discussions about the assumptions underlying assessments is not yet clear, but some such process is needed to overcome the difficulties that students have in understanding the feedback they are given.

Development of the *Experiences of Teaching and Learning Questionnaire* (ETLQ)

The preceding review of the literature provided an emerging description of some of the aspects of a powerful teaching-learning environment within higher education that are likely to encourage engagement with the subject matter, a deep approach, and high-quality learning within the discipline or professional area. The second ETL questionnaire was designed to capture students' approaches to studying on the *specific course unit*, and their perceptions of that particular teaching-learning environment. This *Experiences of Teaching and Learning Questionnaire* (ETLQ) has five sections. The first contains a short form of the *Approaches to Learning and Studying Inventory* in which the students are asked to describe how they actually had been studying within the target course unit (in contrast with the first questionnaire which asked about their more *general* approaches to studying). The second section is another inventory that covers the students' perceptions of the teaching and learning experienced on the course unit, and is described below. The third section asks about the demands that students felt the course unit made in terms of knowledge requirements and learning processes, while the fourth section parallels those aspects in relation to what they felt they had actually gained from the unit (knowledge gains and learning process gains). The final section is again a single item asking students how well they felt they had done in the course unit they had just been taking.

The items describing students' perceptions of the teaching-learning environment were derived partly from the review of the literature, the main aspects of which were identified in the conceptual map (Figure 1), and partly from an examination of previous inventories (not included here). Some of the aspects were not suitable for assessing in an inventory format and were sought through qualitative analyses of group interviews with students. To provide an initial structure for the students, the items were set out in a logical framework, which was then checked through the item factor analysis shown in Table 1. The five factors were quite closely correlated, indicating a single general factor of favourable responses towards the course unit.

Maximum likelihood factor analysis was carried out with rotation to simple structure; five factors were indicated by the scree plot and presented the clearest pattern matrix, explaining 41% of the variance. Factor loadings above 0.25 are shown, with only one item (20 — web pages) failing to have any sizeable loading. Factor I loaded on *aims, organisation and alignment*, but also picked up organisational aspects of teaching (items 9 and 15), together with an item indicating alignment of assessment (item 31). Factor II describes *encouraging learning* with an emphasis on "ways of thinking" in the discipline, with the items on "choice" also forming part of this factor in conceptually understandable ways. The third factor picks up most of the items related to *assessment, assignments and feedback*, with the strongest loadings in this sample relating to the provision of good feedback on student work. Factor IV brings together all the items relating to staff and students and seems to describe a *supportive climate* within the course unit, although in one sub-group analysis peer support separated out from staff support, and was less closely related to the other factors. The final factor describes *evoking interest*, with weaker loadings relating to a perception of relevance.

Altogether, these initial item analyses are very encouraging in suggesting a set of coherent scales describing perceptions of the aspects of the teaching believed to be influential in encouraging a deep approach and high-quality learning. The set of items may seem, at first sight, to be similar to those found in the conventional student course evaluation forms. The crucial difference, however, is that our items focus on particular teaching and learning activities and so draw attention to specific aspects of these activities that are worth considering further.

Table 1: Item factor analysis of students' perceptions of the teaching-learning environment.

	I	II	III	IV	V
			Factor		
ORGANISATION AND STRUCTURE OF THE COURSE (N = 472)					
Aims and organization					
1. It was clear to me what I was supposed to learn in this course unit.	**0.61**				
2. The topics seemed to follow each other in a way that made sense to me.	**0.60**				
4. The course unit was well organized and ran smoothly.	**0.43**				
Alignment					
6. What we were taught seemed to match what we were supposed to learn.	**0.59**				
14. The different types of teaching (lectures, tutorials, labs, etc.) supported each other well.	0.36				
18. How this unit was taught fitted in well with what we were supposed to learn.	**0.53**				
Choice					
3. We were given a good deal of choice over how we went about learning.		0.32			
5. We were allowed some choice over what aspects of the subject to concentrate on.		0.38			
TEACHING AND LEARNING					
Teaching for understanding					
7. We were encouraged to look for links between this unit and others.		0.29			
9. The handouts and other materials we were given helped me to understand the unit.	**0.40**				
13. The teaching encouraged me to rethink my understanding of some aspects of the subject.		0.42			
15. Plenty of examples and illustrations were given to help us to grasp things better.	**0.46**				
20. The web pages provided by staff helped me to understand the topics better.					

Table 1: Continued.

	Factor				
	I	**II**	**III**	**IV**	**V**
TEACHING AND LEARNING (Continued)					
Awareness of learning skills and ways of thinking					
10. On this unit I was prompted to think about how well I was learning and how I might improve.		0.29			
12. We weren't just given information; staff explained how knowledge is developed in this subject.	0.31	0.33			
16. This unit has given me a sense of what goes on 'behind the scenes' in this subject area.		**0.51**			
17. The teaching in this unit helped me to think about the evidence underpinning different views.		**0.67**			
28. Staff helped us to see how you are supposed to think and reach conclusions in this subject.			0.33		
Evoking interest and enjoyment					
8. I can imagine myself working in the subject area covered by this unit.					**0.61**
11. I could see the relevance of most of what we were taught in this unit.	0.33				0.35
19. This unit encouraged me to relate what I learned to issues in the wider world.		0.33			0.38
22. I found most of what I learned in this course unit really interesting.					**0.74**
26. I enjoyed being involved in this course unit.					**0.75**
STUDENTS AND TEACHERS					
Teachers' enthusiasm and responsiveness to students					
23. Staff tried to share their enthusiasm about the subject with us.				0.30	
25. Staff were patient in explaining things which seemed difficult to grasp.			0.30	0.35	
27. Students' views were valued in this course unit			0.33	0.36	

Table 1: Continued.

	I	II	III	IV	V
			Factor		
STUDENTS AND TEACHERS (Continued)					
Climate and relationships					
21. Students supported each other and tried to give help when it was needed.				**0.74**	
24. Talking with other students helped me to develop my understanding.				**0.65**	
29. I found I could generally work comfortably with the other students on this unit.				**0.61**	
30. This course unit provided plenty of opportunities for me to discuss important ideas.				0.37	
ASSESSMENTS AND OTHER SET WORK					
Alignment and clarity					
31. It was clear to me what was expected in the assessed work for this course unit.	**0.45**		**0.45**		
33. I could see how the set work fitted in with what we were supposed to learn.	0.42		0.37		
Focusing on understanding					
34. You had to really understand the subject to get good marks in this course unit.			(0.23)		
36. Doing the set work helped me to think about how evidence is used in this subject.			**0.52**		
38. To do well in this course unit, you had to think critically about the topics.			0.36		
39. The set work helped me to make connections to my existing knowledge or experience.			0.37		
Supporting learning and awareness of learning skills					
32. I was encouraged to think about how best to tackle the set work.			**0.55**		
35. The feedback given on my work helped me to improve my ways of learning and studying.			**0.67**		
37. Staff gave me the support I needed to help me complete the set work for this course unit.			**0.58**		
40. The feedback given on my set work helped to clarify things I hadn't fully understood.			**0.72**		

Table 1: Continued.

Intercorrelations between factors		I	II	III	IV	V
Factor I	Organization, structure and alignment	—				
Factor II	Encouraging learning	0.34	—			
Factor III	Assessments, assignments and feedback	0.35	0.41	—		
Factor IV	Supportive climate	0.45	0.41	0.24	—	
Factor V	Evoking interest	0.50	0.33	0.32	0.34	—

Relationships Between Scales

As data has so far only been collected from a small number of departments, only preliminary analyses can be reported. So far, complete sets of data from both questionnaires have been obtained from 216 students, and these have been used to examine correlations between the various sub-scales (reported at http://www.ed.ac.uk/etl) and to carry out an exploratory factor analysis. To provide an indication of our early findings, we selected scales from both questionnaires to cover the main aspects being investigated, drawing on all of the sections (see the earlier description of the development of ETLQ). The scales used were based on item factor analyses with the exception of the extrinsic orientation, which did not form a clear factor. Instead, a single item was chosen to indicate a lack of purpose. The approaches to studying items produced five factors, as described previously, but for this analysis the six factor solution for the perceptions items was preferred to bring out the distinction between staff and peer support.

Table 2 presents the pattern matrix for the three-factor solution of a maximum likelihood analysis rotated to simple structure, being the most readily interpretable solution, although only accounting for 37% of the variance. Loadings below 0.25 have been omitted, with the exception of self-ratings on attainment that were retained to aid interpretation. Factor I covers all the aspects of students' perceptions of the teaching-learning environment previously identified (although very weakly in peer support), together with a rating of the course unit as having relatively light demands for knowledge, combined with strong perceived gains in both knowledge and learning processes. It is also associated with a deep approach, accompanied by monitoring studying and a low level of surface approach. The second factor has its major loadings on the most positive aspects of studying, with weaker positive loadings on intrinsic orientation, on light demands on study processes combined with gains in them, and on attainment, together with negative loadings on both surface approach and a lack of purpose. The inter-correlation between these two factors shows a strong link between perceptions of the teaching learning environment and approaches to studying, although not necessarily just in that direction.

The final factor is created through the strong inter-correlation between the two self-ratings of attainment and shows low self-ratings being associated with a perception of

Table 2: Factor loadings from a factor analysis of selected scales.

Scales	Factor I	Factor II	Factor III
LSQ — Learning orientations/reasons for taking unit			
Intrinsic orientation		0.29	
Negative orientation — lack of purpose		–0.34	
Intrinsic reasons for choosing course unit			
Extrinsic reasons for choosing course unit			0.26
ETLQ — Approaches to studying specific to the unit			
Deep approach	0.29	0.51	
Surface approach	–0.29	–0.33	0.33
Monitoring studying	0.26	0.55	
Organized studying		0.65	
Effort management		0.80	
Perceptions of the teaching-learning environment			
Organization, structure and alignment	0.78		
Encouraging learning	0.83		
Assessments, assignments and feedback	0.74		
Staff supportive	0.70		
Peers supportive	0.26		
Evoking interest	0.73		
Light knowledge demands perceived	0.41		–0.29
Light demands for learning processes perceived		0.25	
Perceived knowledge gains	0.60		
Perceived learning process gains	0.40	0.30	
Self-rating of attainment prior to taking the unit (LSQ)		0.31	–0.64
Self-rating of attainment on the unit (ETLQ)	(0.21)	(0.22)	–0.51

(Loadings less than /0.25/ have been omitted except for those relating to attainment).

Inter-correlation between factors	I	II	III
I Positive perceptions of the unit	—		
II Positive aspects of studying	0.41	—	
III Low self-ratings on attainment	–0.16	–0.05	—

heavy knowledge demands from the unit, combined with extrinsic reasons for choosing the unit and a surface approach to studying. Correlations with the other two factors indicate that the self-rating of attainment is linked, although quite weakly, with perceptions of the teaching-learning environment, but insignificantly with approaches to studying.

Although this analysis is based on a relatively small, unrepresentative sample, the findings are promising, suggesting that the questionnaires are working effectively. If these findings are confirmed from the much larger samples now available, we should have good evidence of the relationships between approaches to studying and perceptions of teaching. The interviews and the investigation of the effects of the collaborative initiatives are then intended to help in unravelling the nature of these relationships.

Discussion and Conclusion

In a continuing programme of research in Leuven, Janssen (1996) has explored ways of describing the different ways of studying adopted by students. A parsimonious and theoretically justifiable framework has been developed to reflect the main components of effective learning and studying by students, and the range of study behaviours it describes overlaps considerably with what is now included within our *LSQ*. As a result of extensive work with lecturers (De Neve 1991), it was also possible to create an equivalent framework describing teaching behaviours that are perceived by both students and staff as supporting high-quality learning. This work has demonstrated the importance of thinking about teaching in relation to the specific kinds of learning staff wish to encourage, and Janssen's ideas informed our thinking in considering those components of a supportive teaching-learning environment related to teaching.

It proved difficult, however, to bring together ideas within that specific theoretical perspective and relate them directly to the conceptual frameworks used in our own study. Ongoing research by Vermetten *et al.* (2002) is closer to our own approach. They have been investigating the effects of introducing *student-oriented education* in several degree courses in Tilburg University in The Netherlands, comparing the inventory responses of students who had experienced the innovation with students who had not. In their first study, they found rather weak evidence of differences, but it did suggest that authentic materials worked on in groups would be an important element of a "powerful learning environment". The effect was, however, detectable only where this approach formed a prominent part of the curriculum. The weak effects otherwise found were attributed to the different ways in which the notion of "student-oriented education" had been implemented by staff. The possibility, noted in the literature, that there would be marked individual differences in the ways in which students responded to any teaching-learning environment was confirmed in another study (Vermunt & Verloop 1999), with individual students appreciating

> aspects of the environment which suited their own way of learning. For example, deep and highly self-regulated learners indicated that they do not need detailed manuals, whereas surface/undirected learners would like to have them more often . . . (The former group) are inclined to apply

their own methods, and find their own answers, and use instructional measures merely as a check … This study makes it clear that direct influence of instructional measures does not take place, which may explain the … generally … unsatisfactory impact of educational reforms on the learning processes of students. It seems that students prefer, and act, as if there is "congruence" between the learning environment and their own learning habits. However, (constructive) "friction" between teaching and learning is often necessary to make students change and to develop their learning strategies (p. 281).

It is still too early in our own project to carry out equivalent analyses, but it is an aspect which will become important as we seek to interpret any possible effects of teaching-learning environments on students' approaches to studying (or the lack of such general effects). However, insights derived from our current study and other recent work are already leading us to re-conceptualise our own view of the influences of teaching-learning environments on student learning. Specifically, we are becoming more aware of the difficulty, through any single conceptual framework, of adequately representing the complexity and the social dynamics of the inter-relationships that exist in everyday teaching and learning.

We have also become more concerned about the match between research findings and everyday reality in the descriptions in the research literature of both deep and surface approaches to studying and the teaching-learning environment. In an earlier contribution, we reflected on the contrast between ways of describing approaches to studying and attempts at understanding the individual circumstances affecting the likelihood of a student changing a well-established approach (Entwistle *et al.* 2001). The concepts and categories used to describe general differences in studying provide a valuable analytic framework for considering the ways individuals study, but also tend to disguise the complexity of the everyday situation. In the current study, a similar pattern is beginning to emerge in describing the context within which studying takes place. We have outlined a conceptual framework and indicative research findings that suggest how various aspects of a teaching-learning environment may affect student engagement with the course, a deep approach, and high-quality learning outcomes. But the notion of constructive alignment reminds us that any such environment is a complex composite of many interacting influences that need to be aligned towards supporting deep active learning, if there is to be any overall effect.

Finally, it is worth drawing attention to the contrast between the research reported here and much of the other work on powerful learning environments. Rather than using theory to suggest interventions which are then implemented by teachers, here we are working *with* university teachers to draw from previous research, and from the initial findings within a specific course setting, a mutually agreed collaborative initiative for improving the learning environment. This approach has the considerable advantage of ensuring that the changes introduced are fully understood and are wholly acceptable to the teacher, although it sacrifices the experimental control of the more conventional investigations.

Acknowledgments

The ideas being developed in the ETL project are a product not only of the whole project team, but also of colleagues in our collaborating departments. Besides the authors, the researchers on the project team, at the time this paper was written, were Charles Anderson, Liz Beaty (Coventry Centre Director), Glynis Cousin, Kate Day, Dai Hounsell (Project Co-Director), Ray Land, and Nicola Reimann. Erik Meyer (Durham Centre Director) was a member of the sub-group that worked on the preparation of both questionnaires, while Hilary Tait (Napier University) was also involved in the early stages of developing the LSQ.

References

Anderson, C. D. B. (1997). Enabling and shaping understanding through tutorials. In: F. Marton, D. J. Hounsell, & N. J. Entwistle (Eds), *The experience of learning* (2nd ed., pp. 184–197). Edinburgh: Scottish Academic Press.

Beaty, E., Gibbs, G., & Morgan, A. (1997). Learning orientations and study contracts. In: F. Marton, D. J. Hounsell, & N. J. Entwistle (Eds), *The experience of learning* (2nd ed., pp. 72–88). Edinburgh: Scottish Academic Press.

Biggs, J. B. (1987). *Student approaches to learning and studying*. Melbourne: Australian Council for Educational Research.

Biggs, J. B. (1999). *Teaching for quality learning*. Buckingham: SRHE and Open University Press.

Collins, A., Brown, J. S., & Newman, S. E. (1989). Cognitive apprenticeship: Teaching the crafts of reading writing and arithmetic. In: L. B. Resnick (Ed.), *Knowing, learning and instruction: Essays in honor of Robert Glaser* (pp. 453–494). Hillsdale, NJ: Erlbaum.

De Corte, E. (1995). Fostering cognitive growth: A perspective from research on mathematics. *Educational Psychologist, 30*, 37–46.

De Corte (2000). Marrying theory building and the improvement of school practice. *Learning and Instruction, 10*, 249–266.

De Neve, H. M. F. (1991). University teachers thinking about lecturing: Student evaluations of lecturing as an improvement perspective for the lecturer. *Higher Education, 22*, 63–91.

Eley, M. G. (2002). *Changes in teachers' conceptions of teaching. Do they prompt teacher development or are they outcomes from teacher development?* Paper presented at the 22nd Annual Conference of the Society for Teaching and Learning in Higher Education, McMaster University, Hamilton, Canada, June 12–15, 2002.

Entwistle, N. J. (1998a). Improving teaching through research on student learning. In: J. J. F. Forest (Ed.), *University teaching: International perspectives* (pp. 73–112). New York: Garland.

Entwistle, N. J. (1998b). Approaches to learning and forms of understanding. In: B. Dart, & G. Boulton-Lewis (Eds), *Teaching and learning in higher education* (pp. 72–101). Melbourne: Australian Council for Educational Research.

Entwistle, N. J. (2000). Approaches to studying and levels of understanding: The influences of teaching and assessment. In: J. C. Smart (Ed.), *Higher education: Handbook of theory and research* (Vol. 15, pp. 156–218). New York: Agathon Press.

Entwistle, N. J., & McCune, V. S. (in press). The conceptual bases of study strategy inventories in higher education. *Educational Psychology Review*.

Entwistle, N. J., McCune, V. S., & Walker, P. (2001). Conceptions, styles, and approaches within higher education: Analytical abstractions and everyday experience. In: R. J. Sternberg, & L.-F. Zhang (Eds), *Perspectives on thinking, learning and cognitive styles* (pp. 103–136). Mahwah, NJ: Erlbaum.

Entwistle, N. J., & Ramsden, P. (1983). *Understanding student learning*. London: Croom Helm.

Entwistle, N. J., & Tait, H. (1990). Approaches to learning, evaluations of teaching, and preferences for contrasting academic environments. *Higher Education, 19*, 169–194.

Entwistle, N. J., & Walker, P. (2002). Strategic alertness and expanded awareness within sophisticated conceptions of teaching. In: N. Hativa, & P. Goodyear (Eds), *Teacher thinking, beliefs and knowledge in higher education* (pp. 15–40). Dordrecht: Kluwer.

France, L., & Beaty, L. (1998). Layers of motivation: Individual orientations and contextual influences. In: S. Brown, S. Armstrong, & G. Thompson (Eds). *Motivating students* (pp. 113–122). London: Kogan Page.

Hofer, B. K., & Pintrich, P. R. (1997). The development of epistemological theories: Beliefs about knowledge and knowing and their relation to learning. *Review of Educational Research, 67*, 88–140.

Hounsell, D. (1987). Essay writing and the quality of feedback. In: J. T. E. Richardson, M. W. Eysenck, & D. Warren Piper (Eds), *Student learning: Research into education and cognitive psychology* (pp. 109–119). Milton Keynes: OUP.

Janssen, P. J. (1996). Studaxology: The expertise students need to be effective in higher education. *Higher Education, 31*, 117–141.

Marton, F. (1976). What does it take to learn? Some implications of an alternative view of learning. In: N. J. Entwistle (Ed.), *Strategies for research and development in higher education* (pp. 32–43). Amsterdam: Swets & Zeitlinger.

Marton, F., & Säljö, R. (1976). On qualitative differences in learning. I — Outcome and process. *British Journal of Educational Psychology, 46*, 4–11.

Marton, F., & Säljö, R. (1997). Approaches to learning. In: F. Marton, D. J. Hounsell, & N. J. Entwistle (Eds), *The experience of learning* (2nd ed., pp. 39–58). Edinburgh: Scottish Academic Press.

Mentowski, M., & Associates (2000). *Learning that lasts. Integrating learning, development, and performance in college and beyond*. San Francisco: Jossey-Bass.

Meyer, J. H. F. (1991). Study orchestration: The manifestation, interpretation and consequences of contextualised approaches to studying. *Higher Education, 22*, 297–316.

Meyer, J. H. F. (2000). Variation in contrasting forms of "memorising" and associated observables. *British Journal of Educational Psychology, 70*, 163–176.

Morgan, A., & Beaty, L. (1997). The world of the learner. In: F. Marton, D. J. Hounsell, & N. J. Entwistle (Eds), *The experience of learning* (2nd ed., pp. 217–237). Edinburgh: Scottish Academic Press.

Pask, G. (1976). Styles and strategies of learning. *British Journal of Educational Psychology, 46*, 128–148.

Perry, W. G. (1970). *Forms of intellectual and ethical development in the college years: A scheme*. New York: Holt, Rinehart & Winston.

Phillips, D. C. (Ed.) (2000). *Constructivism in education*. Chicago, IL: National Society for the Study of Education.

Prosser, M., & Trigwell, K. (1999). *Understanding learning and teaching: The experience of higher education*. Buckingham: SRHE & Open University Press.

Provost, S. C., & Bond, N. W. (1997). Approaches to studying and academic performance in a traditional psychology course. *Higher Education Research and Development, 16*, 309–320.

Ramsden, P. (1997). The context of learning in academic departments. In: F. Marton, D. J. Hounsell, & N. J. Entwistle (Eds), *The experience of learning* (2nd ed., pp. 198–216). Edinburgh: Scottish Academic Press.

Säljö, R. (1979). *Learning in the learner's perspective. I. Some common-sense conceptions.* (Report 76). Gothenburg: University of Gothenburg, Department of Education.

Säljö, R. (1982). *Learning and understanding.* Gothenburg: Acta Universitatis Gothoburgensis.

Schunk, D. H., & Zimmerman, B. J. (1998). *Self-regulated learning: From teaching to self-regulated practice.* New York: Guilford Press.

Scouller, K. (1998). The influence of assessment method on students' learning approaches: Multiple choice question examination versus assignment essay. *Higher Education, 35,* 453–452.

Snyder, B. R. (1971). *The hidden curriculum.* New York: Knopf.

Tait, H., Entwistle, N. J., & McCune, V. (1998). ASSIST: A reconceptualisation of the *Approaches to Studying Inventory.* In: C. Rust (Ed.), *Improving student learning: Improving students as learners* (pp. 262–271). Oxford: Oxford Centre for Staff and Learning Development.

Taylor, M. (1986). Learning for self-direction in the classroom: The pattern of a transition process. *Studies in Higher Education, 11,* 55–72.

Trigwell, K., & Prosser, M. (1991). Improving the quality of student learning: The influence of learning context and student approaches to learning on learning outcomes. *Higher Education, 22,* 251–266.

Trigwell, K., Prosser, M., & Waterhouse, F. (1999). Relations between teachers' approaches to teaching and student learning, *Higher Education, 37,* 57–70.

Tynjälä, P. (1997). Towards expert knowledge? A comparison between a constructivist and a traditional learning environment in the university. *International Journal of Educational Research, 31,* 357–442.

Van Rossum, E. J., & Schenk, S. (1984). The relationship between learning conception, study strategy and learning outcome. *British Journal of Educational Psychology, 54,* 73–83.

Vermetten, Y. (1999). *Consistency and variability of student learning in higher education.* Ph.D. Thesis, Katholieke Universiteit Brabant.

Vermetten, Y. J., Vermunt, J. D., & Lodewijks, H. G. (2002). Powerful learning environments? How university students differ in their response to instructional measures. *Learning and Instruction, 12,* 263–284.

Vermunt, J. D. (1996). Metacognitive, cognitive and affective aspects of learning styles and strategies: A phenomenographic analysis. *Higher Education, 31,* 25–50.

Vermunt, J. D. (1998). The regulation of constructive learning processes. *British Journal of Educational Psychology, 68,* 149–171.

Vermunt, J. D., & Verloop, N. (1999). Congruence and friction between learning and teaching. *Learning and Instruction, 9,* 257–280.

Volet, S. (2001). Understanding motivation and learning in context: A multi-dimensional and multi-situative perspective. In: S. Volet, & S. Jarvela (Eds), *Motivation in learning contexts.* London: Pergamon.

Webb, G. (1997). Deconstructing deep and surface: Towards a critique of phenomenography. *Higher Education, 33,* 195–212.

Wenger, E. (1998). *Communities of practice: Learning, meaning and identity.* London: Cambridge University Press.

Wiske, M. S. (1998). What is teaching for understanding? In: M. S. Wiske (Ed.), *Teaching for understanding: Linking research with practice* (pp. 61–85). San Francisco, CA: Jossey-Bass.

Chapter 7

The Power of Learning Environments and the Quality of Student Learning

Jan D. Vermunt

Introduction

Today's society is characterized by an enormous growth in the available knowledge and information. In earlier times, education was aimed at teaching students the knowledge and skills of a subject domain with which they could practice a profession for the rest of their lives. Nowadays, it is impossible to master a subject domain completely at graduation. There is too much to know and to be skilled in, and what we know and can do today is out of date in a couple of years. Simons *et al.* (2000) therefore advocate the view that graduates should foremost have acquired skills that enable them to keep on learning throughout their lives, to think independently, to work together and to regulate one's own learning and thinking. They describe this "new learning" as new learning outcomes, new types of learning processes, and new teaching methods that are both demanded by today's society and stressed by contemporary psychological and instructional theories. Thus, new scholars are people that have good knowledge of their discipline and good competence to keep on growing and developing. They have the knowledge, attitudes and skills needed to continuously update one's knowledge of the discipline and develop one's own professional competencies, independently and in cooperation with others, also after graduation from the educational institute. New scholars never stop learning!

This chapter explores which learning environments are suitable to foster this new learning. The focus will be on a number of innovative teaching methods and practices that all claim to represent powerful learning environments and that all are applied already on a rather large scale in higher education. More specifically, the question will be addressed whether these innovative teaching methods suffice to realize new forms of learning. An attempt will be made to identify major components and dimensions of powerful learning environments for the acquisition in students of educational objectives focusing on conceptual understanding, higher-order cognitive and metacognitive skills, and self-regulated learning.

The Quality of Student Learning

Discussions about the quality of education focus ever more on the quality of students' learning processes. In ancient times "good teaching" meant that the teacher explained the subject matter well. Whether students also understood the subject matter well was mainly seen as their own responsibility. Nowadays we only speak of good teaching when the teacher has brought the students to good learning. But what is "good learning"?

The last decade our research team has done a series of studies on the way students learn and the factors that influence that way of learning. Again and again four qualitatively different forms of learning were found. Reproductive learning means that students study the subject matter thoroughly, in detail, and try to remember it as well as possible so they can reproduce it on a test. In meaning-directed learning a student tries to discover connections in the study materials, to gain an overview, to be critical towards the material and to understand it as well as possible. A student who learns in an application-directed way especially tries to imagine the subject matter concretely and to think about how it can be used in practice. Undirected learning means that students actually do not know well how to approach their studies best. For example, they fall back on learning habits from secondary education that no longer work in higher education. Teachers generally consider meaning- and application-directed learning as "good" for students in higher education and undirected learning as undesirable. Conversations often get heated when the value of reproductive learning is discussed: some consider that a necessity, others reprehensible.

What way of learning, students practice in their studies turns out to be related to their beliefs about learning and teaching (learning conceptions) and their study motivation and attitudes (learning orientation) (see also Entwistle & McCune, in press). This probably explains why Vermetten *et al.* (1999) found students' way of learning to be relatively stable over time and over different courses, but certainly not unchangeable. This means that the way of teaching, or the learning environment in general, also matters.

Another dimension on which learning processes can be scaled is the degree of independence with which they are conducted. All kinds of learning and regulation activities can, to a more or less degree, be performed by the students themselves or by agents in the learning environment, such as teachers, tutors, computers, and textbook authors. Independent learning means that students mainly perform those learning and regulation activities themselves. When students work together on learning tasks one may speak of cooperative, or collaborative learning. In this type of learning, teaching can be more or less directive, and so the degree of independence that is expected from groups of cooperating students may vary. Learning alone is the opposite of learning together and is certainly not the same as independent learning.

Our research group has investigated various aspects of students' learning processes, mainly in higher education. In qualitative and quantitative studies we have investigated, among other things, what cognitive, affective and metacognitive learning and thinking strategies students employ in their studies and how that usage is associated with personal and contextual factors (Vermunt 1996, 1998). Vermetten *et al.* (1999) studied the degree to which students' learning strategy use is consistent or variable over time and across situations, and the degree to which that strategy use is influenced by factors like goal orientation, personality, perception of the learning environment and interpretation of instructional measures. Ajisuksmo & Vermunt (1999) compared Dutch and Indonesian students in their learning patterns and found cultural differences in the way both groups study and regulate their learning processes. Schellings *et al.* (1996) focused on one particular cognitive learning strategy, selecting information from text, and found individual differences in the way students adapt that strategy to different types of learning tasks. In another study we could identify forms of dissonance between students' approaches to studying, their conceptions of learning and their study motivation: the phenomenon that study behavior does not correspond to study beliefs and motives. Students who showed evidence of dissonance often achieved low examination scores (Vermunt & Verloop 2000).

Recently, our research group has broadened it's focus to include teachers' and student-teachers' learning processes. For example, Oosterheert & Vermunt (2001) identified the learning patterns of student-teachers in training programs that combine learning and working, with special attention for the role of emotions in this learning. Zanting *et al.* (2001) studied whether, and in what way, student-teachers try to utilize the practical knowledge of experienced teachers at their practice schools. A study of Van Eekelen *et al.* (submitted) showed that experienced teachers do not, as is often thought, stop learning new things after some time. However, their learning turned out to be far less planned than is usually the case in regular educational situations.

So far, we have been able to discern various qualities of learning: undirected, reproduction-directed, meaning-directed, application-directed, self-directed and cooperative. Questionnaire research shows that students generally appreciate it very much when they can work independently with tasks or assignments that are derived from daily practice (e.g. Steenkamp *et al.* 2000).

The Case of Problem-Based Learning

A couple of years ago the present author took up a position as professor of educational development and research at the Faculty of Health Sciences of Maastricht University in the Netherlands. One of the main responsibilities was to initiate a process of educational innovation in the faculty. From its start in 1976, this university has adopted the model of problem-based learning (PBL) in all its faculties. PBL was initially developed in 1974 at McMaster University in Canada (Barrows & Tamblyn 1980). The approach has been very successful in Maastricht: the university attracted large numbers of students and in national surveys the students rated the university as first or among the first in quality of teaching for many years. Basically, the PBL-method as practiced at the university has not changed during the 25 years of its success. However, the last decade other universities have begun innovating their traditional teaching models too, and have copied parts of the successful problem-based learning formula. Moreover, students seemed to get a bit bored with the system after some years. Therefore, the dean of the faculty asked our department to critically evaluate the PBL-method against new insights from learning and educational theory and to propose innovations in the educational practices based on that analysis. In view of what has been said in the introduction of this chapter, the leading question was formulated as follows: "Does problem-based learning represent a learning environment to educate people to new scholars, to people who never stop learning?" (Vermunt 2000).

In problem-based learning students work in small groups of about ten persons, the tutorial group, at trying to understand and explain problems. The starting point for the learning process is a problem: a short description of a phenomenon about which students should acquire knowledge. The problem-based way of working is systematically structured into seven steps, the "seven-jump": (1) clarify terms and concepts not readily understood; (2) define the problem; (3) analyze the problem; (4) summarize the various explanations of the problem into a coherent model; (5) formulate learning objectives; (6) individual study activities outside the group; and (7) report and synthesize the newly acquired information. In the tutorial group students analyze the problem and generate learning objectives: questions to which they should find an answer through individual study. After a period of individual study, the students meet again and report what they have learned about the problem. The acquired information is discussed, critically evaluated and integrated. During their work in the tutorial group the students are guided by a tutor, whose main task is to facilitate the learning and group processes (Barrows & Tamblyn 1980; Schmidt & Moust 1998). Mostly, the tutorial group meets twice a week for sessions of two hours. During the first hour of such a meeting students try to understand and explain the problem discussed previously and report what they have found when studying the literature (step 7). During the second hour students discuss a new problem and formulate learning objectives for individual study with regard to this new problem (step 1 to 5). Besides these tutorial group meetings, students also attend practicals, skills trainings and a few lectures. At the end of a block period, that typically lasts between five to eight weeks, a block test is administered, after which a new block period starts with another theme. In the remainder of this chapter this form of problem-based learning will be called "classical PBL".

What types of learning does this classical PBL environment foster? PBL is a rather structured, small scale teaching method, that counteracts undirected learning by students. In its original set-up PBL is also explicitly aimed at discouraging reproductive, test-directed learning. PBL certainly seems aimed at promoting deep-level, meaning-directed learning, because students have to search for explanations and understandings for mostly meaningful problems. To a certain extent PBL also encourages application-directed learning, since the tasks and problems are to a more or lesser extent derived from professional practice. As one may expect, these matters strongly depend however on the quality and variety of the tasks and problems used. What PBL certainly encourages is cooperative learning, because students work together in the tutorial group at analyzing, discussing, and explaining problems. At first sight PBL also stimulates self-directed learning, because students have, for example, to formulate learning objectives, search for relevant resources, and study these individually.

Teaching methods that aim to teach students to learn and think independently, are characterized by a gradual transfer in the task division in the learning process from teaching agents (teachers, books, computers, study materials, etc.) to the students

Regulation of learning processes

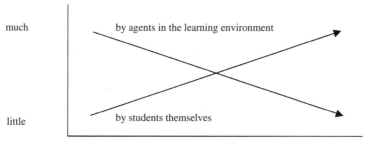

Figure 1: Gradual transfer of control over students' learning processes from agents in the learning environment (teacher, tutor, book, computer) to the students during their university studies.

(Vermunt & Verschaffel 2000). In the beginning, explicit external regulation and support are offered to the students. This support is gradually withdrawn as students' mastery increases. At the same time, students are taught how to perform this control over their learning processes themselves. Learning to learn and think independently then means a gradual transfer of learning functions from the learning environment to the students, a gradual transition from external to internal (self-)regulation of learning (see Figure 1). Typically, the teaching method changes while students' self-regulatory skills increase. In this way students are continuously challenged to get a step further in the self-regulation of their learning and thinking. The ultimate goal is that students are willing and capable to keep on learning and developing in their professional domain and to never stop learning, also after finishing their school career.

Characteristic of most learning environments is that the teaching methods used *do not* change with the students' increasing self-regulative competencies. For example, in classical PBL the pattern of two tutorials a week, two problems a week, problems of a certain size, blocks of a fixed number of weeks, tutorial groups of a particular size, the regulating role of the tutor, and the "seven-jump" procedure to structure the problem-based way of working, stay about the same throughout the years. For first year students this learning method generally still constitutes a great challenge, since at secondary school they were not used to self-directed learning involving formulating learning objectives, looking for relevant resources, reporting back the learning results, and the like. And as it should be, during the first year many students get better in these skills that correspond to the degree of independence that is expected from them in PBL. But after the first year little changes: the learning method becomes a routine and the challenge stops to be there (see Figure 2).

Educational Innovation

The basic idea that underlies problem-based learning, namely that students acquire knowledge through active learning and trying to understand real-life problems, is still as

Regulation of learning processes

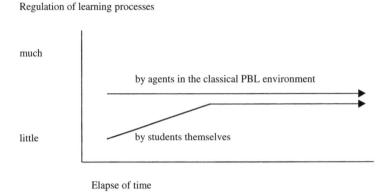

Figure 2: Constant control over stundents' learning processes by a classical problem-based learning environment.

topical as at the time the method was developed more than 25 years ago. What needs revitalizing and renovation are, in our view, the "hands and feet" with which this idea is made concrete in practice. A "seven-jump", two tutorials a week, rather small problems that can be explained or solved within two days of individual study, problems that are invented by the teachers, the size of tutorials groups of about ten students, the kind and degree of regulation exerted by the tutor, are all *certain realizations* of this basic idea that are, however, often raised to doctrine and presented as the only right way PBL should be conducted. But classical problem-based education is only one form of encouraging independent learning, besides other possibilities. Bouhuys (2000), for example, states that originally the "seven-jump" was mainly meant to offer support to students who had little experience with PBL.

At the annual conference of the American Educational Research Association in San Diego a couple of years ago, a dual educational program (combining learning and working), designed according to principles of problem-based learning (see above), was presented (Fessler & Ingram 1998). Student-teachers gave practice lessons at a school and attended classes at the university. The university's teaching method was problem-based in nature, but, contrary to what is usually the case in PBL, the problems were not invented by the university staff members but brought in by the students. They were based on problems the students had experienced in real-life teaching practice. Sometimes these problems were small, sometimes they were large. In the tutorial group meetings these problems were discussed and analyzed from the different practical experiences of the group members. Those aspects the group could not handle yet, learning objectives were formulated for, followed by search and study of the literature and a report meeting. An essential difference with classical PBL is the *ownership* of the problems that are dealt with: in this case the students owned the problems.

At an international conference on "Innovations in higher education" held in Helsinki in 2000, it was striking to see how creative some teachers had been in inventing new "hands and feet" for PBL. For example, especially for faculties with large numbers of students, the number of tutors needed for the small group tutorials may represent a problem. At the Faculty of Psychology of the University of Helsinki the rule that every tutorial meeting should be guided by a tutor was abandoned. Study groups of about four students were formed. These groups worked without a tutor or teacher at explaining problems that were introduced, discussed and reported in one meeting a week supervised by a staff member. Dependent on the goal of the meeting, the size of the group of students was varied in multiples of four (Nieminen & Pruuki 2000).

Eight Types of Learning Environments

Let us examine a number of widely used learning environments, or teaching methods, more in detail with regard to the degree of self-regulation, own initiative and responsibility they foster in students.

Traditional Teaching

This type of teaching was dominant at many universities in the previous century. The subject matter was determined completely by the teacher, often not in the form of cases, problems or tasks, but as books or chapters of which the content had to be known. The subject matter was explained and clarified in lectures. Sometimes there were seminars where the subject matter was deepened, problems were clarified, feedback on assignments was given, etcetera. At the end of a semester, or of a whole academic year, there was an exam period in which all subjects of the past period were assessed. In the sciences there were also quite a lot of practicals. The subject matter, learning objectives, study resources, criteria for the learning outcomes, assessment and feedback were all completely determined by the teachers. Students only had some freedom in the choice of their learning activities: their approaches to studying.

Assignment-Based Teaching

In assignment-based teaching, the main learning concept is guided self-study. Compared to traditional teaching there are less lectures, more assignments for self-study and more small working groups. The number of teaching hours is reduced to 30 to 40% of the total study time, thereby offering students more time for individual study. Students conduct their self-study guided by precise instructions in the assignments. In working groups students' results of their assignments are discussed and their learning is adjusted by the teachers. In this way, students actively and independently process the study materials in which they are intensively supervised by the course team (e.g. University of Limburg 2002). The regulation of students' learning processes is still mainly in the hands of the teachers: they largely decide about the subject matter, learning objectives, criteria for learning outcomes, assessment and feedback. In choosing the learning activities and study resources, students have more freedom and responsibility.

Classical Problem-Based Learning

In this teaching method, learning processes proceed in about the way as sketched above in the paragraph on "the case of problem-based learning". Students work in small groups of about ten persons, guided by a tutor, at understanding and explaining problems. In the tutorial group students analyze a problem and generate learning objectives. After a period of individual study they meet again and report to each other what they have learnt about the problem. Most often, the tutorial group meets twice a week; during such a meeting students report what they have learnt about one problem and they discuss the next new problem. At the end of a block period, a block test is administered.

PBL with Self-Directing Study Teams

In this type of learning environment, more self-regulation and initiative are expected from students than in classical PBL, as well as a more complex form of collaboration between students. Therefore, the difficulty level of this teaching method is higher. Groups of about four students are formed that work at study tasks of a varied nature, among which are the understanding and explanation of problems. They work according to the principles of collaborative learning: small groups, positive interdependency, individual responsibility, and equal contributions (Slavin 1996). During the small group work no tutor is present, and students take turns in fulfilling roles like chair and minutes writer. Once a week there is a class meeting guided by a teacher, where a number of those study groups are combined. In this meeting the learning progress is discussed, difficulties are solved, products of the different groups are compared, unclear matters are clarified and the acquired information is discussed, critically evaluated and integrated. Besides, the study work of the next week is discussed in advance. In comparison with classical PBL, the problems are bigger and more complex, students are more self-directive as a study team, tasks and problems do not necessarily need to be completed in one week, and group products need to be made besides individual products. Students also attend practicals, skills training and a few lectures. Assessment is based on the products that the students, individually and as teams, have made during the block as a result of working on the tasks (Vermunt 2000).

Project-Centered Learning

Project-centered learning is another rung further on the ladder of self-regulated learning and thinking: the problems addressed are again more complex in nature and the degree of self-regulation in learning and working expected from students is larger. The starting point of the learning process in project-centered learning is a project assignment or problem. This concerns authentic, real-life assignments that are often directly derived from professional practice. Sometimes students can choose from a number of assignments or problems to work on; they work in small groups (mostly 4–5 students) independently at the project assignment. Prior or parallel to the actual project work, often a phase of knowledge acquisition is designed via other methods, like PBL or lectures. The knowledge, understandings and skills of the domain that students acquire in this way, have to be applied to the project assignment.

Often, once a week the project group meets the supervising staff member, in which meeting progress is discussed, difficulties are solved and the next project phase is previewed. The project proceeds in phases that are rounded off with an assessment of process and product (see for example Kirschner 2000). The project results in a group product, for example a design, an advice, a plan, a proposition, and the like. At the end of a project block the products or outcomes made by the students are often presented to the whole group of students in the presence of the teachers and sometimes also the clients. The product is assessed along criteria that are made in advance. Often, also the project presentation is assessed in terms of content and form. Sometimes the knowledge acquisition is assessed separately and individually. Sometimes also individual portfolios are used to be able to assess the individual learning achievements and the contribution of the individual students to the group processes and products (see e.g. Westerterp 2000).

Self-Directed Specialization Learning

In the later years of studies in higher education often forms of self-directed specialization learning are applied that are individually supervised. A well-known example is the Master Thesis in the form of a report of empirical, literature or resources research. By then, students have acquired the common, basic knowledge base of the discipline and specialize in certain aspects of it, often based on individual interests. Sometimes also two or three students work together on such a project, when there are students with shared interests. Typically, projects like these have a somewhat longer duration (3–6 months) and knowledge acquisition about the specific subject is part of the project.

One or two staff members function as supervisors. Students write a research proposal in which the research problem, goals, activities, resources to be used, the projects outcomes aimed at, and the way of supervision are described. In essence this comes down to a study task or project assignment that the students formulate for themselves. This proposal is discussed with the supervisors, and based on their comments students revise the proposal before executing it. Further supervision is often tailor-made, depending for example on the research phase the student is in, the difficulty level of the project and the need for supervision, or the degree of self-regulation a student is capable of. After finishing the research report, it is evaluated based on criteria that were formulated beforehand. Sometimes also process criteria are included in the evaluation.

Dual Learning

In dual forms of learning, students combine two types of learning environments: studying at the university with learning from practice (e.g. Kirschner 2000). All university-based teacher education programs in the Netherlands, for example, are designed according to this teaching method, and have the format of one-year, postgraduate programs. From the beginning to the end student-teachers do teaching practice at a secondary school for about half of their study time. There they observe lessons from experienced teachers, conduct lessons themselves, do practice research, supervise pupils, consult their mentor teachers, and form part of the school organization as a whole. The other half of their study program consists of the theoretical part of their studies at the university. In this way, students have three important sources to learn from: their own practical experiences, the practical knowledge of the mentor teacher and the other experienced teachers in the school, and the "theories" of learning, teaching and pedagogy offered and discussed at the university (see e.g. Zanting *et al.* 2001).

The crucial issue in such training programs is how the different kinds of knowledge students acquire, can be brought together into a coherent knowledge base. This requires another teaching concept than with a singular, non-dual trajectory. The sequence in which the subject matter should be dealt with is, for example, no longer mainly based on subject-logical arguments, but much more on concerns and learning needs that students develop during their practice work. When an inappropriate educational model is used, students develop three separate knowledge bases that are hardly interconnected. Especially Korthagen (2001) has done pioneering work in this area. In view of integrating theoretical and practical knowledge, on the one hand, and developing a subjective theory of the discipline or profession, on the other, he gives a central role to reflection on practical experiences. Many current Master programs are designed according to this model. Boud (1999) speaks of "work-based learning" in this context. Evaluation of learning progress sometimes takes place with portfolios (Driessen *et al.* 2003). When the theoretical part of the program is designed according to principles of problem-based learning, students bring cases or problems into the tutorial group that they have experienced in practice, as a starting point for a problem-based learning cycle.

Autodidactic Learning

In autodidactic learning, learners themselves decide about all aspects of their learning processes: the problems addressed, the learning objectives, the learning activities, the resources to be consulted, the learning outcomes aimed at, and assessment and feedback. Learners are their own teachers, so to speak. Of course, people can choose to share some aspects of this learning with colleagues or others, and decide to give feedback to each other (Van der Linden *et al.* 2000). In education, at least in the formal curriculum, fully autodidactic learning will hardly show up, if only because students' learning achievements will ultimately always be evaluated by the institution, that, in doing so, guarantees the quality of her diplomas.

The Construction of a Curriculum in Terms of Learning Environments

When we categorize the eight types of learning environments discussed above, according to the degree of regulation that is conducted over the course of students' learning processes, the following picture emerges (see Table 1).

All seven last-mentioned learning environments encourage active learning on the basis of problems, cases or assignments, but they show an increasing pattern in the degree of self-regulation demanded from the students and in the size and complexity of the problems students work on. They vary in the kind of cooperation and the degree of interdependence that is expected from the students. From all aspects of the learning process, learning activities are the first to be put into the hands of the students. Assessment and feedback are the last ones. Learning environments 3 to 7 are small-scale and student-oriented in nature. Of these five learning environments, classical problem-based learning demands the lowest degree of self-regulated learning. When we consider it important that students learn to learn and think ever more independently, it seems imperative that the teaching methods change as students' skill in self-regulated learning increases over time.

More specifically, this leads to a curriculum that is typified by a gradual, systematic decrease in external regulation by agents in the learning environment, and a gradual increase in students' self-regulation (transfer of regulation and control from environment to students). In the successive study years the types of learning environments may succeed one another: in the beginning assignment-based teaching, then successively classical problem-based learning, PBL with self-directing study teams, project-centered learning, self-directed specialization learning and dual learning. This principle should,

Table 1: The way various aspects of students' learning processes are regulated in the eight[a] learning environments on a dimension from teacher-regulated to student-regulated.

Learning process	Teacher-regulated		Shared regulation			Student-regulated
Problems/tasks/cases/ assignments	1 2 3		4 5	6	7	8
Learning objectives	1 2		3 4 5		6 7	8
Learning activities		1	2 3	4	5 6 7	8
Study (re)sources	1	2	3 4	5	6 7	8
Criteria learning outcomes	1 2 3 4		5	6	7	8
Assessment and feedback	1 2 3 4		5 6	7		8

[a]: 1 = traditional teaching; 2 = assignment-based teaching; 3 = classical PBL; 4 = PBL with self-directing study teams; 5 = project-centered learning; 6 = self-regulated specialization learning; 7 = dual learning; 8 = autodidactic learning.

of course, not be applied too rigidly, since variation is the source of all learning (Marton 1999). Getting acquainted with professional practice through small dual trajectories may also be very useful in the first years of some types of studies (for example, the medical curriculum), and self-directing study teams can evolve silently into project teams of project-centered learning. On the other hand, classical PBL may be the best teaching method in a block with difficult and new subject matter in the third year.

In this way, the development of self-regulation in student learning is fostered in two parallel tracks. First, in the course of the curriculum students are confronted with progressively more comprehensive and complex tasks, problems or assignments, that force them to use an ever bigger and more integrated array of competencies. Secondly, the amount of external regulation in the tasks and learning environments gradually decreases, so students get an ever more important role in deciding on the problems they want to work on, the learning objectives to pursue, the choice of learning activities, the search for appropriate resources, the criteria the learning outcomes should meet, and in monitoring the learning progress and evaluating the learning outcomes.

Elsewhere we named such an educational concept "process-oriented teaching", because it is aimed at the processes of knowledge acquisition and utilization (Simons 1997; Vermunt & Verschaffel 2000; Volet *et al.* 1995). It is based on an analysis of the interplays that may occur between the method of teaching and the way students learn and approach their studies (Vermunt & Verloop 1999). It is characterized by a gradual cutting down of the instructional regulation of learning processes, and calls increasingly for students' self-regulation of learning processes, individually and in groups. In our view this educational concept offers a good solution for the dissatisfaction that can be observed among university staff members where there is only one education model for a whole curriculum, as is the case in classical problem-based learning (e.g. Kuipers 2000). Besides, it is a model that offers a perspective to simultaneously improve the academic goal of "learning to think independently".

Bachelor — Master

As a result of the Bologna-declaration, in which the ministers of education of 29 European countries have agreed in 1999 to better tune their systems of higher education to each other, nowadays at many places in European higher education curricula are being reformed in terms of the Bachelor — Master model: a (three year) Bachelor phase that is mostly rather broad in nature, followed by a (one to two year) Master phase with a more specialized character. In this reform process, choices have to be made with regard to, among other things: the final objectives for both phases; the broadness versus specialization of both phases; the freedom of choice for students concerning their study package; working according to a major-minor system or not; the methods of learning, teaching and assessment; the civil effect of the Bachelor degree; and the open versus restricted admission to the Master phase.

The choice of teaching and assessment methods, or stated more generally, of the types of learning environments to be used, should in our view be based on the principles described above. This means, for example, assignment-based teaching, classical PBL,

PBL with self-directing study teams and project centered learning subsequently as dominant learning environments in the Bachelor phase, self-directed specialization learning and dual learning as dominant environments in the Master phase, and a general increase in the size and complexity of the problems students deal with. When the Bachelor degree also aims at a civil effect, in this phase also practice-directed, preferably dual components should be included. Offering freedom of choice to students generally promotes a deep approach to studying (Ramsden 1992) and self-regulation in learning. The final objectives of so-called "Colleges", broad Bachelor studies in which students can study a wide variety of disciplines, can be partly described in terms of cognitive, regulative and affective competencies ("learn to think academically").

Major Components and Dimensions of Powerful Learning Environments

All chapters in this book in some way attempt to identify major components and dimensions of powerful learning environments for the acquisition in students of educational objectives focusing on conceptual understanding, higher-order cognitive and metacognitive skills, and self-regulated learning. This chapter focused on a number of innovative teaching methods that all claim to represent powerful learning environments and that are all applied already on a rather large scale in higher-education practices.

A key feature of powerful learning environments resulting from this analysis is that they foster high-quality learning. Drawing on research in the field of student learning, in this chapter various qualities of student learning could be identified. High-quality learning leading to the attainment of conceptual understanding, higher-order cognitive and metacognitive skills, and self-regulated learning is meaning-directed, application-directed, and self-directed in nature, many times also involving student collaboration in small groups. Undirected and reproduction-directed learning represent lower-quality learning not likely leading to the acquisition in students of these educational objectives. Therefore, essential for learning environments to be powerful is that they foster students to adopt high-quality approaches to learning and discourage them to adopt lower-quality approaches.

A second key feature of powerful learning environments identified in this chapter is that the teaching method changes in response to students' increasing metacognitive, self-regulatory skills. Although this principle sounds very logical, it is not commonly practiced in innovative teaching methods like problem-based learning. Often, after a long time of exposure to a particular teaching method, a kind of ceiling effect seems to occur: students reach a point where they master the regulatory skills needed to be effective in that particular teaching method, and when the method does not change any further, students' self-regulatory skills do not further develop either. This was shown to be the case with classical PBL, but it is also the case with every teaching method, innovative or not, that is typified by an invariant, constant type of control over students' learning processes during a long time.

Unraveling this key feature of powerful learning environments, six components could be identified that together define the degree of control exerted over students' learning. All six may vary along a dimension from teacher-regulated via shared regulation to student-regulated: (1) the problems, cases, assignments or tasks students work on; (2) the learning objectives that direct the learning; (3) the learning activities students employ to learn; (4) the sources that are consulted; (5) the criteria the learning outcomes should conform to; and (6) the assessment and feedback procedures. The innovative learning environments that were analyzed in this chapter can all be characterized by their unique position on these six dimensions. The successive application of these learning environments in response to students' increasing metacognitive, self-regulatory skills may be a good operationalization of this second key feature.

A third key feature of powerful learning environments is the increasing complexity of the real-life problems used as an impetus for learning. The complexity of problems may vary along dimensions like clarity (many to few cues in the problem), abstraction (concrete to abstract), structuring (well-structured to ill-structured problems), size (a few days to a few months needed to solve, understand or explain the problem, and longer), distance to prior knowledge (small to large distance), number of aspects in the problem (unidimensional to multidimensional) and amount of irrelevant information in the problem description (little to much). To achieve educational objectives focusing on conceptual understanding and higher-order cognitive skills, the complexity of problems should increase in the run of a curriculum. This, again, is not an automatic practice in many of the innovative teaching methods we encountered in our analysis.

Educational Research and Development

In the years to come, a central issue in both theoretical and practical respect is the design and development of novel powerful learning environments, that are demanding towards students and that change with the increasing self-regulation and collaboration students are capable of. This means that research is needed to further unravel the learning processes, depth of processing, way of regulation and study behavior of students, the factors that influence these phenomena, and the consequences from this all for the design of powerful learning environments for the distinct stages of university studies. In addition, the learning processes of teachers being part of those learning environments should also be the subject of research, as well as the issue what constitutes powerful learning environments for (experienced) teachers to keep on learning in their professional practice. In cooperation between teachers, students and researchers novel forms of student-oriented education should be designed and developed for the different study phases as described above. These new types of learning environments have to be tried out in experiments and their effects on the quality and outcomes of student learning in those environments should be studied. In addition, new forms of powerful learning environments for teachers should be designed and developed, be tried out in experiments and be studied on their effects on the quality and outcomes of teacher learning processes.

References

Ajisuksmo, C. R. P., & Vermunt, J. D. (1999). Learning styles and self-regulation of learning at university: An Indonesian study. *Asia Pacific Journal of Education, 19* (2), 45–59.

Barrows, H. S., & Tamblyn, R. M. (1980). *Problem-based learning: An approach to medical education.* New York: Springer.

Boud, D. (1999, August). *Is problem-based learning sufficiently robust to meet the new challenges of professional work?* Paper presented at the 8th Conference of the European Association of Research on Learning and Instruction, Göteborg, Sweden.

Bouhuys, P. (2000, September). *Developing the learner's potential to learn.* Keynote address given at the international conference on "Innovations in higher education 2000", Helsinki, Finland.

Driessen, E. W., Van Tartwijk, J., Vermunt, J. D., & Van der Vleuten, C. P. M. (2003). Use of portfolios in early undergraduate medical training. *Medical Teacher, 25* (1), 18–23.

Entwistle, N., & McCune, V. (in press). The conceptual basis of study strategy inventories in higher education. *Educational Psychology Review.*

Fessler, R., & Ingram, R. (1998, April). *Assessing the impact of a school immersion-MAT program in the United States.* Paper presented at the annual conference of the American Educational Research Association, San Diego.

Kirschner, P. (2000). *The inevitable duality of higher education: Cooperative higher education.* Inaugural address, Maastricht University, The Netherlands.

Korthagen, F. (2001). *Linking practice and theory. The pedagogy of realistic teacher education.* Mahwah, NJ: Erlbaum.

Kuipers, H. (2000). *Het PGO is aan vernieuwing toe! Discussie notitie* [PBL is in need of renewal! Discussion paper]. Maastricht University, The Netherlands: Faculty of Health Sciences.

Marton, F. (1999, August). *Variatio est mater studiorum.* Opening address given at the 8th Conference of the European Association of Research on Learning and Instruction, Göteborg, Sweden.

Nieminen, J., & Pruuki, L. (2000, September). *How to support self-regulated learning? A report on an experimental course — applications of the PBL-method.* Paper presented at the international conference on "Innovations in higher education 2000", Helsinki, Finland.

Oosterheert, I. E., & Vermunt, J. D. (2001). Individual differences in learning to teach – relating cognition, regulation and affect. *Learning and Instruction, 11*, 133–156.

Ramsden, P. (1992). *Learning to teach in higher education.* London: Routledge.

Schellings, G. L. M., Van Hout-Wolters, B. H. A. M., & Vermunt, J. D. (1996). Individual differences in adapting to three different tasks of selecting information from texts. *Contemporary Educational Psychology, 21*, 423–446.

Schmidt, H. G., & Moust, J. H. C. (1998). *Probleemgestuurd onderwijs: Praktijk en theorie* [Problem-based learning: practice and theory]. Groningen, The Netherlands: Wolters-Noordhoff.

Simons, P. R. J. (1997). From romanticism to practice in learning. *Lifelong Learning in Europe, 1*, 8–15.

Simons, R. J., Van der Linden, J., & Duffy, T. (2000). New learning: Three ways to learn in a new balance. In: R. J. Simons, J. van der Linden, & T. Duffy (Eds), *New learning* (pp. 1–20). Dordrecht: Kluwer Academic.

Slavin, R. E. (1996, April). *Cooperative learning among students: Theory, research, and implications for active learning.* Paper presented at the annual conference of the American Educational Research Association, New York.

Steenkamp, F., Maljaars, W., & Blankesteijn, E. (Eds) (2000). *Keuzegids hoger onderwijs. Editie 2000–2001* [Choice guide higher education. Edition 2000–2001]. Amsterdam: Balans.

University of Limburg (2002). *Onderwijsontwikkelingsplan LUC/tUL. Bijlage 2: Actieplannen van faculteiten en schools* [Educational development plan University of Limburg. Appendix 2: Action plans of faculties and schools]. Diepenbeek, Belgium: University of Limburg.

Van der Linden, J., Erkens, G., Schmidt, H., & Renshaw, P. (2000). Collaborative learning. In: R. J. Simons, J. van der Linden, & T. Duffy (Eds), *New learning* (pp. 37–54). Dordrecht: Kluwer Academic.

Van Eekelen, I., Boshuizen, H., & Vermunt, J. (submitted). *Learning at work: Examples from the teaching profession.* Manuscript submitted for publication.

Vermetten, Y. J., Lodewijks, H. G., & Vermunt, J. D. (1999). Consistency and variability of learning strategies in different university courses. *Higher Education, 37*, 1–21.

Vermunt, J. D. (1996). Metacognitive, cognitive and affective aspects of learning styles and strategies: A phenomenographic analysis. *Higher Education, 31*, 25–50.

Vermunt, J. D. (1998). The regulation of constructive learning processes. *British Journal of Educational Psychology, 68*, 149–171.

Vermunt, J. (2000). *Studeren voor nieuwe geleerden: Over de kwaliteit van het leren* [Studying for new scholars: About the quality of learning]. Inaugural address, Maastricht University, The Netherlands.

Vermunt, J. D., & Verloop, N. (1999). Congruence and friction between learning and teaching. *Learning and Instruction, 9*, 257–280.

Vermunt, J. D., & Verloop, N. (2000). Dissonance in students' regulation of learning processes. *European Journal of Psychology of Education, 15*, 75–89.

Vermunt, J., & Verschaffel, L. (2000). Process-oriented teaching. In: R. J. Simons, J. van der Linden, & T. Duffy (Eds), *New learning* (pp. 209–225). Dordrecht: Kluwer Academic.

Volet, S., McGill, T., & Pears, H. (1995). Implementing process-based instruction in regular university teaching: Conceptual, methodological and practical issues. *European Journal of Psychology of Education, 10*, 385–400.

Westerterp, M. *et al.* (2000). *Electronische project omgeving voor Gezondheidswetenschappen. Activiteit 1: Onderwijskundig ontwerp* [Electronic project environment for Health Sciences. Activity 1: Instructional design]. Maastricht University, The Netherlands: Faculty of Health Sciences and McLuhan Institute.

Zanting, A., Verloop, N., & Vermunt, J. D. (2001). Student teachers eliciting mentors' practical knowledge and comparing it to their own beliefs. *Teaching and Teacher Education, 17*, 725–740.

Part III

Design and Application of Technological Tools to Support Learning in Powerful Learning Environments

Chapter 8

Informational Support in Designing Powerful Learning Environments

Jules Pieters, Renate Limbach and Ton de Jong

Introduction

In current practice of designing powerful learning environments (De Corte 1994), a constructive process of learning is emphasized, in which both environment and learner play an active role metaphorically addressed as participation (Sfard 1998). This contrasts with the classical instructional mode based on expository teaching that focuses on the provision of information. This change of focus has its impact on instructional design (e.g. Reigeluth 1999) and on the instructional design process (Hannafin *et al*. 1997).

Usually, instructional design models for expository teaching aim at the identification and classification of operational learning goals and the design of instructional material that brings learners to achieve these goals (e.g. Dick & Carey 1990; Rothwell & Kazanas 1992). In powerful learning environments this is clearly different. In discovery learning, the learning approach in our study, learners are invited to take the initiative in their learning process. When designing powerful discovery learning environments the designer does not always know which end goals the learner will achieve. More emphasis is placed on the development of learning tasks that will be carried out by the learner. Learners are expected to be increasingly responsible for their own knowledge construction process, and the designer does not need to specify in detail the learning path from begin-state to end-state.

This change in instructional design also influences the design process. Without normative learning goals, a linear design process seems less feasible. In the design practice a movement away from linear models is already visible. Considerable differences have been reported between the traditional normative approaches to designing instructional systems and how practitioners actually design instruction (Pieters & Bergman 1995; Rowland 1992; Tessmer & Wedman 1995). Whereas almost all models have a linear (waterfall) structure, research shows that the actual design process may not be linear at all (e.g. De Hoog *et al.* 1994; Jonassen *et al.* 1996; Richey 1995).

Our study addresses the design of powerful learning environments with a constructive and discovery perspective. Discovery learning is a highly self-directed and constructive way of learning with the purpose of acquiring deep, flexible, and transferable knowledge. Learners are invited to construct their knowledge by extracting the required information from the learning environment by stating hypotheses, doing experiments, and drawing conclusions, in short by acting as a scientist (De Jong & Van Joolingen 1998).

The study is conducted in the context of the SimQuest authoring system. SimQuest is an authoring system for creating educational computer simulations embedded in a powerful environment. A typical learning environment (application) created with SimQuest allows learners to engage in an activity of discovery learning with a simulation, supported by instructional measures (e.g. assignments, explanations, process monitoring facilities) embedded in the environment. SimQuest supports the full process of authoring simulation-based learning environments by templates in an object oriented way, from creating the simulation model to defining the instructional interaction of the learning environment with the learner. For an extensive description of SimQuest, see Van Joolingen and De Jong (in press). In SimQuest, both aspects of instructional design as discussed above are taken into account. First, the instructional design process can be followed in a very flexible way, without predetermined starting points. This flexibility in designing with the SimQuest system is extensively described in Kuyper *et al.* (2001). The current study focuses on the second aspect, the instructional design itself. In this study we aim to develop, within SimQuest, support for the instructional design of discovery learning environments. This support takes the form of an on-line information system that gives the designer background information and examples on the many aspects of discovery learning and discovery learning environments. Our assumption was that designers are not familiar with this kind of environment and would therefore need additional information. We investigated the use, satisfaction, and efficacy of this on-line information system.

Method

In our method we followed Yin's approach of a multiple-case study (Yin 1994) with three phases. In the first phase, three cases of designing a simulation-based discovery learning environment using SimQuest with a first version of the information system are observed. In the second phase, a "control study" is performed in which the designers designed without the help of the information system. If a comparison of the results after the first and the second phase encourages the idea that the information system supports the designer during the design task, a shift to the third phase is made. This third phase is similar to the first phase, but now with a larger number of participants and with an information system that has been improved on the basis of the experiences in the first phase.

Participants

Students of the Educational Science and Technology Programme at the University of Twente participated in all three phases. In the first and second phase three designers participated, and in the third phase nine designers participated. Participants were experienced in the practical educational field (some of them were teachers). All were supposed to have some prior knowledge in the physics subject "kinematics" since this was the topic of the SimQuest application that was developed. This prior knowledge was a prerequisite for participation in the study.

Design Task

The authoring environment SimQuest was used for designing a discovery learning session in the field of kinematics for students in middle vocational training. The task was performed in an adaptable SimQuest application that contained an archive with domain-related elements. This means that designers not only had "empty" building blocks in the library of the SimQuest authoring environment but also ready made models and assignments in the domain of kinematics.

Information System

The information system is a hypertext-based part of SimQuest that presents all kinds of information on discovery learning and the design of discovery learning environments. The specific content of the information system was based on an analysis of questions designers may have (see Limbach 2001; Pieters *et al.* in press). From this analysis we also inferred that the information presented should be short, goal-directed, and just-in-time. The information system was created as a two-dimensional card-tray, with two dimensions: (a) the (sub) topics on which information is available; and (b) a classification of the information. Based on the results of previous studies (Limbach 2001), we decided upon a classification of the information about powerful learning environments consisting of four categories indicated by four different "questions": "What is?" provides information of a definition, description or explanation of a (sub)design aspect; "Example" provides textual or visual example(s) of a (sub) design aspect; "Considerations" provide suggestions about a (sub) design aspect; and "Background" provides information for example about results of studies on the use of assignments in discovery learning environments. The complete information system contained 12 topics about discovery learning, approximately 50 subtopics, and 500 information cards.

Figure 1 presents the upper level topics (and not the subtopics) of the information system.

Designers were able to get access to the information system through a general "advice" button. They also had direct context sensitive access to the information system from specific editors in SimQuest (e.g. when editing a "specification assignment" and

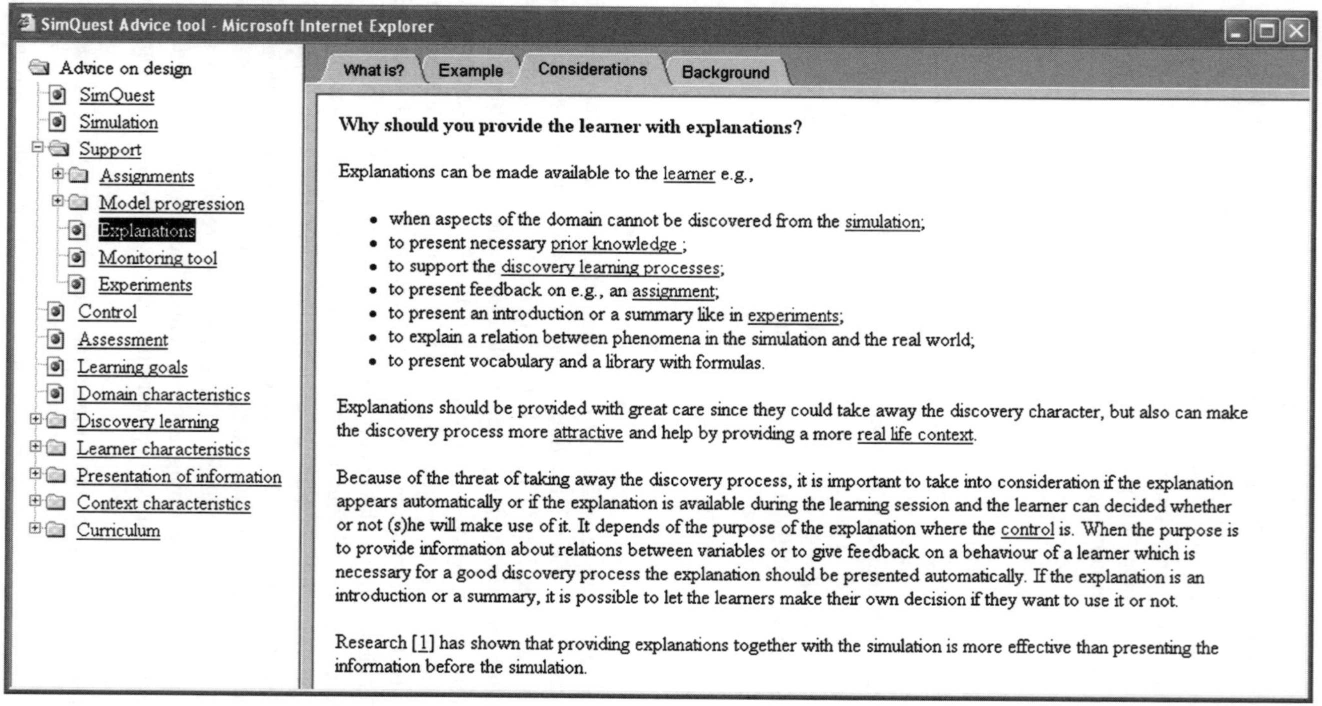

Figure 1: The lay-out of the information system.

pressing the "advice button" designers were immediately taken to the relevant part of the information system).

Tests

In this study we used tests to measure declarative, structural, and functional components of knowledge (e.g. Jonassen *et al.* 1993). Also, log-files and qualitative data were gathered by observing the design process (including the use of the information system) and by analyzing the products that were developed.

The *declarative knowledge test* was administered before and after the design session. The test consisted of a list of educational terms, partly related to discovery learning (e.g. self-directed learning, constructivism, learning goal). The task of the participants, hereafter referred to as designers, was to describe the terms in their own words. In addition, the relevance of concepts and the relations between concepts were assessed. Three raters scored both tests. They assigned to each of the items either: (a) an improvement in the post-test (+); (b) a decline in the post-test (–); or (c) no difference between pre- and post-test (=). This was decided upon agreement between these three raters. An improvement was noticed when the description was more precise or better described. A score of no difference did not only imply that there was no difference at all, but could also mean that, even though the description was different, no improvement or decline was apparent.

The *structural knowledge test* was also administered before and after the design session. Structural knowledge is knowledge about semantic relations between concepts. This relation could change after visiting the information system. The scaling technique used measured the proximity judgments of designers for pairs of concepts, between 0 (no relation) and 7 (high presumed relation). Each value in this proximity matrix corresponded to the strength within a single pair of the concepts. A change in strength of three or more out of a range of seven was decided to be a significant change.

The purpose of using the *functional knowledge test* was to assess the knowledge, which participants applied in relation to specific design cases and to see how this knowledge developed as a function of the design task. This functional knowledge test was a free generation session of ideas. Participants were presented two short cases on the teaching of nursing, one expository based and the other discovery based, with which they could generate objects and ideas relevant for instructional design. The assignment was to design a lesson (A and B; one for each case), taking into account the instructional design of the lesson, intended learning process, evaluation of the learning process, and the role of the teacher. The results from a pre- and post-test were assessed by two raters. A positive change was noticed when compared to the pre-test more relevant ideas were discussed in the post-test.

Log-files registered performed activities in SimQuest and the time spent on each activity. These patterns revealed relevant characteristics of the design process with the authoring environment SimQuest. Log-files also registered the information-seeking behavior of the designers, the information the designers searched (in relation with the performed design activity), and the way in which the information system was accessed.

Moreover, time was registered throughout the use of the information system to determine the time spent to each topic. After the design session and after the post-test, a questionnaire and an interview were administered for evaluation. The questionnaire only focused on the information system and evaluated the designer's satisfaction of the information system. The interview focused both on the various characteristics of the information system and on the design process.

Phase One

Procedure

Before the design session started, the three subjects received a description of the task, including the purpose and the procedure of the study, a text about the domain, being the prior knowledge of the learners for which they had to design the learning environment, and a list with possible globally formulated, intended learning outcomes. The goals consisted of both knowledge outcomes (e.g. a formula of a law) and skill outcomes (e.g. interpretation of a graph). An introduction about SimQuest was also included. The design session took about five hours: a pre-test of one hour, an introduction of half an hour, the design task of about two hours (designers were allowed to complete the task), and the post-test for one hour. Written information was available during the session, in addition to the information system and a blank piece of paper for making notes.

Results

Designer 1, experienced computer user but moderate experience in instructional design, spent 123 minutes on the design task. Designer 2 was an experienced computer user, but little experienced in instructional design practice and spent 138 minutes on the design task. Designer 3 was a domain expert and frequent user of computers, but less experienced with discovery learning. For designer 3 the design task took 122 minutes.

The designers consulted the information system very differently. Designer 2 spent 30 minutes and 42 seconds in the information system, whereas designer 1 spent 13 minutes and 9 seconds and designer 3 spent only 1 minute and 22 seconds. Designer 1 consulted the information system four times (three times in the beginning of the design process and once in the middle of the design process). The information system was accessed while using an Assignment editor, an Explanation editor (twice), and the Help-menu. Designer 2 also consulted the information system four times (twice in the beginning of the design session, once in the middle of the design process, and once at the end of the design process), and it was accessed twice within an Assignment editor and twice via the Help-menu. Designer 3 consulted the information system only twice (in the beginning and at the end of the design process), via an Assignment editor and an Explanation editor. Designer 1 consulted 63 information cards (more or less equally distributed over the four classifications of information). Designer 2 consulted 99 information cards, especially the "What is?"-information. Designer 3 consulted 12 information cards, especially the ones on the "Considerations" classification. Also the navigation in the information system showed different patterns. Designer 1 and designer 2 used various ways of navigation. Designer 1 used links, tab, back, and structure; designer 2 also used the history, but designer 3 especially used the structure to navigate through the information system.

Designer 1 and designer 3 demonstrated an improvement on one third of the items on the *declarative knowledge test* (an improvement on eight out of the 24 items against a decline on two out of the 24 items). For designer 2 there was improvement on 42% of the items (an improvement on 10 out of the 24 items against a decline on three out of the 24 items). Descriptions of the concepts were more specifically and extensively described. Improvement was shown, especially on the items related to information consulted in the information system. For designer 1, 50% of the items, which were related to the information searched for in the information system, showed an improvement. For designers 2 and 3 this was 53.8% and 57.1% of the items, respectively.

The *structural knowledge post-test* compared to the pre-test results showed a decrease in strength for 22 out of 45 pairs (designer 1) and for 28 out of 45 pairs (designer 2). For designer 3, on the contrary, 22 out of 45 pairs increased in strength. A change in strength of three or more (on a scale of 7) was indicated as a significant change. This resulted in a significant decrease for two pairs out of two (designer 1) and eight out of eight (designer 2), and a significant increase within six pairs out of seven (designer 3). Although a decrease was found for designer 1 and 2 in general, we could observe an increase in strength for those pairs of concepts explicitly related to information cards consulted in the information system. The same pattern could be observed with designer 3.

For the descriptions of lesson A (expository based) no clear differences between pre- and post-scores on the *functional knowledge test* were found. For lesson B (discovery based) the description in the post-test by designer 1 was more domain-independent. Instructional design issues, for instance assessment, were addressed. Information on assignments was consulted in the information system. By designer 2 in the post-test with lesson B, the control-aspect was dealt with differently, simulations were additionally addressed and the instructional measures varied. The information system was consulted on these issues. In the post-test designer 3, describing lesson B, used ideas that substantially differed from the pre-test. Information about applications of simulations was consulted.

The learning environments that were developed varied in completeness. Because designer 1 spent time to get a clear overview of the context before starting with the actual design, the developed product was very premature. Designer 1 displayed a breadth-first design process that linked up best with an instrumental paradigm. Seemingly suitable elements were grouped in a folder and filled in or adapted later on in the design process. The design task was thoroughly analyzed and log-files indicated a clear tendency of analyzing the elements in the archive on their appropriateness. In the information system especially information was consulted about do-it assignments, control, discovery learning, presentation of the information (for instance use of media), and learner characteristics. Like designer 1, designer 2 started analyzing the domain, the authoring environment, and the information system. The design process showed elements of a breadth-first approach. This designer especially consulted information on support, (do-it) assignments, discovery learning, and learner characteristics. Designer 3 displayed a more depth-first oriented design process that linked up best with a pragmatic paradigm. This type of design process was confirmed in the log-files, which indicated repeated try-out and revision of elements. During the design process the information system was consulted at the beginning and at end of the design session. Especially, information on control, explanations, and domain characteristics was consulted.

The content of the information system was positively evaluated. The designers indicated that they were inclined to use the information system next time they would work with SimQuest. Designer 1 and designer 2 experienced free exploration as a benefit, but designer 3 expressed a need for more guidelines. On a 10-point scale, the mean of the quality of the total available information was expressed with the mark 8; the mean of relevance of the information was 7.2; the What is?-classification a mean of 6.7; the Example-classification of 7.5; the Considerations-classification a mean of 7.7, and the Background-classification a mean of 7.5. From the above discussion and the results we may conclude that the content of the information system has been well received.

Conclusions

The information system was used in different ways. The designers walked various routes through the information system, visiting highly divergent information. The log-files revealed that the instructional designers performed both information-seeking behaviors, browsing, and searching activities. The designers with a breadth-first design process consulted the information system especially in the beginning of the design process and used the information system to improve their understanding of the design task to be performed. The information system was, overall, evaluated well. The designers did not spend a long time on each information card. We were able to associate improvements and changes to visited information in the information system. In the declarative knowledge test all designers demonstrated an improvement and the designers improved especially on the items, which were related to consultations of the information system. Also for the structural knowledge test the changes could be related to consultations. For two out of three designers most values in strength between pairs of relationships showed a decrease. For lesson A, the functional knowledge test hardly showed any difference between pre- and post-test. For lesson B, we observed differences in descriptions between pre- and post-test, which could be related to the information visited. The results of the first phase encouraged us to believe that the use of an information system seemed to be a valuable means to provide instructional design support. Therefore, based on the results of the first phase the next phase was started.

Phase Two

In the second phase a "control" study was conducted. The set-up of this phase was identical to the first phase, only the information system was not provided to the designers. In this phase also three designers participated.

Results

All designers (4, 5, and 6) were expert computer users, but not expert instructional designers. Designer 4 and designer 5 considered themselves domain experts; designer 5 was also familiar with discovery learning. On the *declarative knowledge test* designer 4 demonstrated an improvement on 62.5% of the items between pre-test and post-test. The descriptions of the concepts were more related to simulation-based learning environments. On a small number of items designers 5 and 6 demonstrated improvement; almost all items did not show any difference between the pre- and post-test (75% of the items for both designers).

In the *structural knowledge test* the strength of relations between concepts in the pre-test was compared with the post-test. Results indicated that, compared with the pre-test, for designer 5 and designer 6, 19 out of 45 pairs decreased in strength. For designer 4, on the contrary, strength of 18 out of 45 pairs increased, although only two significantly changed. For designer 5, six out of 19 pairs significantly decreased in strength, whereas eight out of 15 increased significantly. The same pattern revealed the descriptions of designer 6: seven out of 19 decreased and three out of sixteen pairs significantly increased.

Results on the *functional knowledge test* did not indicate any noticeable difference between the pre- and post-test with lesson A, which was in line with the results of the first phase. For lesson B, only designers 4 and 5 demonstrated a small positive difference in using learner control; more learner control was addressed in the post-test.

Designer 4 expressed both breadth-first and depth-first behavior, focusing on the structure of the learning environment followed by a strong in-depth approach on different elements. Elements were filled in, adapted, and tested until they suited the wishes of the designer. The developed learning environment started with a video, followed by some general information (how to operate a simulation). Learners received a free exploration assignment, after which an investigation and a specification assignment became available.

The design process of designer 5 demonstrated different results. On the one hand elements of a depth-first approach could be found, but during the design process the designer also expressed a breadth-first approach. The interview revealed that in the beginning of the design process the designer experienced difficulties to manage the design process. Designer 5 developed an environment in which general help, for instance on interpreting diagrams and operating the system, was always available for the learner.

Designer 6 started with the design process right away and did not perform an analysis of available material. Based on the log-files and the interview we concluded that designer 6 demonstrated depth-first behavior. In the learning environment developed by designer 6 the learner was completely free in what to do. A general help and explanations of concepts were available. All assignments were put in a list in a folder. Various assignments were used: investigation, specification and do-it assignments. For investigation assignments the number of attempts was set to two, for the other assignments there was only one attempt by the learners allowed.

Conclusions

In the second phase, designer 4 outperformed the other two designers. Only designer 4 demonstrated an improvement on the declarative knowledge test and developed an extended learning environment. The design processes in the second phase expressed both breadth-first and depth-first design approaches. The structural knowledge showed an increase in values of strength in pairs of relationships. For the functional knowledge test the descriptions for lesson A and lesson B hardly showed any difference between the pre- and post-test.

For the declarative knowledge test, the performance of the designers from the first phase more strongly improved than the performance of the designers from the second phase, in particular for items that were related to information visited in the information system.

For the structural knowledge test the number of values between relations that increased in strength was higher in the second phase, compared to the first phase. The number of values that stayed at the same level was comparable between the first and the second phase. In the first phase for both designers 1 and 2 most values showed a decrease whereas for designer 3 most values showed an increase. The second phase shows the same picture: for designer 5 and designer 6 most values decreased and for designer 4 values increased. In the second phase the relation value showed more often a change of more than three points.

It is interesting to note that only the declarative and structural knowledge tests demonstrated a difference between the first and the second phase, whereas the functional knowledge test with its implicit applied character did not show any clear differences. This discrepancy might be explained by the time available for designing and simultaneously exploring the information system, and secondly, by the opportunity to internalize the acquired knowledge from the information system. The time available for designing was hardly enough to design an adequate learning environment and, as was shown by the results from the characteristics of the designed learning environments, the information acquired from the information system could not adequately be applied in the process of designing. Instead, acquired information did enable the designers to perform better on the declarative and structural knowledge test. As these tests are designed to measure the knowledge in an immediate way, performance can be improved when visiting the information system. On the other hand, on the functional knowledge test, the designer has to show the application in the context of the information acquired. Partly due to the limited time available but also due to the lack of any opportunity for practising the knowledge acquired, the functional knowledge test could not show any difference between the first phase, with the information system available, and the second phase, lacking the information system.

Two designers in the first phase demonstrated a breadth-first design process (they set out a plan and intended to first get an overview of the entire content of the learning environment, before they started with changing the elements). One designer demonstrated a more depth-first design process. In the second phase there was one designer with a depth-first design process and two designers who demonstrated a design process containing both types (they changed their tactics). The design behavior in the second phase, a majority designing without a predefined plan, expressed the lacking of the information system. The one designer in the second phase that showed depth-first behavior obviously had adequate prior knowledge at his disposal.

Phase Three

A difference was noticed in the need and in the application of information support between the first phase and the second phase. Results on the declarative and the structural knowledge tests indicated that consulting the information system does make a difference in the acquisition of the relevant information. Results on the functional knowledge test demonstrated that although relevant knowledge was acquired, designers could not adequately apply this knowledge. Therefore, we decided to further explore the design behavior and the use of the information system. Nine designers (designer 7–15) participated in this third phase. We decided to use the same procedure for the third phase as we did in the first phase. Furthermore, we used the same evaluation tests as in the first phase.

Based on the results from the first phase we decided to change the following aspects of the information system. First, more information was linked to the cards presenting the overview of the information system and unnecessary links on information cards were deleted. Secondly, it was indicated that sometimes still too much information was presented on one information card. Therefore, texts were shortened. Third, the application directed character of the information had to be more prominent. More examples of elements were provided within a specific domain (the Example-classification in the first study seemed as the most important classification, but the results of the first phase showed that this category was consulted least).

Results

Except for designer 7 all designers were experienced or intermediate computer and WWW users. Only designer 8 expressed having knowledge about discovery learning. Designers 7, 13, and 14 appreciated the subject as difficult. Time spent on the design task ranged from 110 minutes (designer 7) to 134 minutes (designer 10).

All designers, except designer 11, demonstrated improvement on the post-test of the *declarative knowledge test*. Improvement was more articulated on the items related to the information consulted in the information system. On the post-test, items were more specifically and extensively described by the designers. For instance the item "prior knowledge" was not only described more precisely, but was also more associated with a personal knowledge construction process by the learner. Another example is the support measure "explanation" in discovery learning. In the pre-test it was stated that explanations provide information on the learning method. In the post-test it was stated by several designers that explanations explain unknown concepts or provide other knowledge necessary for the learning process. In the post-test the tasks were considered providing explanations, guidance, support on hypothesis generation, and feedback. In the pre-test only the provision of explanations was mentioned.

On the *structural knowledge test* in this third phase, the number of values that showed an increase in strength in relations was higher (six designers) than the number of values that showed a decrease in strength of relation (three designers). The number of values with an increase in strength of relation of three or more was even higher; for seven designers most changes of three or more were an increase and for two designers most changes of three or more were a decrease. We were not able to relate changes in the structural knowledge test to visited information for three designers.

Though almost all descriptions in the post-test were more elaborately described, no qualitative differences could be observed between the *functional knowledge* pre- and post-test. Except for designer 11 whose descriptions on the pre-test of lesson A and B were more specifically described and for designer 12 whose descriptions of lesson A were more profound in the pre-test, although no changes could be related to the information consulted by the designer in the information system.

Designers consulted the information system very differently. Overall, the "What is?" category was consulted most, followed by the "Considerations" category, the "Example" category, and the "Background" category. The structure and tabs were used most. For the access to the information system the Help was used most (15 times), but 13 times there was a context sensitive option used. The same pattern was observed in the first phase.

The information system was consulted 39 times, 15 times at the beginning of the design process, 10 times in the middle of the design process, 5 times at three-quarter of the design process, and 9 times at the end of the design process. Overall, the information card "What is SimQuest?" was consulted most, followed, in order, by "Considerations of learning goals", "Considerations of SimQuest", and "Considerations of Learner characteristics".

The information system was considered very useful but in many instances it was consulted too late, after the lesson was designed. Some designers preferred a more directive use of the system. According to the participants, the information system generated new ideas for the design of a powerful discovery learning environment.

With the evaluation questionnaire designers appraised the information system on a scale of one to seven. Except designer 11, all other designers positively judged the content of the information system. The purpose and profit of the information system were clear (means 5.9 and 5.7). Most designers expressed a need for more guidelines. Statements on specific topics, which were in general or specifically available in the information system, were also measured (scale 1 to 10). A low score was given when the corresponding information was not consulted in the information system. The mean of the quality of the total available information was expressed with the mark 8.0, the mean of the relevance of the information was 7.1, the What is?-classification a mean of 8.3, the Example-classification of 7.5, the Considerations-classification a mean of 7.4, and the Background-classification a mean of 7.6. In addition to the content of the information system, we also asked for the quality of the interface of the system and its navigation options. The layout was experienced as logical (mean 6.3) and consequential (mean 6.1). The results show that navigating and monitoring was considered to be easy (mean 6.0). The results encouraged our idea that the information system should be adapted to both information-seeking behaviors, because the information system was successfully consulted for both browsing and searching activities (more often for browsing activities).

From the interviews several positive reactions could be recorded. Generation of ideas as a main advantage of the information system, having relevance for executing the task and supported the design process, was mentioned several times. Also the quality of the support, especially about discovery learning specifically as well as generally, was mentioned as a main advantage of the information system. Moreover, the system provided information about designing powerful discovery learning environments and made the designer more aware of the complexity of the task. Also the model with the overview of all elements involved in discovery learning was positively addressed. The just-in-time provision of information about assignments and explanations was experienced useful and well appreciated.

Five designers started with the design process right away and did not perform an analysis of available material. Based on the log-files and the interviews we concluded that these designers showed depth-first behavior. For the other four designers the design process demonstrated elements of a breadth-first approach. For instance, some approaches consisted of an extensive analysis of the available material with the design task read thoroughly before starting to work with the authoring environment, whereas by others elements were carefully analyzed and the seemingly suitable elements were grouped in a folder and filled in or adapted later on in the design process.

Conclusion and Discussion

The goal of this study was to establish the use, satisfaction, and efficacy of the information system developed to support designers of powerful learning environments.

Results about the use of the system indicate that the information system was flexible in use. Every designer walked through an individual discovery route. The information cards that were visited and consulted and the navigation used differed among designers. Also, the time spent in the information system varied. Most designers were satisfied with the information system; the purpose and benefit of the information system were clear. The marks graded to different information categories were quite high. Pertaining to the developed products, previous research (e.g. De Vries & De Jong 1997) has revealed that it is difficult to objectively judge the products. We also encountered this problem, because the developed products did not give adequate insight into the design process itself. Therefore, we also used other measures (e.g. the interview and the log-files) for the interpretation of the products and we especially focused on the role of the information system in relation to the developed product. In the phases of our study in which the information system could be consulted, that is, the first and the third phase, the use of a breadth-first and a depth-first design approach were equally distributed. Compared to designers with a depth-first design approach, the designers with a breadth-first design approach consulted the information system more often, especially in the beginning of the design process, and they spent more time in the information system. The designers with a breadth-first approach encountered the design task as less difficult compared to the designers with a depth-first approach. For the designers with a breadth-first approach an analysis of the design task seemed to be important. These designers demonstrated various ways for navigating through the information system, and especially used the functions tabs, structure, hyperlinks and back. The What-is?-tab and Considerations-tab were most frequently consulted by these designers. For the designers using a depth-first design approach, the Considerations-tab turned out to be most popular. These designers most often used the tabs and structure and more often consulted the information system through the context sensitive "advice" button in an editor.

We used various measures to assess the efficacy of the information system. First, we used different knowledge tests to get a better understanding of knowledge gains. For the declarative knowledge test all designers of the first phase improved from pre- to post-test. Also, only one designer in phase 2 (without information system), and all designers except one in the third phase improved on the declarative knowledge test. The results of the third phase indicated that for seven out of the nine designers, strength of relations between pairs of concepts increased. This is in contrast to the first phase where for one out of three designers relations increased in strength. Changes could be linked to the visited information, but there was also a link between the changes and the design task. For lesson A (expository based) and B (discovery based), the functional knowledge test hardly measured any difference between pre- and post-test.

In conclusion, the results of the three phases demonstrated that the information system proved to be an adequate instrument to provide support for designing powerful learning environments. The results of the interviews and questionnaires indicated an even more positive picture than could be expected from the results on the pre- and post-tests. From the results on the knowledge tests it turned out that the use of the information system affected the declarative and the structural knowledge of the designer, but did not have a significant effect on the functional knowledge and the developed products. Reasons could be that the post-test was administered immediately after the design task, that the time spent in the information system was too short, and that there was a lack of experience with designing discovery learning environments.

Because of the time limits by which designers were not able to adequately acquire and apply knowledge from the information system, future improvements should focus on the opportunity of compiling knowledge appropriately. For knowledge compilation to be effective, the use of domain related analogies and examples are important. In the system used in our study only the "Example" information category obtained domain-related information. The results on the evaluation demonstrated that there is a need for more domain related information. Especially, the instructional designers who were experienced computer and WWW users, experienced instructional designers, and those who had prior knowledge about discovery learning and about the domain and did not encounter the design task as difficult, preferred to receive information and no guidelines. Especially in the "Considerations"-tab the information system should make explicitly clear that guidelines do not give enough credit to the specific context for which the designer develops the learning environment.

Further studies will be carried out on the distributed use of information systems. Through collaboration it becomes possible to divide work over several individuals assuming different roles and possessing different skills and knowledge. Using computer mediated communication, designers can exchange relevant information and share the design space, independently from their actual location. Naturally, the design of instruction is often done collaboratively, for instance in sections of schools or in teams that design instructional materials and delivery systems for educational publishers. Extension for collaboration among designers and consecutively for supporting designers comes available, like storing and structuring communication traces. Supportive databases with information on the design process can be part of a collaborative design network. However, still little is known about the ways collaborative processes for design take place, and how collaborative design activities act as a supportive environment for the design process and as a learning environment for teachers on the design and use of constructivistic learning environments.

References

De Corte, E. (1994). Toward the integration of computers in powerful learning environments. In: S. Vosniadou, E. De Corte, & H. Mandl (Eds), *Technology-based learning environments. Psychological and educational foundations* (pp. 19–25). NATO ASI Series, Series F: Computer and Systems Sciences, Vol. 137. Berlin/New York: Springer.

De Hoog, R., De Jong, T., & De Vries, F. (1994). Constraint driven software design: An escape from the waterfall model. *Performance Improvement Quarterly, 7* (3), 48–63.

De Jong, T., & Van Joolingen, W. R. (1998). Scientific discovery learning with computer simulations of conceptual domains. *Review of Educational Research, 68,* 179–201.

De Vries, E., & De Jong, T. (1997). Using information systems while performing complex tasks: An example from architectural design. *International Journal of Human-Computer Studies, 46,* 31–54.

Dick, W., & Carey, L. (1990). *The systematic design of instruction* (3rd ed.). New York: Harper Collins College Publishers

Hannafin, M. J., Hannafin, K. M., Land, S., & Oliver, K. (1997). Grounded practice in the design of learning systems. *Educational Technology, Research and Development, 45* (3), 101–117.

Jonassen, D. H., Beissner, K., & Yacci, M. (1993). *Structural knowledge: Techniques for representing, conveying, and acquiring structural knowledge.* Hillsdale, NJ: Lawrence Erlbaum Associates.

Jonassen, D. H., Myers, J. M., & McKillop, A. M. (1996). From constructivism to constructionism: Learning with hypermedia/multimedia rather than from it. In: B. G. Wilson (Ed.), *Constructivist learning environments: Case studies in instructional design* (pp. 93–106). Englewood Cliffs, NJ: Educational Technology Publications.

Van Joolingen, W. R., & De Jong, T. (in press). SimQuest: Authoring educational simulations. In: T. Murray, S. Blessing, & S. Ainsworth (Eds), *Authoring tools for advanced technology educational software: Toward cost-effective production of adaptive, interactive, and intelligent educational software.* Dordrecht: Kluwer Academic Publishers..

Kuyper, M., De Hoog, R., & De Jong, T. (2001). Modeling and supporting the authoring process of multimedia simulation based educational software: A knowledge engineering approach. *Instructional Science, 29,* 337–359.

Limbach, R. (2001). *Supporting instructional designers: Towards an information system for the design of instructional discovery learning environments.* Unpublished dissertation. Enschede: University of Twente.

Pieters, J. M., & Bergman, R. (1995). The empirical basis of designing instruction: What practice can contribute to theory. *Performance Improvement Quarterly, 8* (3), 118–129.

Pieters, J. M., Limbach, R., & De Jong, T. (in press). Designing discovery learning environments: Process analysis and implications for designing an information system. *International Journal of Computer Applications in Technology.*

Reigeluth, C. M. (Ed.) (1999). *Instructional-design theories and models: A new paradigm of instructional theory* (Vol. 2). Hillsdale, NJ: Lawrence Erlbaum Associates.

Richey, R. C. (1995). Trends in instructional design: Emerging theory-based models. *Performance Improvement Quarterly, 8* (3), 97–111.

Rothwell, W. J., & Kazanas, H. C. (1992). *Mastering the instructional design process: A systematic approach.* San Francisco, CA: Jossey-Bass.

Rowland, G. (1992). What do instructional designers actually do? An empirical investigation of expert practice. *Performance Improvement Quarterly, 5* (2), 65–86.

Sfard, A. (1998). On two metaphors for learning and the dangers of choosing just one. *Educational Researcher, 27* (2), 4–13.

Tessmer, M., & Wedman, J. (1995). Context-sensitive instructional design models: A response to design research, studies, and criticism. *Performance Improvement Quarterly, 8* (3), 38–54.

Yin, R. K. (1994). Case study research: Design and methods. *Applied Social Research Methods Series, 5.* Thousand Oaks, CA: SAGE Publications, Inc.

Chapter 9

Computer Technologies in Powerful Learning Environments: The Case of Using Animated and Interactive Graphics for Teaching Financial Concepts

Mireille Bétrancourt, Pierre Dillenbourg and Cécile Montarnal

Introduction

What is a powerful learning environment? Simply stated, it is an environment that generates high learning gains for its users. Does this means that the label "powerful" can only be allocated a posteriori through empirical testing? No, otherwise we would simply call it an "effective" learning environment. The term powerful refers to potential learning outcomes and is hence based on the learning theory that supports this prediction. Subsequently, the meaning of powerful varies according to learning theories. A powerful learning environment is built on a hypothetical causal relationship between the environment features and the learning processes. For instance, a socio-cultural designer would qualify an environment as being powerful according to the forms of social interactions that are supported. Within a mastery learning perspective, it is rather the possibility to adapt instruction to the learner needs that would legitimate the word powerful. For a behaviorist, the controlled delivery of information and the possibility to deliver immediate feedback would justify the same label. The purpose of this book is precisely to articulate the tuning of technology issues with the learning process.

From a cognitive science perspective, powerful refers to many aspects, but a core issue is the mapping between the computational model of the domain and the mental model to be constructed by the learner. The relationship between these two models is of course not a simple 'copy-from-disk-to-brain' mechanism but a complex process based on interactivity and visualization. Interactivity is the core "powerful" mechanism in pedagogical simulations. Nevertheless, learners have multiple difficulties with efficiently conducting this hypothetico-deductive process (de Jong & van Joolingen 1998).

What about visualization? One key advantage of technology is to be able to visualize dynamic models as animated pictures. Do animations and interactive animations contribute to make computers into powerful learning environments? Intuitively, the answer is positive but empirical findings are contradictory. This contribution addresses the cognitive benefits of using animated pictures in a course.

This effectiveness of animated pictures belongs to basic research since, as we will show in this chapter, it questions the way dynamic processes are mentally represented. At the same time, this concerns a very practical point in the design of virtual learning environments, namely, the added value of electronic lecture notes. Electronic documents provide powerful search facilities, links to other documents, possibilities to compile pieces of text and so forth, but they suffer from several drawbacks such as navigation difficulties (Rouet 2000), poor annotation facilities and poor readability both in terms of speed and tiredness (compared to paper). One of the specific advantages of electronic documents is the possibility to include animated pictures and interactive animations. However, the intuitive superiority of animated and/or interactive pictures over static ones has failed to be confirmed by empirical studies. We report here an empirical comparison of animated and static pictures, interactive or not, in a course on financial analysis.

Learning from Multimedia Instruction

A considerable body of research has demonstrated the benefits of adding graphics for comprehending text instructions (Mandl & Levin 1989; Schnotz & Kulhavy 1994). However, the underlying cognitive processes have not been clearly identified yet. The theoretical explanation generally admitted assumes that graphics help people constructing a mental model of the described object or concept, insofar as they provide an analogical support upon which the mental model can be elaborated (Mayer 1989; Schnotz 2001).

With rapid computer technology advances, multimedia instructional materials and resources are becoming increasingly available from primary to higher education. However, multimedia design features are more often based on aesthetic or practical considerations than on concerns about how people actually learn. In the last decade, research carried out in the mental model theoretical frame has begun to provide guidelines for designing multimedia instruction based on cognitive theories and experimental results (Hegarty *et al.* 1999).

In the mental model paradigm, learning performance is investigated using retention and transfer tests. A retention test aims at controlling the memorization of explicit information in surface representations (i.e. propositional representation and mental image of the text and pictures explanation). A transfer test, which requires learners to infer new information from the explanation, aims at measuring the construction of a correct mental model of the content presented. The mental model theoretical frame admits that text and pictures are processed in order to build surface representations, which are then integrated with previous knowledge to form the mental model of the concept conveyed (Mayer 2001; Schnotz 2001). In this paradigm, deep learning means the construction of a "usable" mental model that enables people to solve transfer problems.

Dynamic Visualization Devices and their Effect on Learning

Computer animation cannot be considered as one clearly defined visualization device. There can be many types of animation, going from the movie-like video clip to the abstract simulation of the results of an equation. Just as various forms of graphics can have various effects on learning, we claim that different types of animation may lead to different cognitive effects. In order to be able to generalize the findings, research must precisely define the type of animation used in terms of delivery issues (e.g. interactivity, information displayed) as well as in terms of content (e.g. realistic vs. schematized). Gonzales (1996) defined animation as: "*a series of varying images presented dynamically according to user action in ways that help the user to perceive a continuous change over time and develop a more appropriate mental model of the task*" (Gonzales 1996: 132).

Two issues arise from this definition. First, animation is a continuous flow of information, which may generate cognitive difficulties for learners (Lowe 1999). Second, computer animation requires users to interact with the device. The level of users' interaction is a key factor in animation effectiveness (Rieber 1989).

Sequential Display as an Alternative to Continuous Animation

Animation should be expected to be effective for conveying processes such as weather patterns, electric circuits, biological mechanisms or the mechanics of a bicycle pump. However, the literature reports many outright failures to find benefits of animation, even when animation is used for conveying change over time (Bétrancourt & Tversky 2000). Tversky *et al.* (2002) examined these intriguing findings in terms of cognitive processes and found that animation can overwhelm human perceptual and conceptual capacities. Moreover, animation is cognitively demanding, since it requires learners to simultaneously construct a mental model, attend to the animation and memorize previous states. Principles to enhance the conceptual value of animation and to decrease cognitive load are proposed in Bétrancourt & Tversky (2000).

The research carried out so far failed to demonstrate clear advantages of using animated graphics over static ones on learning. Another way to take advantage of the dynamic features of computer technologies is to display sequentially the elements of text and picture instruction. The sequential display is then used to convey the organization and inherent logic of the instruction, just as a teacher draws and explains a schema on the blackboard in a carefully chosen sequence. Moreover, according to Mayer's integration model (2001), gradually providing elements enables learners to construct local representations and then to integrate them in a coherent mental model, whereas providing all information at once could lead to cognitive overload. Previous research has demonstrated that the order in which elements of a spatial configuration were mentioned in the text had a dramatic effect on the quality of the mental model participants elaborated (Denis & Cocude 1992). As for graphics, the findings of our first studies (Bétrancourt *et al*. 2000) tended to show that sequential display had no effect on pure memorization but did positively affect the performance on transfer tasks.

Interactivity in Practice and Instruction?

Computer animation usually entails user interaction. Interactivity can occur on two levels: In practice and in instruction. In practice, the level of interactivity, defined as learners' activity, increases when the information displayed varies as a function of the learners' input. The animation then aims at encouraging learners to generate and test hypotheses. According to constructivist theories, deep learning is more likely to occur when learners are engaged in active interaction with the instructional material. Gonzales (1996) designed a study to evaluate interactivity in an animated instruction and found that an increased level of interactivity significantly improved the learners' accuracy and enjoyment in a decision-making task. However, Kettanurak *et al*. (2001) found that the higher the level of interactivity, the lower the improvement in performance, though learners found the high interactivity mode the most enjoyable. This result called into question the ability of students to effectively monitor their learning activity.

Secondly, interactivity in instruction can be defined as the possibility to act on the pace of the animation. In two experiments, Mayer & Chandler (2001) investigated the effects of simple user-controlled interaction on learning: The animation was segmented into meaningful 8-second-sequences, and, after each sequence, learners had to click on a button to run the next sequence. The results of the two experiments showed that learners performed better on a transfer test when they controlled the pace of the presentation. Moreover, students who first received the presentation with control followed by the presentation without control performed better than students who received the two presentations in the reverse order. Thus, inserting interactivity per se did not improve learning. Rather interactivity improved learning only when it is inserted in a way that is consistent with how people learn. The control over pacing enabled learners to incorporate all information of a frame before proceeding to the next. In other words, interactivity decreases cognitive load and enables the formation of a local mental model, which can subsequently be integrated when the whole presentation is provided. These results are consistent with cognitive load theory (Sweller & Chandler 1994), which states that cognitive overload impairs learning, as well as with the two-stage construction of a mental model, which claims that learners first build local mental models, and then incorporate these local models into one integrated representation.

Research Hypotheses

An experimental study was carried out in order to compare three display conditions, according to whether the elements were displayed all at once or sequentially, and to whether the computer or the learner had the control over the display order. The learning material was a multimedia lesson on financial analysis, containing graphics and corresponding text. The study took place within a regular class session.

A main assumption of this study is that sequentially displaying the elements of a multimedia explanatory document will facilitate learning for two reasons. First, presenting information sequentially avoids perceptual and cognitive overload, since learners can gradually integrate the given information. Second, the display order acts as a processing guide, with information displayed sequentially in a meaningful order, just as a teacher draws a schema on the blackboard while explaining its different elements. Taken together, these two advantages will facilitate the construction of a mental model of the concept conveyed in the instruction.

Regarding interactivity, we distinguished two levels. Interactivity in instruction was set to the minimal control mode: after each element was displayed, the presentation stops until the learner chooses to resume. Mayer & Chandler (2001) showed that this minimal level of control had a dramatic positive effect on learning, compared with no control. As for interactivity in practice, two alternative hypotheses may be raised. A previous study on the sequential display of graphics (Bétrancourt *et al.* 2000) showed that when the display order was relevant, learners tended to elaborate a mental model consistent with the organization conveyed. According to this view, providing learners with a relevant order will help them to more easily construct a coherent mental model of the concept, than if they were to choose the order in which elements should be displayed themselves. Alternatively, previous research on interactivity has shown that when learners studied in an exploratory mode, they are more inclined to engage in an active learning strategy. According to this view, learners who are given the control over the next element to be explained will learn more deeply than learners who do not.

Method

Participants

Participants were 81 undergraduate students engaged in the first year of a business school in Grenoble (ESCG). They were randomly assigned to a static group ($n = 26$), a sequential non-interactive group ($n = 27$), and a sequential interactive group ($n = 28$). The experiment took place during a regular course but the participation was on a voluntary basis. All students had followed a class on the basics of accounting balance the semester before, but none of the learners was acquainted with financial analysis.

Material

The material was made up from the teaching materials of two teachers in financial analysis at ESCG. The material consisted of 13 pages. Four pages contained texts and graphics explanations and nine pages contained test questions. The explanation pages described the construction of an accounting balance sheet and its transformation into a financial balance sheet, using the proper computation of financial indicators.

Three versions of the material were designed. The test pages were identical across conditions, but the pages with explanations varied:

- In the sequential non-interactive condition, the order in which elements were displayed was defined by the instructional designer and computer-controlled.
- In the sequential interactive condition, the order in which elements were displayed was under learner's control.
- In the static condition the elements appeared simultaneously on the screen with all text available in an adjacent window (with a scroll bar if necessary).

In the two sequential conditions, elements of the graphics were displayed in a random order at the bottom of the screen (see Figure 1). In the non-interactive condition, when the learner clicked on the *Next* button, one of the elements moved to the correct location in the graphics and the corresponding explanatory text appeared on the right-hand part of the page. In the interactive condition, the learner had to click on each one of the elements instead of the *Next* button to have it moved to the correct location and receive the explanation.

In the sequential conditions, the text built up gradually in the right-hand frame, whereas it was displayed all at once in the static condition. However, for page 1, only the text corresponding to the last selected item was displayed in the sequential condition, because the complete text was more than one page long.

Procedure

Participants were tested in groups of 15 to 18 students during the regular class slot, individually seated in front of a computer. The students first signed a consent form explaining the purpose of the study. Then they followed the instruction given on the computer screen and proceeded at their own pace. After they indicated their age and previous courses, they read the instructions explaining the five phases of the study. The first phase consisted of three pages that explained the construction of an accounting balance, the computation of a financial indicator, and the transformation from an accounting balance to a financial balance sheet. Then followed four multiple-choice questions, for which they could read the explanation pages again. In the second phase, participants were asked to compute the financial index of a company from the accounting balance sheet. They could *not* refer back to the explanation pages. In the third phase, a second set of explanation pages on financial analysis was provided. The fourth phase consisted of two tests and was identical for all conditions. The first test was an interactive manipulation task for which students had to graphically reconstruct a financial balance sheet by direct drag-and-drop of the items provided on the bottom of the screen. If the location of the item was not correct, it was moved back to its original place. After three trials it was moved automatically to its correct location. The second test was a set of four transfer questions about the comparison of two companies in terms of financial analysis. In the fifth and final phase, participants were asked to rate the material according to three parameters: enjoyment, difficulty and pedagogical value. The whole experiment took 30 to 45 minutes to be completed. The program

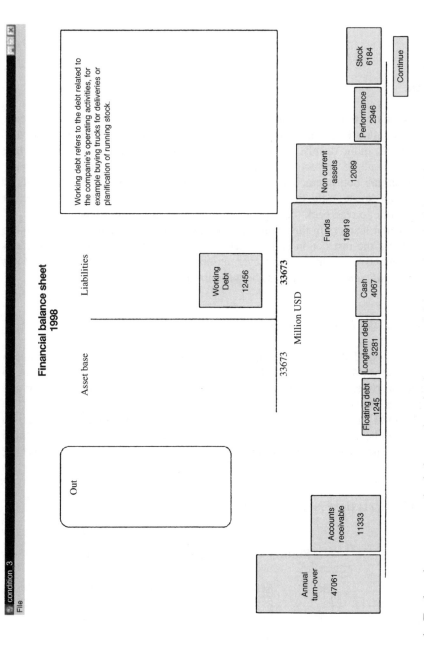

Figure 1: Explanation page on the balance sheet in the sequential interactive condition. The learner has clicked on the element "Working debt". The corresponding block has moved to its location in the schema and the explanatory text has appeared in the right-hand frame.

automatically recorded time on explanation pages and time and answers to test pages. In the manipulation task, the order in which items were selected was also automatically recorded.

Results

Study Time

Study time includes time to read the first three explanation pages and to answer the four multiple-choice questions. The four questions aimed at helping students in processing the explanations more deeply. As they could refer back to the explanations while answering, the rate of correct responses was very similar across conditions (static: 67.3%; sequential non-interactive: 67.3%; sequential interactive: 67.9%). Table 1 displays the time spent on the first phase, making a distinction between the initial study time and the time to read back the explanations and answer the questions.

Data show that learners in the sequential non-interactive condition spent some more time at studying the instruction and answering the questions than both the static and sequential interactive conditions. However, an analysis of variance (ANOVA) did not confirm the significance of differences between groups ($F(2,78) = 0.873$, NS).

Computation of the Financial Index

After they answered the four multiple-choice questions, learners had to compute a financial indicator (Working Capital Need or WCN). Now, they could *not* refer back to the explanation pages. Table 2 displays the time required to compute the indicator and the percentages of correct answers.

Table 2 shows that learners in the sequential interactive condition were fastest to compute the indicator ($M = 113$ secs), followed by learners in the static condition ($M = 131$ secs) and, finally, learners in the sequential non-interactive condition ($M = 152$

Table 1: Time spent (in secs) on studying the explanations.

	Static		Sequential non-interactive		Sequential interactive	
	M	*SD*	*M*	*SD*	*M*	*SD*
Initial reading	190	*111*	259	*91*	195	*74*
Questions	179	*64*	191	*84*	201	*80*
Total	368	*159*	450	*147*	396	*103*

Table 2: Time (in secs) and performance on computing the financial index (WCN).

	Static		Sequential non-interactive		Sequential interactive	
	M	*SD*	*M*	*SD*	*M*	*SD*
Computing time	131	42	152	72	113	50
Percentage of correct answers	81%	—	89%	—	68%	—

secs). ANOVA indicated a significant effect ($F(2,78) = 3.26$, $MSE = 23834.46$, $p < 0.05$). A post-hoc test using Fisher's PLSD indicated a significant contrast between the two sequential conditions, $MSE = 38.79$, $p < 0.05$. The percentage of correct answers seemed to show the reverse pattern, but this difference is not statistically significant ($\chi^2 = 3.74$, *NS*).

Time and Performance for Constructing a Financial Balance

The second test task consisted of an interactive drag-and-drop task, in which learners had to construct a financial balance sheet. The time spent on the task and the number of errors are displayed in Table 3.

Table 3 shows that learners in the sequential non-interactive condition spent less time and committed fewer errors than learners in the other two conditions. An analysis of covariance (ANCOVA) computed on the time spent on the task with the number of errors as a covariate indicated a significant effect ($F(2,75) = 3.22$, $MSE = 6739.76$, $p < 0.05$). A post-hoc test using Fisher's PLSD yielded a significant difference between the two sequential conditions and the static condition (sequential non-interactive vs. static: $MSE = 37.41$, $p < 0.05$, sequential interactive vs. static: $MSE = 29.38$, $p < 0.05$).

Table 3: Mean time (in secs) and number of errors in constructing the financial balance sheet.

	Static		Sequential non-interactive		Sequential interactive	
	M	*SD*	*M*	*SD*	*M*	*SD*
Manipulation time	146	56	109	37	117	51
Number of errors	7.00	2.84	5.18	2.73	6.96	3.07

Table 4: Time (secs) and performance for the four transfer questions.

	Static		Sequential non-interactive		Sequential interactive	
	M	*SD*	*M*	*SD*	*M*	*SD*
Answering time	820	*270*	969	*297*	898	*373*
Mean score[a]	0.29	*0.28*	0.61	*0.34*	0.52	*0.47*

[a] Answers were rated on a 3-point-scale. 0 = incorrect or missing; 1 = correct but incomplete; 2 = correct.

Transfer Test

The last test task consisted of four transfer questions on financial analysis. Two independent evaluators rated the answers on a 3-point scale according to the correct answers given by an expert in financial analysis. The agreement was 95% and cases of disagreement were cleared up by a short discussion. Time data for one student were lost due to technical problems. Table 4 displays the answering times and the mean scores for the four questions.

As displayed in Table 4, learners in the sequential non-interactive condition spent more time to solve the inference questions than learners in the sequential interactive condition, but the differences were not statistically significant. (ANOVA computed on answering times with questions (1 to 4) as a repeated measures, $F(2,77) = 1.30$). Regarding the accuracy of learners' answers, participants in the sequential non-interactive condition and, to a lesser degree, the sequential interactive condition outperformed participants in the static condition. Figure 2 displays the mean scores for each separate question.

Though mean scores were quite low, a similar pattern of performance can be observed for each question, with learners in the two sequential conditions outperforming learners in the static condition. ANOVA computed on individual scores with question (1 to 4) as a repeated measure indicated a significant difference between conditions, $F(2,78) = 5.16$, $MSE = 2.95$, $p < 0.01$. A post-hoc test (Fisher's PLSD) showed that the sequential groups differed significantly from the static group (static vs. sequential non-interactive: $MSE = 0.323$, $p < 0.001$; static vs. sequential interactive: $MSE = 0.238$, $p < 0.01$).

Subjective Evaluation

Finally, learners were asked to rate the instructional material according to three criteria: enjoyment, difficulty and pedagogical value. Table 5 displays the results of this evaluation.

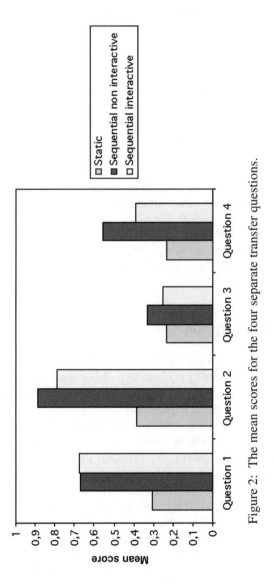

Figure 2: The mean scores for the four separate transfer questions.

Table 5: Subjective ratings of the material on a 6-point Lickert scale (1 = very low and 6 = very high) according to three criteria: enjoyment, difficulty and pedagogical value.

	Static		Sequential non-interactive		Sequential interactive	
	M	*SD*	*M*	*SD*	*M*	*SD*
Enjoyment	3.38	*0.94*	3.86	*1.22*	3.06	*1.60*
Difficulty	3.74	*0.89*	3.25	*0.81*	3.39	*1.36*
Pedagogical value	2.86	*1.45*	3.35	*1.50*	2.04	*1.66*

Regarding *enjoyment*, ANOVA showed that the effect of the format was not statistically significant ($F(2,77) = 2.62$). The ratings of *perceived difficulty* were quite similar across groups and the differences were not statistically significant ($F(2,77) = 1.5$). As for pedagogical value, the sequential non-interactive group was the most positive, compared to the static and the sequential interactive group. ANOVA showed that the effect of the format was statistically significant ($F(2,77) = 4.96$, $MSE = 11.76$, $p < 0.01$) and Fisher's PLSD indicated a significant contrast between the two sequential conditions ($MSE = 1.31$, $p < 0.005$).

Discussion and Conclusion

The experimental study reported above aimed at studying the effects of animated and interactive instruction on learning performance and subjective evaluation. The study was integrated as an actual session in a regular course on financial analysis, so that the results can be expected to be as ecologically valid as possible given the experimental setting. The results showed no significant difference in the learning phase regarding the time spent to study the instructions, though the mode of interaction with the material was very different between groups. We expected that learners in the sequential non-interactive condition would take more time to read the instruction, and especially to re-inspect it, since they could not change the display order of the items. We did indeed observe this trend, but it did not reach statistical significance. Thus computer-controlled instruction display did not dramatically hinder students' search strategies.

Two application tasks followed the study phase. Application tasks aim at measuring the extent to which the learned procedures can be reproduced from memory. They assess the construction of a correct surface representation of the concepts conveyed in the instruction. The first test task concerned the computation of a financial indicator (WCN), according to the procedure given in the instructions. Learners in the sequential interactive condition needed significantly less time than learners in the sequential non-interactive condition to compute the indicator, but they performed worse though this difference was not statistically significant. The second application problem concerned the construction of a financial balance sheet from accounting items, as shown in the instructions. Learners in the two sequential conditions performed this task significantly faster and more accurately than learners in the static condition. To sum up, little can be concluded from the first test task because performance did not significantly differ between conditions and trends in performance were not in agreement with differences in time investment. In contrast, the results of the second test task reinforce the idea that using sequential display facilitates the construction of a mental representation of the learned concepts.

The test phase ended with four transfer questions. Transfer problems aim at measuring the extent to which the learned concepts and procedures are integrated in a "runnable" mental model (Mayer 1989), which can be correctly used in similar situations to draw inferences on what is going to happen and why. Results showed that the learners in the two sequential conditions performed significantly higher than learners in the static condition. This result reinforces the assumption that sequentially displaying information facilitates the construction of a runnable mental model from which inferences can be drawn to understand similar situations.

Finally, the subjective evaluation showed, surprisingly enough, that interactivity significantly decreased the perceived pedagogical value of the document. This result seems in contradiction with the "active learning model" which states that learners must be actively engaged in learning activities in order to improve motivation and learning outcomes. An alternative explanation is offered by cognitive load theory (Sweller & Chandler 1994). Discovery-based learning environments require learners to simultane-ously handle the manipulation of the tool, the management of their learning strategies and the to-be-acquired knowledge, which often leads to cognitive overload. As Mayer *et al.* (2002) noticed, discovery-based learning environments can be beneficial for learning under the conditions that sufficient cognitive scaffolding is provided to students. The material used in this experiment was a multimedia document and not a simulation environment, but learners in the sequential interactive condition yet had to face more cognitively demanding instructional material. This could be the reason that students in the sequential interactive condition had a less positive attitude toward the instruction and tended to show lower performance than students in the sequential non-interactive condition. A second possible explanation is provided by Kettanurak *et al.* (2001): Novices in a domain can hardly efficiently manage their learning strategy because they do not have the knowledge required to have a meta-cognitive attitude. As in the Kettanurak *et al.* (2001) study, we observed that learners in the sequential interactive condition spent less time on the instructions than learners in the sequential non-interactive condition. This observation reinforces the idea that students in the interactive condition did not know in which order items ought to be activated, and how much time they should spend on a given instruction page.

A main assumption of this study was that sequentially displaying the elements of a multimedia explanatory document would facilitate learning. The results clearly supported this assumption, irrespective of the fact if the order was computer-controlled or user-controlled. Our first explanation was that sequential display was decreasing cognitive load since elements could be gradually processed and mentally integrated. Learners' performance in application and transfer tasks did not contradict this explanation, but the subjective evaluation data did not confirm it either. Our second explanation was that the display order would act as a processing guide, with information displayed sequentially in a meaningful order, just as a teacher draws a schema on the blackboard while explaining its elements. In that case, the sequential non-interactive condition, with a predefined order, should be more beneficial than the sequential interactive condition. Overall the results did not confirm this explanation, except for the performance on the manipulation task, in which learners in the sequential non-interactive condition could have just mimicked the display order. Sequential non-interactive display thus appears to be adequate when learning outcomes entail mimicking manipulation procedures, as in software demonstration.

In conclusion, we think there is strong evidence to consider dynamic features offered by computer environments as an effective tool to promote deep learning. Sequential display seems adequate to teach procedures that will be mimicked and to build runnable mental models. The case for interactivity is not yet clear: Though the sequential interactive display was as beneficial to learning as the computer-controlled display, learners' evaluation of the pedagogical value of the instruction was significantly lower in this condition than in the other two conditions. Further research is needed to assess whether this effect is due to cognitive overload in managing the tool, to inadequate learning strategies for acquisition of knowledge, or to actual interface features. An important challenge for the future of education is to identify the most effective combination of features offered by computer technologies and instructional strategies to promote the emergence of powerful learning environments.

Acknowledgments

This study was conducted in collaboration with Dominique Thevenin and Michel Albouy, professors at the Grenoble Business School (ESCG), who provided support for designing adequate pedagogical content on financial analysis. We are grateful to Christophe Seguin and Camille Roche for their contribution in running the experiment. We also acknowledge the work of Nathalie Pezio who designed the material and ran the study for her master thesis. Finally, we thank Jeroen van Merriënboer for thoughtful comments on a first draft of this paper.

References

Bétrancourt, M., Bisseret, A., & Faure, A. (2000). Sequential display of pictures and its effect on mental representations. In: J. F. Rouet, J. J. Levonen, & A. Biardeau (Eds), *Multimedia learning: Cognitive and instructional issues* (pp. 112–118). London, U.K.: Elsevier Science.
Bétrancourt, M., & Tversky, B. (2000). Effects of computer animation on users' performance: A review. *Le Travail Humain, 63*, 311–329.
De Jong, T., & van Joolingen, W. (1998). Scientific discovery learning with computer simulations of conceptual domains. *Review of Educational Research, 68*, 179–201.
Denis, M., & Cocude, M. (1992). Structural properties of visual images constructed from poorly or well structured verbal descriptions. *Memory and Cognition, 20*, 497–506.

Gonzales, C. (1996). Does animation in user interfaces improve decision making? In: *Proceedings of CHI'96* (pp. 27–34). Vancouver, Canada: ACM Press.

Hegarty, M., Quilici, J., Narayanan, N. H., Holmquist, S., & Moreno, R. (1999). Designing multimedia manuals that explain how machines work: Lessons from evaluation of a theory-based design. *Journal of Educational Multimedia and Hypermedia, 8*, 119–150.

Kettanurak, V. N., Ramamurthy, K., & Haseman, W. D. (2001). User attitude as a mediator of learning performance improvement in an interactive multimedia environment: An empirical investigation of the degree of interactivity and learning styles. *International Journal of Human-Computer Studies, 54*, 541–583.

Lowe, R. (1999). Extracting information from an animation during complex visual processing. *European Journal of the Psychology of Education, 14*, 225–244.

Mandl, A., & Levin, J. (Eds) (1989). *Knowledge acquisition from text and pictures*. Amsterdam, The Netherlands: Elsevier North-Holland.

Mayer, R. E. (1989). Models for understanding. *Review of Educational Research, 59*, 43–64.

Mayer, R. E. (2001). *Multimedia learning*. Cambridge, MA: Cambridge University Press.

Mayer, R. E., & Chandler, P. (2001). When learning is just a click away: Does simple interaction foster deeper understanding of multimedia messages? *Journal of Educational Psychology, 93*, 390–397.

Mayer, R. E., Mautone, P., & Prothero, W. (2002). Pictorial aids for learning by doing in multimedia geology simulation game. *Journal of Educational Psychology, 94*, 171–185.

Rieber, L. P. (1989). The effects of computer animated elaboration strategies and practice on factual and application learning in an elementary science lesson. *Journal of Educational Computing Research, 5*, 431–444.

Rouet, J. F. (Ed.). (2000). Learning from hypermedia systems: Cognitive perspectives. *Journal of Computer Assisted Learning, 16*, Whole Issue.

Schnotz, W. (2001). Sign systems, technologies, and the acquisition of knowledge. In: J. F. Rouet, J. Levonen, & A. Biardeau (Eds), *Multimedia learning: Cognitive and instructional issues* (pp. 9–29). Amsterdam, The Netherlands: Elsevier.

Schnotz, W., & Kulhavy, R. W. (Eds) (1994). *Comprehension of graphics* (Advances in Psychology, Vol. 108). Amsterdam, The Netherlands: Elsevier.

Sweller, J., & Chandler, P. (1994). Why some material is difficult to learn. *Cognition and Instruction, 12*, 185–233.

Tversky, B., Bauer Morrison, J., & Bétrancourt, M. (2002). Animation: can it facilitate? *International Journal on Human Computer Studies, 57*, 247–262.

Chapter 10

Computer Support for Collaborative and Argumentative Writing

Gijsbert Erkens, Gellof Kanselaar, Maaike Prangsma and Jos Jaspers

Introduction

Secondary school students in The Netherlands are doing increasingly independent science projects in preparation for college studies. The projects vary from doing an informational research assignment for History classes to doing an experiment in the context of Biology. Generally these projects are carried out in small groups. This is the result of recent changes in the curriculum of the final years, called the "study house". The focus has shifted towards working actively, constructively and collaboratively, as this is believed to enhance learning.

A groupware learning environment has been developed that supports collaborative writing, which should fit well within this curriculum because the task and communication oriented tools involved can emphasize both the constructivist and collaborative aspects through its active and interactive nature (Erkens *et al.* 2002). Tools in a groupware environment are shared and accessible to all participants. In this way they cannot only support task related constructive activities, but also the collaborative deliberation about these activities. The basic components in a Computer Supported Collaborative Learning (CSCL) environment are the tasks and activities, the learning resources and the shared tools that support the collaborative performance of the task. So, collaboration and the support of argumentation processes between students and the use of shared tools are important aspects of a powerful learning environment in this study. The purpose of this study is to investigate the effect of the developed computer supported writing environment and its tools on the final written product through differences in the participants' collaboration processes. The results discussed here deal with the influence of Computer Mediated Communication (CMC) tools on the argumentation and collaboration processes in writing an argumentative text.

Argumentation and Collaboration

One of the main principles of constructivist learning theory is that the construction of knowledge is negotiated in the dialogue between participants of the learning situation. Such learning through negotiation can consist of testing understanding and ideas against each other as a mechanism for enriching, interweaving and expanding understanding of particular phenomena (Kanselaar & Erkens 1996). Active engagement in collaborative argumentation during problem solving fits this principle by giving prominence to conflict and query as mechanisms for enriching, combining and expanding under-standing of problems that have to be solved (Savery & Duffy 1995). After all, as Von Glaserfeld (1989) has noted, other people are the greatest source of alternative views to challenge our current views and hence to serve as the source of cognitive conflict that stimulates learning.

Knowledge is actively constructed, connected to the individual's cognitive repertoire and to a broader, often team-based and interdisciplinary context in which learning activities take place (Salomon 1997). Constructivism is not only influenced by a Piagetian perspective on individual cognitive development through socio-cognitive conflict, but also by the socio-cultural approach emphasizing the process of interactive knowledge construction in which appropriation of meaning through negotiation plays a central role (Greeno 1997). From a constructivist perspective, collaborative argumenta-tion during problem solving can be regarded as an activity encouraging learning through mechanisms such as externalizing knowledge and opinions, self-explanation, reflecting on each other's information and reconstructing knowledge through critical discussion.

An argument is considered to be a structured connection of claims, evidence and rebuttals. A minimal argument is a claim for which at least doubt or disbelief is expressed (van Eemeren *et al*. 1995). Such doubt or disbelief can be expressed by an individual (if working alone) or by a partner in an argumentative dialogue. In response to such doubts a complex structure may be produced potentially including features such as chaining of arguments, qualifications, contra-indications, counter-arguments and rebuttals. Hence the argument is the product, the structure linking claims, the evidence or rebuttals. Argumentation is the process by which the argument is produced.

The interest of this research lies in argumentation structures that are built by groups of students involved in collaborative problem solving and writing (Kanselaar *et al*. 2000). During problem solving, students are bound to make various claims about the domain and the potential solutions. It is possible that during the problem-solving process no doubt is expressed regarding claims and solutions and hence no argument emerges in the dialogue. However, such a situation seems unlikely and would not produce the best solution to the problem. Certainly if the students have not produced reasons to support the claims and solutions during the problem-solving process itself then there is no reason to believe that they will be able to produce such reasons at a later date. Therefore we believe that students should be encouraged to use argumentation processes to build argument structures during problem solving.

The TC3 Environment

In the COSAR project (acronym for COmputer Supported ARgumentative writing) the groupware program TC3 (Text Composer, Computer supported & Collaborative) was developed with which students carry out the main writing task (Erkens *et al.* 2002). This environment is based on an earlier tool called Collaborative Text Production (CTP; Andriessen *et al.* 1996), and it combines a shared text editor, a chat facility, and private access to a notepad and to information sources to encourage collaborative distance writing. The participants worked in pairs within TC3, each partner working at his/her own computer, and wherever possible partners were seated separately in different classrooms. The main screen of the program displays several private and shared windows. The basic TC3 environment, shown in Figure 1, contains four main windows of which the upper two windows are private and the lower two windows are shared:

(1) INFORMATION (upper right window): This private window contains tabs for the assignment ("i"), sources ("bron") and TC3 operating instructions ("handleiding"). Sources are divided evenly between the students. Each partner has 3 or 5 different sources plus one — fairly factual — common source. The content of the sources cannot be copied or pasted.
(2) NOTES (upper left window, "AANTEKENINGEN"): A private notepad where the student can make non-shared notes.
(3) CHAT (lower left, 3 small windows): The student adds his/her chat message in the bottom box. Every letter typed is immediately sent to the partner via the network, so that both boxes are WYSIWIS: What You See Is What I See. The middle box shows the incoming messages from the partner. The scrollable upper chat box contains the discussion history.
(4) SHARED TEXT (lower right window, "GEMEENSCHAPPELIJKE TEKST"): A simple text editor (also WYSIWIS) in which the shared text is written while taking turns.

Text from the private notes, chat, chat history and shared text can be exchanged through standard copy and paste functions. To allow the participants to focus more on private work or on the collaboration, three layout buttons were added in the left-hand corner: The middle layout button enlarges the private windows, the rightmost button enlarges the shared windows, and the leftmost layout button restores the basic layout. The buttons search ("zoek"), mark ("markeer"), and delete ("wis") can be used to mark and unmark text in the source windows and to search through the marked texts. The number of words ("aantal woorden") button allows the participants to count the number of words in the shared text editor at any given moment. The stop ("stoppen") button ends the session. The traffic light button serves as the turn taking device necessary to take turns in writing in the shared text editor.

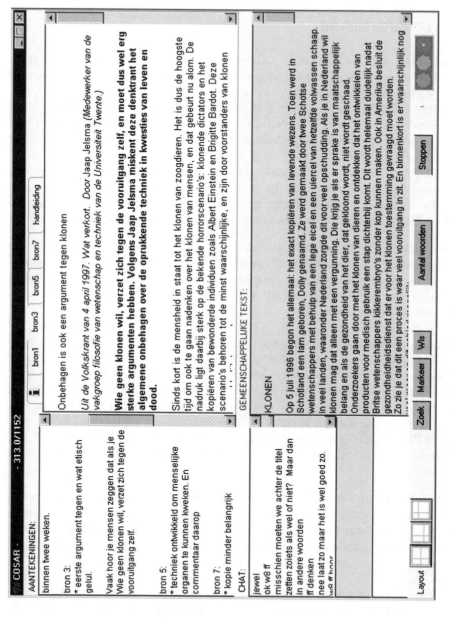

Figure 1: The interface of the basic TC3 environment.

In addition, two planning tools and a helping facility were developed in the TC3 program for the experimental conditions: the diagram, the outline and the advisor. The *diagram* (see Figure 2) is a shared tool for generating, organizing and relating information units in a graphical knowledge structure comparable to Belvédère (Suthers & Hundhausen 2001; Suthers *et al.* 1995). The tool was conceptualized to the students as a graphical summary of the information in the argumentative essay. Students were told that the information contained in the diagram had to faithfully represent the information in the final version of their essay. This requirement was meant to help students to notice inconsistencies, gaps, and other imperfections in their texts, and encourage them to review and revise. In the diagram, several types of text boxes can be used: information ("informatie"), position ("standpunt"), argument pro ("voorargument"), support ("onderbouwing"), argument contra ("tegenargument"), refutation ("weerlegging"), and conclusion ("conclusie"). Two types of connectors were available to link the text boxes: arrows and lines. The diagram can be used to visualize the argumentative structure of the position taken by the students. The effects of the diagram are expected mainly to concern the consistency and completeness of the argumentation of the text (Veerman *et al.* 2000).

The *outline* (see Figure 3) is a shared tool in the TC3 program for generating and organizing information units as an outline of consecutive subjects in the text. This tool was conceptualized to the students as producing a meaningful outline of the paper, and as for the diagram, the participants were required to have the information in the outline faithfully represent the information of the final text. The outline tool was designed to support planning and organization of the linear structure of the texts. The tool allows students to make an overview or hierarchical structure of the text to be written. This should help them in determining the order of content in the text. In addition, the outline tool has the didactic function of making the user aware of characteristics of good textual structure, thus allowing the user to learn to write better texts. The outline has a maximum of four automatically indented, numbered levels. Both planning windows are WYSIWIS. Using the outline is expected to result in a better and therefore more persuasive argumentative structure and a more adequate use of linguistic structures such as connectives and anaphors (Chanquoy 1996).

The *advisor* is a help facility that gives advice on how to use the diagram and/or outline. Participants in the advisor condition received extra instructions before writing about organizing and linearizing ideas in writing an argumentative text. Furthermore, an advisor tab sheet was added to the information window with tips and instructions for optimum use of the planning tools. All communication and activities of the participating students during the collaboration in the TC3 groupware environment are logged automatically in a chat and activity protocol.

Method

Design

For answering the research question about the influence of the shared planning tools on the interaction and argumentative text, an experiment was set up. The experiment was

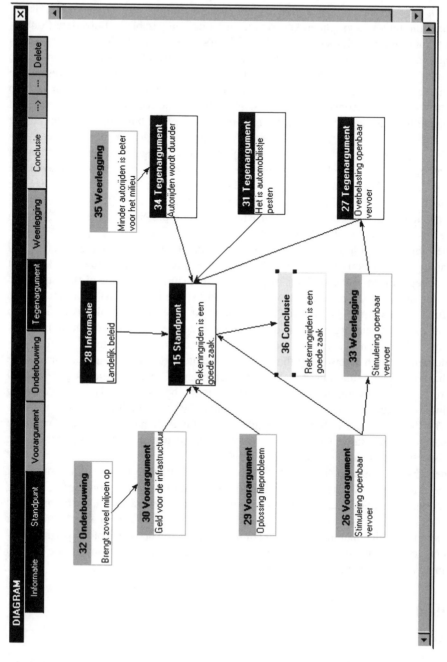

Figure 2: The diagram window in the TC3 program.

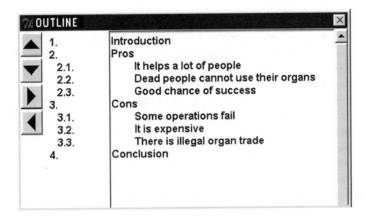

Figure 3: The outline window in the TC3 program.

executed in two separate studies: the control group and the experimental groups. The control condition refers to the basic TC3 environment, whereas the planning tools and advising facility were experimentally varied, resulting in seven experimental conditions (see Table 1).

Logistically, it was not possible to assign students to the experimental conditions at random; so entire classes were assigned to the conditions. To control for school effects, classes from different schools were assigned to each condition. To control for differences in writing and argumentation skills two pre-tests were administered before executing the writing task.

Participants

Participants were 290 Dutch students aged 16 to 18 from six secondary schools in the Netherlands. The assignment was completed during four to six lessons. The initial

Table 1: Experimental design.

Condition	Tools & facilities
Control	Basic TC3
Diagram	Basic TC3 + Diagram
Diagram Advisor	Basic TC3 + Diagram + Advisor
Diagram Outline	Basic TC3 + Diagram + Outline
Diagram Outline Advisor	Basic TC3 + Diagram + Outline + Advisor
Outline	Basic TC3 + Outline
Outline Advisor	Basic TC3 + Outline + Advisor

sample was about 50% larger: dyads who were partially absent during the experiments were excluded from the final sample, as were dyads caught using sources other than those given, communicating through mobile phones or chat programs external to TC3, as well as a few dyads who logged on under each others names to read their partner's information sources.

The analyzed samples included 151 girls and 139 boys. The students worked in pairs that were put together randomly. Pairs were assigned by the experimenter on the basis of the list of names provided by the teacher. Mixed gender dyads comprised 58 pairs of the total sample, while 46 dyads were all female, and 41 were all male.

In order to be able to participate in the experiments, schools had to meet certain criteria. The experiments required one computer per student preferably separating students who were collaborating in two computer labs. The computers should be connected to the school network and have Internet access. Currently, most Dutch schools will meet these criteria, but at the start of these experiments mostly schools selected as official "frontrunners" responded.

The Writing Task

The main task in this study was a collaborative writing task: to write an argumentative text of 600 to 1000 words in Dutch on cloning or organ donation. The assignment was to convince the Minister of Health, Welfare and Sport of the position the students choose to defend on the issue. The arguments pro or con the position had to be based upon facts and discussions about the issue presented in external information sources. The sources were taken from the Internet sites of Dutch newspapers. For organ donation each partner had five private sources plus one common source, so there were eleven sources in total. For cloning the partners each had three sources and one common source, so there were seven sources in total. By splitting the sources among the partners, the students had to exchange and to discuss the relevance of the information presented in the sources. In all groups, partners were seated in separate computer rooms, to encourage them to communicate only through TC3. Naturally, communication during breaks and in between sessions could not be prevented. The students received teacher grades for their texts as part of their normal curriculum.

MEPA: A Tool for Multiple Episode Protocol Analysis

The program Multiple Episode Protocol Analysis (MEPA) was used to analyze all the data the students produced in the TC3 environment. The purpose of MEPA[1] is to offer a flexible environment for creating protocols from verbal and non-verbal observational data, and annotating, coding and analyzing these data. Examples of suitable data within education are class discussions, collaborative discussions, teaching conversations,

---

[1] MEPA was developed as a general program for protocol analysis and is being used in several research projects at Utrecht University, as well as abroad. For further information, please contact G. Erkens.

thinking-aloud protocols, e-mail forums, electronic discussions and videotape transcriptions. The program is multifunctional in the sense that it allows for the development of both the coding and protocolling systems within the same program, as well as direct analysis and exploration of the coded verbal and non-verbal data using several built-in quantitative and qualitative methods of analysis. In its current version, MEPA can execute frequency and time-interval analyses; construct cross-tables with associative measures; perform lag-sequential analysis, interrater reliability, visual charts, word frequency and word context analyses, and carry out selecting, sorting and search processes. Also, some aids for inductive pattern recognition have been implemented. MEPA uses a multidimensional data structure, allowing protocol data to be coded on multiple dimensions or variables. To minimize the work associated with coding protocols and to maximize coding reliability, MEPA contains a module that can be used to program complex structured if-then rules for automatic coding.

The Writing Product: Analysis of the Argumentative Texts

Each of the 145 student pairs produced one argumentative text, and this was analyzed on several dimensions. As a preparation for the final assessment, the texts were imported in MEPA, with a single sentence — defined by a period — per line. The sentences with potential multiple argumentative functions were split into smaller units using an automatic splitting filter, so that the constituents of sentences such as "Cloning is good, but it can also have side effects" could be properly coded as position and argument contra. The sentences were split automatically where necessary on the basis of argumentative and organizational markers, such as *but, however, although, therefore, unless*. Before coding, the experimenters manually divided the texts into segments, largely based on the existing paragraph structure. The final argumentative texts were scored on five variables: (1) The textual structure, which is the formal structure of the text as defined by introduction, body, and conclusion; (2) the segment argumentation, which is the quality of the argumentation within the paragraphs; (3) the overall argumentation, which is the quality of the main line of argumentation in the text; (4) the audience focus, which is the presentation towards the reader and the level of formality of the text, and (5) the mean text score, which is the mean of the four scores above.

Analyses of the Chats

The chat discussions between the students were analyzed by coding every utterance with regard to type and function. The dialogue act coding indicates the type of action and the communicative function of an utterance. The dialogue acts were based on the Verbal Observation System (VOS) and were mainly derived from discourse markers (Erkens 1997). Discourse markers are characteristic words, intonations or grammatical forms showing the function of the phrase in a dialogue. The coding system distinguishes between five communicative functions that can be further subdivided into several dialogue acts. Table 2 shows these communicative functions, and their main dialogue acts with descriptions and examples of discourse markers.

Argumentatives are utterances indicating a line of argumentation or reasoning. Reasoning is used to clarify, but also to convince the partner. Elicitatives are all utterances that are meant to elicit a response: questions or proposals. Imperatives are commanding utterances: commands to take action and summoning to draw the attention of the partner. Informatives serve to transfer information through a statement or an evaluative remark. Responsives are mostly answers to questions and proposals, but they can also be reactions to other utterances from the partner.

The dialogue act coding of the protocols was done almost fully automatically with the help of MEPA. In the program a filter file was made that could label the chat utterances with the dialogue acts. A filter is like a sieve that sifts the protocols for typical words or phrases (discourse markers) through if-then rules. The filter file for the dialogue acts contained more than 700 of these if-then rules. With the filters, some 80 to 85% of the protocol lines were coded automatically. The remaining lines were checked and coded manually: in most cases in one of only two categories. The reliability of the automatic coding filters is naturally high, but the manual correction makes the procedure slightly less reliable.

Results

Tools Condition and Quality of Texts

The COSAR research project was set up as a process-oriented study. However, the end results, that is, the argumentative texts are a vital ingredient for understanding the creative and collaborative processes that are our main interest. In this section the analyses of the argumentative texts are presented and discussed. Table 3 shows the means and standard deviations for all conditions separately and for the sample as a whole.

The table shows that the scores were quite close together for all groups. Independent samples T-tests showed no differences between the two topics — organ donation and cloning — and there were no significant gender differences either. The quality of the texts was not very high: an average of 6.2 on a scale of 1–10 is not very impressive. We found a few differences in a multiple comparison analysis on the conditions: the diagram-advisor group had slightly lower scores on textual structure and segment argumentation, especially in comparison with the control, the diagram, and the diagram-outline-advisor condition. In general we can say that the planning tool conditions in themselves did not have a positive effect on the quality of the resulting texts. However, we must not confuse the availability of a planning tool with the proper use of it. Further analyses showed that using the diagram to specify supports and refutations of positions and to state new arguments was positively related to the quality of the texts. Furthermore, a strong positive influence was found of the proper use of the outline (especially in outline-text congruence) and its advisor on textual structure and segment argumentation in the resulting argumentative text.

Table 2: Communicative functions and dialogue acts in chat discussions.

Communicative function	Code	Dialogue act	Description	Example of discourse marker
Argumentative	ArgRsn	Reason	Explaining by giving a reason	"..., because..."
	ArgCnt	Contra	Giving a counterargument	"But..."
	ArgCon	Conditional	Giving a condition	"If..."
	ArgThn	Consequence	Giving a consequence	"Then..."
	ArgDis	Disjunctive	Disjunctive argument	"Or..."
	ArgCcl	Conclusion	Concluding	"So,..."
Elicitative	EliQstVer	Verification	Yes/no question	"Ready?"
	EliQstSet	Set question	Set question/multiple choice	"...or...?"
	EliQstOpn	Open question	Open question	"Why?"
	EliPrpAct	Proposal	Proposing a action	"Let's..."
Imperative	ImpAct	Command	Ordering a action	"Wait!"
	ImpFoc	Focus signal	Summoning for attention	"Hey!"
Informative	InfPer	Performative	Action performed by saying it	"Thanks"
	InfEva	Evaluation	Pos., neg. or neutral evaluation	"I think..."
	InfStm	Statement	Informative statement	"It is..."
	InfSoc	Social	Social statement	"See you"
Responsive	ResCfm	Confirmation	Confirming information	"Yes"
	ResDen	Denial	Refuting information	"No"
	ResAcc	Acceptance	Accepting information	"Oh,..."
	ResRplStm	Reply	Informative response	"It is..."

Table 3: Descriptive statistics for text quality per condition.

Condition	N	Textual structure		Segment argument		Overall argument		Audience focus		Mean text score	
		Mean	SD	Mean	SD	Mean	SD	Mean	SD	Mean	SD
Control	39	6.76	1.13	6.19	1.36	5.75	2.37	6.20	2.10	6.22	1.43
Diagram	17	6.71	0.97	5.63	1.34	6.81	2.29	5.81	1.84	6.29	1.09
Diagram + Advisor	26	6.03	0.82	5.49	1.34	6.41	2.07	6.01	1.64	6.00	1.01
Diagram + Outline	23	6.44	0.83	5.64	1.32	6.16	2.25	6.20	1.60	6.17	1.03
Diagram + Outline Advisor	11	7.15	0.88	5.42	0.84	5.76	1.69	5.57	1.00	6.19	0.75
Outline	18	6.59	1.00	5.90	1.06	5.74	1.80	6.04	1.95	6.17	0.96
Outline + Advisor	11	6.49	0.83	6.34	0.94	5.76	1.52	6.59	1.90	6.38	0.74
Total	145	6.56	1.00	5.83	1.28	6.06	2.13	6.08	1.81	6.19	1.11

Structural Characteristics of the Chat Dialogue

This section[2] contains a description of the results for the structural characteristics of the dialogue in terms of communicative functions and dialogue patterns within the collaboration dialogues, and the relationship between these features and the final product, the argumentative text. Table 4 shows the distribution for the five communicative functions for the control group and for each experimental condition.

The distribution for all groups together shows that informatives occur most frequently (37.66%), followed by responsives (24.06%). Argumentatives make out an encouraging 10% of the communicative functions, and imperatives are the least frequent with 8%.

Compared to the other conditions, the control group uses significant fewer argumentatives, especially in comparison to the diagram, diagram-advisor and outline conditions. Imperatives are more frequent in the diagram-outline-advisor condition, but less frequent in the diagram and diagram-advisor conditions. The diagram-outline-advisor condition also used fewer informatives, and the outline-advisor group used relatively few responsives.

In general, the distributions within the communicative functions are very similar as well for all conditions, so only the total sample will be discussed here. Within the argumentatives, the relatively most frequent dialogue act refers to counterarguments (3.86%). This is a nice surprise, as relatively novice writers are usually thought to use counterarguments quite sparsely. Verifying questions (9.53%) are relatively most frequent in the elicitatives, followed by proposals (5.75%) and open questions (4.66%). Urging the partner to take action or fulfill a task is the more frequent imperative with 4.91%, although asking for attention follows closely behind at 3.00%. Task information is exchanged relatively often (informative statement = 26.00%), while evaluative informatives are used less frequently (3.74%). Finally, within responsives the most frequent dialogue acts are confirmations (13.46%) and plain replies (3.78%).

Transitions Between Dialogue Acts

Figure 4 shows the transition diagrams made by the MEPA program for the control condition and the diagram condition. The other transition diagrams will be discussed too, but they are not shown here. The transition diagrams result from lag-sequential analyses (Wampold 1992). In lag-sequential analysis the number of transitions of one event to the next (lag = 1) is tested for significance with regard to the expected number of transitions of that type based on the distribution of probability. In the diagrams, only the significant transitions are shown, with the width of the arrows indicating the level of significance. A large number of different transitions in the diagrams points towards unstructured dialogues: the fewer arrows, the more structured the dialogues were for that condition. A relatively high number of autocorrelations — indicated by the circular

---

[2] Floor Scheltens assisted in the data analyses.

Table 4: Distribution of communicative function in the dialogue in mean percentages.

	Total	Control	Diagram	Diagram Advisor	Diagram Outline	Diagram Outline Advisor	Outline	Outline Advisor
	Mean	**Mean**	**Mean**	**Mean**	**Mean**	**Mean**	**Mean**	**Mean**
Argumentatives	9.80	8.98	10.74	10.51	9.72	9.03	10.70	9.04
Elicitatives	20.55	20.46	21.26	20.39	20.92	19.30	20.11	21.30
Imperatives	7.93	8.06	6.40	6.36	7.68	10.74	9.18	9.18
Informatives	37.66	38.65	36.04	38.28	37.93	33.94	36.50	40.22
Responsives	24.06	23.84	25.56	24.45	23.75	26.99	23.51	20.26
	SD	**SD**	**SD**	**SD**	**SD**	**SD**	**SD**	**SD**
Argumentatives	2.82	2.89	2.98	2.77	2.39	2.89	2.51	2.71
Elicitatives	3.97	5.08	3.72	4.04	3.27	1.84	2.74	4.20
Imperatives	3.45	3.31	1.82	1.69	2.50	4.99	5.08	2.69
Informatives	5.65	6.09	4.73	5.51	5.64	3.02	6.11	4.67
Responsives	4.71	4.33	4.48	5.08	3.62	5.18	5.23	3.48
Total number of contributions	425.37	421.15	312.59	441.81	518.00	460.27	401.72	385.91
N (dyads)	145	39	17	26	23	11	18	11

See first column in Table 1 for description of categories and Table 2 for description of conditions.

(A) Transition diagram of Dialogue Acts: control condition

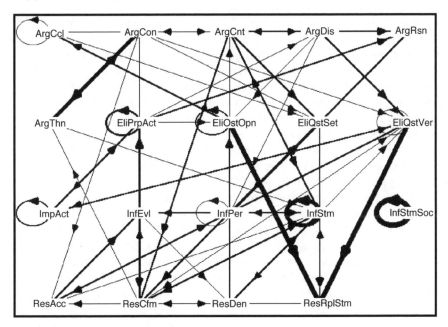

(B) Transition diagram of Dialogue acts: diagram condition

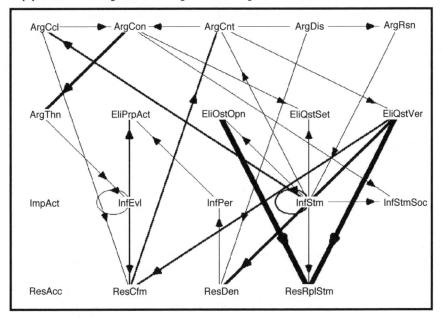

Figure 4: Transition diagrams of dialogue acts in control and in diagram condition.

arrows — also indicates relatively unstructured dialogues. For readability reasons, a number of categories were merged in these analyses.

The control group with only the basic TC3 environment, shown in Figure 4a, differs from the experimental conditions with extra tools: this group shows a lot more different significant transitions between the dialogue acts. The control group displays relatively more different patterns than the experimental groups (i.e. the diagram condition in Figure 4b), and 8 out of 19 of its dialogue acts show autocorrelations, which means that the dialogue is less structured in the control group. Probably, the planning tools in the experimental groups stimulate structuring of the dialogue.

All transition diagrams show one typical pattern in particular: the arrows from open questions (EliQstOpn) and verifying questions (EliQstVer) to statement replies (ResRplStm). Although the obvious answer to a verifying question would be a denying or accepting reply (ResDen or ResAcc) in all seven conditions verifying questions are relatively often answered with an elaborated statement.

Another characteristic pattern is the strong presence of argumentative sequences throughout the conditions (see upper half in Figure 4a and 4b). Only the diagram-advisor condition differs on this point, as it shows fewer transitions between argumentatives than any other condition. The diagram-advisor condition generally differs from the other experimental conditions in its transitions. There are more significant transitions and these transitions are different from the ones that occur in the other experimental groups. For example, argumentative conclusions (ArgCcl) are followed significantly by social statements (InfStmSoc); conditionals (ArgCon) are followed significantly by imperative actions (ImpAct), and there are relatively many transitions to accepting responsives like *mmm* or *oh* (ResAcc). Just like the control group, the diagram-advisor condition contains relatively many autocorrelations.

The transition between 'if'-argumentatives (ArgCon) and 'then'-argumentatives (ArgThn) is not significant for the outline and outline-advisor conditions, whereas the transition *is* significant in the control group and the conditions with the diagram. Possibly, the diagram stimulates the use of if-then patterns, whereas the outline suppresses these patterns.

Conclusions and Discussion

Education can be viewed as an ongoing process of argumentation (Petraglia 1997). It is the process of discovering and generating acceptable arguments and lines of reasoning underlying scientific assumptions and bodies of knowledge. In collaborative learning, students can negotiate different perspectives by externalizing and articulating them, and learn from each other's insights and different understandings. Thus, through negotiation processes, including argumentation, they can construct, re-construct, and co-construct knowledge in relation to specific learning goals. With regard to computerized learning environments, the research indicates that students particularly need facilitation in co-ordinating electronic and text-based communication and in keeping track of the main issues while producing network-based discussions. Technical disturbances and a loss of thematic focus easily occur, especially in synchronous CMC systems, and have a negative effect on collaborative learning processes. Additional tools to keep a graphical overview of the issues at hand can be helpful, such as the diagram construction tool provided by the Belvédère system (Suthers *et al.* 1995) and the TC3 program.

In research by Erkens (1997), focusing, checking and argumentation were revealed as essential factors in collaborative learning processes. In addition, parallel studies aimed at argumentation, epistemic interactions and grounding processes contributed to gaining more understanding of the mechanisms that can support collaborative learning through (electronic) dialogue. In this chapter, a study was presented that explored those relations more in depth. The diagram, outline and diagram-advisor conditions were all found to have a positive effect on the number of argumentatives. This suggests that the moderate availability of extra tools has a positive influence on the number of arguments in the chat and also on some aspects of the quality of the argumentative text.

The transition patterns show that the experimental groups are more structured in their direct communication than the control group. This suggests that the planning tools (diagram and outline) stimulate a more structured dialogue. The same difference in the structure of dialogues can be observed when comparing high scoring and low scoring dyads. This leads us to conclude that the experimental condition (extra tools) has a direct effect on text quality, but also an indirect effect through the communicative function in the chat dialogues.

The analyses of chat dialogues about the diagrams suggest that for some participants this tool did not serve as a basis for discussion or a tool for idea generation, as it was intended, but rather functioned as a visual representation. The correspondence of arguments between the diagram and the final text reveals a discrepancy between the two: Only about a third of the arguments are found both in the final text and the diagram. Although the use of wholly original arguments seems to be slightly positively related to text quality, these are hardly used, and most of the arguments are taken directly from the given sources.

With respect to these results a study of Veerman (2000) can be mentioned in which students used the Belvédère environment to chat electronically and to visualize their discussion about a computer-based design by the use of an argumentative diagram construction tool. It showed that the students only gained from the Belvédère environment, when they linked their chat discussions closely to their diagrams. A significant relationship was found between the amount of overlapping information between chats and diagrams, and the amount of constructive activities produced. However, student groups varied in linking information between chats and diagrams. This appeared to depend heavily on student groups' task approaches and preparation activities.

Using the private — hence non-collaborative — notes window (the upper left window in TC3, see Figure 1) was found to be detrimental to the quality of the collaborative product. This confirms the idea that collaboration is necessary on all subtasks, including planning, idea generation, coordination and information processing. Furthermore, explicit argumentation on content, coordination, and meta-cognitive strategies is related positively to text quality, whereas argumentation on technical aspects of the task and on non-task related topics is related negatively to text quality. The relation between non-task chat and text quality is negative throughout the groups, although the relation is most clear for the control group.

Comparing the diagram (Figure 2) with the outline (Figure 3), the outline tool was more successful. Availability and proper use of this planning tool have a positive effect on the dialogue structure, and on the coordination processes of focusing and argumentation, as well as on text quality. The diagram often functions as a visual representation, and not as a basis for discussion or a tool for idea generation. When a diagram reflects the discussion itself, it can be a valuable starting point for writing the text, and of benefit to textual structure. Students do not have much experience with the use of diagram tools. Perhaps a different approach to the task instruction, for example by giving the students time to practice using the complex diagram tool beforehand, could encourage the students to use the tool as it was intended, and thus lead to different results.

Much is possible in electronic learning environments, but so far not enough is known about the relationships between collaborative learning, argumentation and educational technology. This research has shown that such relationships are neither simple nor very predictable. Hence, much more research is needed that examines the role of (interactive) mechanisms such as argumentation and focusing in relationship to the task, resources and tools offered by a CSCL environment. Instruction and more time to practice using the collaborative tools may help. However, if the goal of education is shared understanding, transmission is not good enough. Design of learning arrangements in which awareness of collaboration is raised and encouraged is then a necessary requirement.

References

Andriessen, J., Erkens. G., Overeem, E., & Jaspers, J. (1996, September). *Using complex information in argumentation for collaborative text production.* Paper presented at the UCIS '96 conference, Poitiers, France.

Chanquoy, L. (1996, October). *Connectives and argumentative text: A developmental study.* Paper presented at the First International Workshop on Argumentative Text Processing, Barcelona, Spain.

Erkens, G. (1997). *Coöperatief probleemoplossen met computers in het onderwijs: Het modelleren van coöperatieve dialogen voor de ontwikkeling van intelligente onderwijssystemen* [Co-operative problem solving with computers in education: Modelling of co-operative dialogues for the design of intelligent educational systems]. Doctoral dissertation. Utrecht, The Netherlands: Brouwer Uithof.

Erkens, G., Prangsma, M. E., Jaspers, J. G. M., & Kanselaar, G. (2002). *Computer supported collaborative and argumentative writing.* Utrecht, The Netherlands: Utrecht University, ICO-ISOR Onderwijsresearch.

Greeno, J. G. (1997). Response: On claims that answer the wrong question. *Educational Researcher, 20*, 5–17.

Kanselaar, G., & Erkens, G. (1996). Interactivity in co-operative problem solving with computers. In: S. Vosniadou, E. De Corte, R. Glaser, & H. Mandl (Eds), *International perspectives on the design of technology-supported learning environments* (pp. 185–202). Mahwah, NJ: Lawrence Erlbaum.

Kanselaar, G., de Jong, T., Andriessen, J. E. B., & Goodyear, P. (2000). New technologies. In: P. R. J. Simons, J. L. van der Linden, & T. Duffy (Eds), *New learning* (pp. 49–72). Dordrecht, The Netherlands: Kluwer Academic Publishers.

Petraglia, J. (1997). *The rhetoric and technology of authenticity in education*. Mahwah, NJ: Lawrence Erlbaum.

Salomon, G. (1997, August). *Novel constructivist learning environments and novel technologies: Some issues to be concerned*. Invited key-note address at the EARLI conference, Athens, Greece.

Savery, J. R., & Duffy, T. M. (1995). Problem based learning: An instructional model and its constructivistic framework. *Educational Technology, 35*, 31–38.

Suthers, D., & Hundhausen, C. (2001). Learning by constructing collaborative representations: An empirical comparison of three alternatives. In: P. Dillenbourg, A. Eurelings, & K. Hakkarainen (Eds), *European perspectives on computer-supported collaborative learning: Proceedings of the first European conference on computer-supported collaborative learning* (pp. 577–584). Maastricht, The Netherlands: University of Maastricht.

Suthers, D., Weiner, A., Connelly, J., & Paolucci, M. (1995, August). *Belvedere: Engaging students in critical discussion of science and public policy issues*. Paper presented at the AI-Ed 95, the 7th World Conference on Artificial Intelligence in Education, Washington, D.C.

Van Eemeren, F. H., Grootendorst, R., & Snoeck Henkemans, A. F. (1995). *Argumentatie* [Argumentation]. Groningen, The Netherlands: Woltersgroep.

Veerman, A. L. (2000). *Computer-supported collaborative learning through argumentation*. Doctoral dissertation. Enschede, The Netherlands: Print Partners Ipskamp.

Veerman, A. L., Andriessen, J. E. B., & Kanselaar, G. (2000.) Enhancing learning through synchronous discussion. *Computers & Education, 34* (2–3), 1–22.

Von Glasersfeld, E. (1989). Cognition, construction of knowledge and teaching. *Synthese, 80*, 121–140.

Wampold (1992). The intensive examination of social interaction. In: T. R. K. J. R. Levin (Ed.), *Single-case research design and analysis: New directions for psychology and education* (pp. 93–133). Hillsdale, NJ: Lawrence Erlbaum.

Part IV

The Role of Peer Tutoring and Collaboration for Promoting Conceptual Change and Intentional Learning in Different Content Domains

Chapter 11

Using Collaborative, Computer-Supported, Model Building to Promote Conceptual Change in Science

Stella Vosniadou and Vassilios Kollias

Introduction

General Design Principles

During the last years a broad consensus has been achieved in instructional psychology on certain basic principles that can guide the design of learning environments within the general theoretical framework of social constructivism (e.g. Bereiter 2002; Brown 1995; Cognition Technology Group at Vanderbilt 1993; Koschmann 1996; Vosniadou 1996). For example, most researchers seem to agree that the support of active learning and the guidance of students towards the acquisition of self-regulated processes are important characteristics of powerful learning environments. The importance of having educational tasks that students find relevant and meaningful is another widely agreed upon principle. Finally, since learning is not an individual but a social affair, researchers usually agree that teachers should encourage children to work with other children and learn from them. Research suggests that collaboration and mutual decision-making can have an important impact on learning outcomes (Howe *et al.* 2000). These and some other design principles of learning environments (from the point of view of instructional psychology) are described in the booklet "How Children Learn", which the first author of this paper wrote for the International Academy of Education and the International Bureau of Education (Educational Practices Series-7; Vosniadou 2001a).

In this chapter we will argue that while principles such as the above are necessary to be taken into consideration when designing learning environments, they are not sufficient by themselves. They need to be supplemented by principles emerging from research on the acquisition of subject matter knowledge, particularly in the case of science teaching. There are at least two good reasons for this argument. First, each discipline has its own unique methods of testing and of argumentation that constitute an important part of the expertise in this discipline and thus of the content and skills that need to be taught. The scientific ways of establishing reliable empirical knowledge, the methods of scientific argumentation and finally the goals of scientific enterprise are different from those of other human activities (e.g. mathematics, history, etc.), and need to be taken into consideration when designing learning environments for teaching science. Second, scientific knowledge is the outgrowth of a long historical development that required significant scientific revolutions to take place. The body of knowledge that constitutes current science contradicts basic presuppositions of our intuitive knowledge about the physical world and requires radical conceptual change to be understood. In order to promote conceptual change in science, we will argue, particular attention needs to be paid to the design of appropriate curricula and the development of metaconceptual awareness and intentional (purposeful, goal-directed) learning.

In the pages that follow we will concentrate on the issue of conceptual change and we will describe our experimentation with two different learning environments designed to promote conceptual change in the learning of science.

The Problem of Conceptual Change in the Learning of Science

Research in cognitive development and science instruction has shown that by the time when systematic instruction starts, most children have already constructed a naïve theory of physics that makes it possible for them to interpret phenomena in the physical world. The term "theory" is used here to denote a relational explanatory structure, and not an explicit, well-formed, and socially shared scientific theory. This naïve theory is based on everyday experience and information coming from lay culture, and it is very different in its structure, in the phenomena it explains, and in its individual concepts, from the scientific theories to which children are exposed in school.

For example, a number of studies investigating children's knowledge about observational astronomy (e.g. Vosniadou 1994; Vosniadou & Brewer 1992; Vosniadou & Brewer 1994) have shown that when children go to school they have already formed a framework theory of the physical world within which astronomical phenomena are interpreted. In the context of this naïve "framework" theory[1] of physics, the earth is interpreted to be a physical object, which obeys all the constraints that apply to physical objects in general. In other words, the earth is conceptualized as a solid, stationary object that is supported (usually) by ground or water, with people living above its flat top and with the solar objects and the sky occupying the space above its top, as shown in Figure 1.

This naïve cosmology is of course very different from the scientifically accepted cosmology to which students are instructed when they go to school; in other words, that

---

[1] The "framework theory" specifies the general ontological and epistemological presuppositions of a naïve theory of physics within which various "specific theories" (such as a theory of astronomy) can be embedded (see Vosniadou 1994, 2002; for more details).

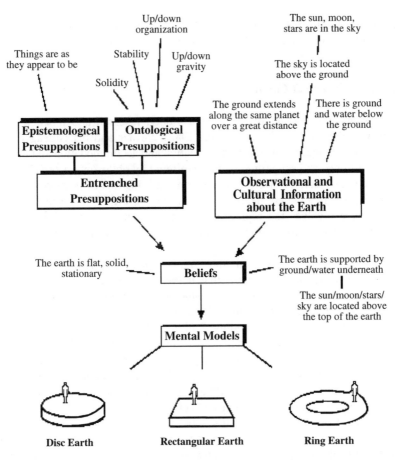

Figure 1: Hypothetical conceptual structure underlying children's concept of the shape of the earth.

the earth is a huge sphere that rotates around its axis and revolves around the sun, in a heliocentric solar system.

Empirical studies in this area have shown that students, not being aware of the fundamental differences between the scientific information and their own prior knowledge, often add the information that the earth is sphere to what they already know, forming misconceptions or "synthetic models" as we call them (Vosniadou & Brewer 1992; Vosniadou & Brewer 1994). For example, they may come to the conclusion that there are two earths: one is a spherical earth which is a planet in space and the other a flat, stationary and supported earth on which people really live. Alternatively, they may think that there is only one earth but that this earth is both round and flat (like a disc), or it is like a truncated sphere or like a hollow sphere with people living inside it, on flat ground. By forming such synthetic models children find a way to assimilate the new information that comes from instruction to their existing knowledge structures. They try to synthesize the information that the earth is a sphere with what they know already about the earth, namely that it is flat and that people live above its top.

Teaching for Conceptual Change

For many years, the leading paradigm that guided research and practice in science education was the work of Posner *et al.* (1982). Posner and his colleagues drew an analogy between Piaget's concepts of assimilation and accommodation and the concepts of "normal" science and scientific revolution offered by philosophers of science such as Kuhn (1970) and derived from this analogy an instructional theory to promote "accommodation" in students' learning of science. According to Posner *et al.* (1982), learning science involves the replacement of persistent misconceptions with correct scientific ideas, using instructional techniques such as the production of cognitive conflict.

Smith *et al.* (1993) criticized the "replacement through cognitive conflict" instructional position on the grounds that it presents a narrow view of learning that focuses only on the mistaken qualities of students' prior knowledge and ignores their productive ideas that can become the basis for achieving a more sophisticated mathematical or scientific understanding. Smith *et al.* (1993) argue that misconceptions should be reconceived as faulty extensions of productive knowledge, that misconceptions are not always resistant to change, and that instruction that "confronts misconceptions with a view to replacing them is misguided and unlikely to succeed" (p. 153). Furthermore, diSessa (1998, 1993) argued that naïve physics is a collection of fragmented pieces of knowledge that he calls phenomenological primitives (p-prims). P-prims originate from superficial abstractions of physical knowledge and slowly get organized into a larger system of complex knowledge structures, which can be a constellation of misconceptions or the scientific laws of physics, depending on the way instruction works out with the students.

We think that diSessa and his colleagues are correct when they point out that the knowledge structures of naïve physics are not a unitary framework that can be replaced by the scientific explanatory framework in gestalt-like shifts, but complex knowledge structures consisting of many interrelated pieces that change gradually over time. We also appreciate their efforts to provide an account of the knowledge acquisition process that captures the continuity one expects with learning and development.

However, we do not agree with the view that naïve physics is a collection of fragmented phenomenological principles that students do not organize in larger conceptual structures until systematic instruction starts. On the contrary, everything we know about naïve physics shows that, although it does not have the systematicity and coherence of a scientific theory, it nevertheless forms an explanatory structure capable of generating predictions and explanations and capable of resisting change and causing misconceptions and synthetic models.

The process of learning science is not simply a process of synthesizing fragmented p-prims, but a process during which the explanatory framework of naïve physics is slowly eroded by pieces of scientific information that are added to it, destroying its limited coherence and creating synthetic models. In the case of some easy concepts (such as the shape of the earth and the day/night cycle) some conceptual change can happen during usual instruction and for most students, but in most cases instruction fails to bring about the required conceptual change and students remain confused and with various misconceptions, even after years of science instruction.

This seems to be the case because currently accepted scientific explanations and concepts have evolved over thousands of years of scientific discovery to become rather elaborate, counter-intuitive theories that differ radically from those originally con-structed on the basis of everyday experience. The learning of science requires fundamental changes in existing conceptual structures that are difficult to take place both because of their complexity and because of their counter-intuitive nature but also because of the lack of appropriate instruction. In this paper we will focus on two aspects of instruction that we think are important for conceptual change. The first has to do with the design of curricula that take into consideration students' prior beliefs and presuppositions. The second centers around the development of students' meta-conceptual awareness in science and more general, the creation of intentional learners.

With respect to the first issue, although it is by now considered to be commonplace that scientific concepts need to be introduced in ways that address students' prior beliefs and presuppositions, this does not usually happen. On the contrary, it is very often the case that students are introduced to counter-intuitive information as a fact. For example, when students are taught about the shape of the earth, they are usually told that the earth is "round like a ball" and they are shown a globe to demonstrate the real shape of the earth. The contradiction between the perceived flatness of the earth and its assumed roundness is not explained. Neither are the students told how it is possible for people to live on a spherical earth without "falling down". This type of instruction that presents the new information as a fact, as opposed to something that needs to be explained, does not take into consideration students' prior beliefs and presuppositions. In accordance to what we mentioned already, some of the things that need to be explained are for example, the following: If the earth is a ball, why does it appear to be flat? Where exactly do people live on this spherical earth? How is it possible for people to live on the sides or bottom of a spherical earth without falling down? As we saw earlier in Figure 1, students' ideas about the shape of the earth are embedded within a larger network of beliefs and presuppositions that form a complex conceptual structure. All of this structure needs to be changed if we would like to have students who really understand the spherical shape of the earth.

Existing science curricula often do not provide explanations that take into consideration students' prior beliefs. We have examined science curricula both in the U.S. and in Greece and we found that in both cases, the information about the spherical shape of the earth was not adequate (Vosniadou 1991). This does not happen only in the case of the earth. It is a widespread phenomenon in science instruction.

In our opinion, it is very important for effective science instruction to design research-based curricula that focus on the deep exploration of a few, key concepts in one subject-matter area and that take into consideration students' prior beliefs and presuppositions in a systematic fashion.

A second but equally important characteristic of learning environments that promote conceptual change in the learning of science, we believe has to do with encouragement of metaconceptual awareness and the development of intentional (purposeful and goal oriented) learning. What we mean by metaconceptual awareness is awareness of one's own beliefs and presuppositions and also awareness that one's beliefs about the physical world are hypotheses that can be subjected to experimentation and can be falsified. Students are often unaware of fundamental presuppositions and beliefs that constrain their understanding of scientific explanations or take these presuppositions to be basic truths about the physical world that cannot be questioned (such as, for example, the presupposition that space is organized in terms of the directions of "up" and "down" and that unsupported objects fall down). An important goal of science instruction is to make students aware of their ideas and beliefs and presuppositions and *also* to make them understand that these beliefs are not unique (other students may have different ones). Understanding that your beliefs can be tested and sometimes that they can be falsified, understanding how to use evidence to evaluate a theory and how to revise a theory in light of disconfirming evidence, are fundamental to understanding science.

We believe that the development of metaconceptual awareness is very much related to the more general problem of creating intentional and purposeful learners who can take control of their own learning, know how to learn and how to correct their mistakes. Intentional learning is important, beyond metaconceptual awareness, because conceptual change is a difficult task and requires motivated and committed learners who know how to guide their learning processes. Teachers need to develop educational environments that emphasize understanding over memorization, inquiry rather than learning by authority, create positive beliefs and attitudes about science and about learning, allow students some control over their learning and support a constructivist epistemology of science. Collaborative learning, class discussions, observations, experiments, and the design of models, are important instructional tools for the development of metaconceptual awareness and intentional learning.

Developing Learning Environments for Science

Experiment 1

In Vosniadou, Ioannides, Dimitrakopoulou & Papadimitriou (2001) an experiment was described to test a learning environment to teach science (mechanics and astronomy) to fifth and sixth grade students. The learning environment consisted of an eight-week problem-based experimental curriculum geared towards addressing some of the major difficulties students face when confronted with scientific ideas in astronomy and mechanics. It was based on prior research in this area and attempted to address most of the prior presuppositions and beliefs of students that can stand in the way of understanding currently accepted scientific explanations in these two subject-matter areas. The students were encouraged to express and support their ideas, make predictions and hypotheses, and test them by conducting experiments. They worked in small groups and presented their work to the classroom for debate. Metaconceptual awareness was promoted by encouraging students to make their ideas overt, to discuss them with the other students, and to compare them with the scientific explanations. Emphasis was also placed on giving the students the opportunity to use models, representational symbols, and measurement tools. Results showed significant differences between the experimental and control groups in pre- and post-test comparisons, confirming our hypothesis that the experimental learning environment would result in cognitive gains for the participating students.

Despite the cognitive gains, the learning environment did not provide the students with many opportunities to have control over their learning and to develop cognitive monitoring skills. The monitoring of the classroom and the decisions about learning content and learning activities was still under the control of the teacher. Given the importance of developing not only metaconceptual awareness but also intentional learning, as was discussed earlier, we were interested in developing a learning environment that gave students more freedom to decide on their own learning activities, and to plan and monitor their learning. We were also interested in supporting the development of a learning community culture in the classroom, and to investigate the interplay between social interactions, collaboration, and learning processes. In the pages that follow we will focus on Experiment 2, which attempted to construct a learning environment to promote students' awareness of their own ideas and to give them more control over their learning.

Experiment 2

Experiment 2 took place in the context of a European project on Computer-Supported Collaborative Learning (CL-Net).[2] In the context of this project, two interventions were planned and took place in two 6th grade classrooms in a big private primary school at the outskirts of Athens (Kollias *et al.* 1999; Kollias *et al.* 2001). A software tool specially designed for the support of a CSCL (Scardamalia & Bereiter 1994), Web Knowledge Forum[3] (WebKF) environment, scaffolded students in creating and using a public database where much of the discussion was taking place (for a review of some of the opportunities and difficulties of these learning environments, see Lehtinen *et al.* 1999; Lipponen 1999; Stahl 1999).

The two interventions of experiment 2 had a similar design. Students had to construct a model of the internal heating system of an average Greek house (The "Hot water heating system") and to explain how such a system works. The specific topic was selected after discussions with the students themselves, in order to supplement a unit on

---

[2] CL-Net: Computer Supported Collaborative Learning Networks in Primary and Secondary Education (is a TSER program, which lasted from 1998 to 2000. http://www.b.shuttle.de/wifo/across/p-cl.htm). The central goal of this program, which was formed by a collaboration of research groups from Italy, Netherlands, Belgium, Greece, and Finland was to investigate the didactical and conceptual aspects of CSCL environments.

[3] Web Knowledge Forum is a software tool specially designed for the support of CSCL. It scaffolds the construction of a shared data base by means that promote reflection on the writing processes and on the ideas expressed.

thermal phenomena that was part of their regular science curriculum at the time. Because of the similarity of the two interventions we consider them as two implementations of the same learning environment. The interventions took place in one of the computer rooms of the school and each one lasted for one hour a week for approximately 12 weeks.

The design of these interventions was directed by the following general goals:

(1) To encourage the expression and use of prior knowledge for knowledge building and conceptual change through the use of Knowledge Forum;
(2) To use collaboration to increase motivation and to promote the development of metacognitive and self-regulation skills. The students worked in dyads to find the information and to design the models. They then formed larger groups to work on their final project presentations to the class;
(3) To promote the teacher's role as a facilitator of students' knowledge-building activities and to move students into a more constructivist epistemology of science. For this purpose, the teacher agreed not to provide direct information to the students but to guide them in their search for information. The emphasis was removed from the memorization of correct science facts and explanations to helping the students find the relevant information themselves;
(4) To transfer planning responsibilities to the students in order to promote the development of self-regulation and metacognitive skills. In order to achieve this goal, the students had to find the relevant information, organize it, design a model of the heating system, and present it to the rest of the class in collaboration with other students.

The following sequences of actions were followed in both interventions:

• The students were divided in dyads and each dyad had access to one computer;
• All the students were taught how to use the software (Knowledge Forum) in the context of some initial activities. After that, they started the project, which was to design a model of a hot water heating system;
• A note by the teacher in Knowledge Forum started the discussion about the hot water heating system. The students started commenting on each other's notes, and the teacher took the role of coordinating the discussion and of pointing out discrepancies and inconsistencies in the students' notes;
• The teacher did not provide direct evaluation of students' work but mostly made suggestions to them to read and discuss the other students' notes and also helped them to locate relevant information (web pages, books, etc.);
• The teacher suggested some web pages and also some books and photocopied material. The students visited the central heating system of their school where the responsible expert described to them how the system works. In addition, they interviewed other experts, and discussed the problem with knowledgeable members of their families;
• The students formed larger groups of approximately six children to prepare a final presentation of their findings. The students presented their projects to their peers and to another 6th grade class of their school in the school's auditorium.

The cognitive and metacognitive effects of these interventions were assessed using pre and post questionnaires, through a comparison of children's models of the heating system at the beginning and at the end of each intervention, through analyzing children's notes in the Knowledge Forum data base and also through an analysis of the children's discourse in the dyads.

The results are too numerous to be presented here in detail (Kollias *et al.* 1999; Kollias *et al.* 2001). In summary, the questionnaires testing for knowledge of subject matter showed significant pre-post differences in specific questions indicating that the students understood better how a hot water heating system works but did not show gains in knowledge about heat and temperature in general (i.e. about thermal equilibrium, heat conductivity and the relation between heat and temperature). This came as no surprise because the intervention did not attempt to help the children generalize on the basis of their model building but was rather designed to help them develop knowledge building skills for independent learning and cognitive monitoring. Indeed, the children were able, with the support of the teacher, to locate the necessary information, to evaluate and organize it and to construct an appropriate model of the hot water heating system. Figures 2a&b and 3a&b show examples of the improvement in children's designs and written explanations during the intervention.

The designs were assessed more formally on the number of critical ideas present and the general understanding of the functioning of the heating system, and significant pre-post test differences were found. The students learned about the different parts that make up an internal heating system and their function, and understood the repetitive and continuous nature of its mechanism. They appreciated the functionality of the oil in producing the heat that is necessary, and understood that the pipes must form closed loops as they distribute the water to the radiators. They incorporated the scientific terminology in the explanations and descriptions and were very interested in the task despite its relatively dry nature. The students did not, of course, understand everything. They had difficulty understanding the role of the expansion tank and how the water comes back to its original temperature.

The Knowledge Forum database was analyzed following a categorization scheme that distinguished the different notes produced by the dyads into "cognitive", "meta-cognitive" and "communicative". *Cognitive* notes consisted of explanations, descriptions, clarifications and specifications. *Metacognitive* notes consisted of exchanges indicating planning, monitoring and evaluation. The *communicative* notes were more socially oriented.

It thus appears that the students were using WebKF mostly to explain, clarify, and describe phenomena, and not to plan and organize what they were going to write in their notes. On the contrary, a great deal of the metacognitive activity seemed to take place in the conversations that took place between the children in the dyads, where the children talked about what they were going to write in the notes. In what follows, we present data that pertain to the relation between collaborative characteristics in the intra-dyad interactions and cognitive and metacognitive characteristics of intra-dyad discourse.

The experimenters observed and videotaped some dyads of students, at various times, as they discussed between themselves how to construct their models and planned what

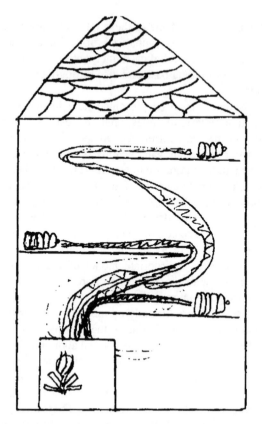

Water gets hot with oil and rises through the pipes to every radiator.
We push the button and this way the place gets warm.

Figure 2a: Design of a model of the hot-water heating system at the beginning of the
intervention (group A).

to write in the Knowledge Forum. Each observation lasted while students completed a
task at hand and had a duration of the order of 5 to 10 minutes. There were 17 such
observations throughout the second intervention (some of the 12 dyads involved were
observed twice). The students' intra-dyad interaction was subsequently analyzed both in
terms of the *Discourse Types* that appeared in the verbal exchanges and the
Collaboration Style of the dyad.

   Three categories of *Collaboration Style* were identified on the basis of the following
criteria: (a) presence of fights or antagonism; (b) mutual exchange of thoughts and
opinions; (c) even division of tasks; and (d) mutual decision making and planning of
activities. The categories were *Reciprocity*, *Forced Collaboration* and *No Collaboration*.
Reciprocity was characterized by peaceful and effective collaboration during which the
two partners mutually decided on the tasks to be completed, discussed their opinions
and thoughts, planned their activities and divided the tasks. *Forced Collaboration* was

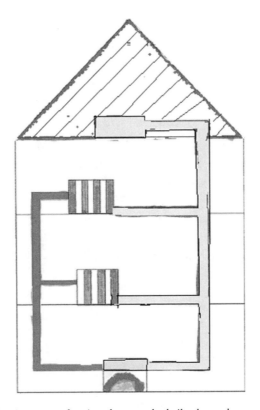

The heating system functions because the boiler heats the water and burns the oil. The heat is transferred from the boiler with various pipes to the radiators. The lighter pipes carry the cold water to the boiler so that it heats it again and the darker pipes carry the hot water from the boiler to the radiators. We repeat this as many times as it needs to warm up. The radiator helps us to keep warm the cold winters.

Figure 2b: Design of a model of the hot-water heating system at the end of the intervention (group A).

characterized by an antagonistic attitude between the partners that prevented efficient collaboration, even when the partners tried to do so. In these dyads, there were some discussions and exchanges of thoughts but there was not an even division of tasks and sometimes the partners went on their own individual course of action. Finally, *No Collaboration* was characterized by complete lack of collaboration. In this case the partners did not share their thoughts and opinions, did not share tasks and responsibilities, and ended up working separately or not working at all.

An analysis of the data from the 17 observations showed 10 instances of *Reciprocity* (60%), 5 instances of *Forced Collaboration* (25%) and 2 instances of *No Collaboration* (15%). From the above we concluded that despite the fact that the students did not have any previous experience in collaborating, most dyads were able to achieve a *Reciprocal* style of interaction.

*Oh! I cannot stand it. We must use the radiators so that we are warm in
the cold winter. Achoo!*

Figure 3a: Design of a model of the hot-water heating system at the beginning of the
intervention (group B).

The analysis of the students' *Discourse Type* allowed us to examine the relationship
between *Collaboration Style* and *Discourse Type*. Four categories of discourse were
identified to take place in the student dyads: (1) *Cognitive*: the children talked about how
to design the model of the heating systems and their remarks could be categorized as
explanatory, descriptive, clarificatory, etc. (2) *Metacognitive*: the children planned their
course of action, evaluated what they had done and evaluated themselves, talked about
the procedures necessary, etc. (3) *Motivational*: the students talked about the need to
further understand why they were doing what they were doing, the need for finding
more information, or the need to impose their opinion. (4) *Collaborative*: the students
talked about how to collaborate and about how to divide the tasks and the procedures.

Figure 4 shows the relationship between *Discourse Type* and *Collaboration Style* in
the dyads. As can be seen, a large% of the discourse in all the dyads centers around
questions of how to collaborate. But this discussion is predominant in the *No
Collaboration* Style, compared to the *Forced Collaboration* and the *Reciprocal*
Collaboration Styles. The children in the *No Collaboration* Style, cannot go beyond

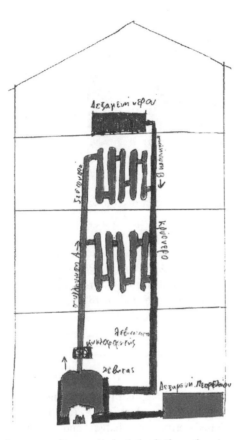

The heating system is composed of the boilers, the pipes and the radiators. The boiler is the place where the water gets hot with the help of the oil. The pipes are made of iron and are covered by plastic or by some bad heat conductor. The hot water passes from the radiators and the room gets warm. In the roof there is a tank with hot water that throws it in the pipes towards the boiler. This is how the radiator works.

Figure 3b: Design of a model of the hot-water heating system at the end of the intervention (group B).

talking about how to collaborate. In the *Forced Collaboration* group, in addition to talking about how to collaborate, the children seem to spend some time on motivational discourse. These children were asking why they were doing what they were doing, what they needed to do in order to complete the task, and negotiated who was going to do what. In contrast to the above, the children in the *Reciprocal* Style talked about the task itself and engaged in the planning and monitoring necessary to do the cognitive work. A great deal of the discourse in this group belonged to the metacognitive category and supplemented the cognitive notes that appeared in the data base of the Knowledge Forum. What is interesting about this discourse is that it is exact and detailed as the

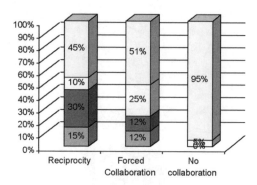

Figure 4: Relationship between discourse types and collaboration styles.

children are discussing in depth specific details of the heating system that are necessary in order to understand its function. Collaborative model building thus, helps students slowly move from their inexact and tacit way of reasoning to the explicit formulation of their ideas whose adequacy can be tested in the context of designing a system that works.

Conclusions

In order to facilitate the kind of conceptual restructuring often required in the learning of science, we need to pay particular attention to: (a) the design of curricula that take into consideration students' prior knowledge; and (b) the development of met-aconceptual awareness, metacognitive skills, and intentional (purposeful and goal-oriented) learning. In this chapter, we focused on the description of a computer-supported collaborative learning environment designed to encourage the development of critical discourse around students' ideas and beliefs and also to give students more control over their learning. We believe that such an environment can be helpful in developing the metacognitive and intentional learning skills that are necessary if we want to make students understand the anomalies behind the counter-intuitive science concepts presented to them through instruction.

An important characteristic of this environment is the technological tool that allows collaboration to be more effective. In Knowledge Forum, the use both of collaboration and of computers opens up the space of possibilities. Collaboration leaves students open to strong social influences that have the potential to "shake" their convictions (by experiencing a variety of alternative opinions), question their sense of understanding (through social pressure when in the minority), and create both contexts of conflict and needs to reach agreement in order to stream operations. Through all these experiences students realize a multifaceted reality in which different opinions can be reasonably supported and challenged and where different forms of resolution have to be tried out to achieve some result they can be proud of. However, the above leave open the possibility of shallow agreements, decisions by majority rule irrespective of the subject as well as the logistic problems of mastering the multiplicity of information and understandings that come forth. The use of computers has the additional advantage of stabilizing information and opinions in a written form and structuring communication so that multiple discussions can be simultaneously pinned on a system of coordinates (i.e. the tree structure of Web Knowledge Forum). In this way, affordances for metacognition created in a collaborative environment can be taken full advantage of, allowing students to think deeper on their own timing, and the teacher to make appropriate comments either to guide interaction or to provide the norms of the discipline under study. In the written collaboratively created data base the student can start comprehending a different meaning for what "learning physics" or "learning history", or "learning mathematics" means. In front of her there is knowledge that has been created painstakingly, with gradual progress, using tools on specific objects, through various contributions.

References

Bereiter, C. (2002). *Education and mind in the knowledge age*. Mahwah NJ: Lawrence Erlbaum Associates.

Brown, A. L. (1995). Advances in learning and instruction. *Educational Researcher, 23* (8), 4–12.

Cognition and Technology Group at Vanderbilt (1993). Anchored instruction and situated cognition revised. *Educational Technology, 33* (3), 42–70.

diSessa, A. A. (1993). Toward an epistemology of physics. *Cognition and Instruction, 10,* 105–225.

diSessa, A. A. (1998). What changes in conceptual change? *International Journal of Science Education, 20,* 1155–1191.

Howe, C., Tolmie, A., Duckar-Tanner, V., & Rattray, C. (2000). Hypothesis testing in science: Group consensus and the acquisition of conceptual and procedural knowledge, *Learning and Instruction, 10,* 361–391.

Kollias, V., Vosniadou, S., & Ioannides, C. (1999). *Designing a computer supported collaborative learning environment for science teaching*. 8th European Conference for Research in Learning and Instruction, August 24–28, Goeteborg, Sweden.

Kollias, V. P., Vlassa, M., & Vosniadou, S. (2001). *Design and evaluation of a CSCL environment for the learning of science*. European Perspectives on Computer-Supported Collaborative Learning, Universiteit Maastricht, March 22–24, Maastricht, The Netherlands.

Koschmann, T. (1996). Paradigm shifts and instructional technology. In: T. Koschmann (Ed.), *CSCL: Theory and practice of an emerging paradigm* (pp. 1–23). Mahwah NJ: Lawrence Erlbaum Associates.

Kuhn, T. (1970). *The structure of scientific revolutions*. Chicago: Chicago University Press.

Lehtinen, E., Hakkarainen, K., Lipponen, L., Rahikainen, M., & Muukkonen, H. (1999). *Computer-supported collaborative learning: A review of research and development* (The J.H.G.I. Giesbers Reports on Education, 10). The Netherlands: University of Nijmegen, Department of Educational Sciences.

Lipponen, L. (1999). Challenges for computer-supported collaborative learning in elementary and secondary level: Finnish perspective. In: C. Hoadley (Ed.), *Proceedings of CSCL '99: The Third International Conference on Computer Support for Collaborative Learning* (pp. 368–375). Mahwah, NJ: Lawrence Erlbaum Associates.

Posner, G. J., Strike, K. A., Hewson, P. W., & Gertzog, W. A. (1982). Accommodation of a scientific conception: Toward a theory of conceptual change. *Science Education, 66*, 211–227.

Scardamalia, M., & Bereiter, C. (1994). Computer support for knowledge-building communities. *The Journal of the Learning Sciences, 3*, 265–283.

Stahl, G. (1999). Reflections on WebGuide. Seven issues for the next generation of collaborative knowledge-building environments. In: C. Hoadley (Ed.), *Proceedings of CSCL '99: The Third International Conference on Computer Support for Collaborative Learning* (pp. 600–610). Mahwah, NJ: Lawrence Erlbaum Associates.

Smith, J. P., diSessa, A. A., & Roschelle, J. (1993). Misconceptions reconceived: A constructivist analysis of knowledge in transition. *The Journal of the Learning Sciences, 3*, 115–163.

Vosniadou, S. (1991). Computer-based learning environments and the problem of conceptual change. In: E. De Corte, M. Linn, H. Mandl, & L. Verschaffel (Eds.) *Computer-based learning environments and problem solving* (pp. 149–162). Heidelberg: Springer-Verlag.

Vosniadou, S. (1994). Capturing and modeling the process of conceptual change. In: S. Vosniadou (Ed.), Special issue on conceptual change, *Learning and Instruction, 4*, 45–69.

Vosniadou, S. (2001). *How children learn* (Educational Practices Series). The International Academy of Education (IAE) and the International Bureau of Education (UNESCO).

Vosniadou, S. (2002). Exploring the relationships between conceptual change and intentional learning. In: G. M. Sinatra, & P. R. Pintrich (Eds), *Intentional conceptual change* (pp. 377–406). Mahwah, NJ: Lawrence Erlbaum Associates.

Vosniadou, S., & Brewer, W. F. (1992). Mental models of the earth: A study of conceptual change in childhood. *Cognitive Psychology, 24*, 535–585.

Vosniadou, S., & Brewer, W. F. (1994). Mental models of the day/night cycle. *Cognitive Science, 18*, 123–183.

Vosniadou, S. (1996). Learning environments for representational growth and cognitive flexibility. In: S. Vosniadou, E. De Corte, R. Glaser, & H. Mandl (Eds), *International perspectives on the design of technology-supported learning environments* (pp. 13–24). Mahwah NJ: Laurence Erlbaum Associates.

Vosniadou, S., Ioannides, C., Dimitrakopoulou, A., & Papademetriou, E., (2001). Designing learning environments to promote conceptual change in science. *Learning and Instruction, 11*, 421–429.

Chapter 12

Analysis of Peer Interaction among Children in a Tutoring Situation Pertaining to Mathematical Problems of the Multiplying Type

Marcel Crahay, Geneviève Hindryckx and Martine Lebé

Introduction

Students can learn through their interactions. Former educationalists' conviction (Dewey 1900; Freinet 1964; Kilpatrick 1922; etc.) became scientific certainty during the second half of the twentieth century. There is now a considerable range of studies showing that pupils or students joint activity situations can be components of powerful learning environments. Especially, research has documented the efficiency of cooperative learning (working group characterized by symmetric interactive roles of participants) as well as peer tutoring (characterized by dissymmetric interactive role with a tutor who has to teach a tutee) (see Crahay 1999, 2000, for an inventory).

Findings from educational studies tally perfectly with psychological research that underscores the impact of peer tutoring interaction on psychological development. Bruner (1996) conceptualizes this phenomenon in terms of scaffolding. Following Vygotsky's and/or Bruner's theory, many researchers investigated the nature of tutor-tutee regulation patterns that lead to learning for both of them (in particular: Beaudichon *et al.* 1988; Berzin *et al.* 1985; Ellis & Rogoff 1982; Radsiszewska & Rogoff 1988; Shute *et al.* 1992; Verba & Wynnikamen 1992).

According to Vedder (1985), a helpful tutoring relationship should satisfy five conditions in order to be effective. Webb (1989) added a first and a last condition to those listed by Vedder:

(1) The learner receiving help must be aware that s/he needs it;
(2) The help received must be relevant to the *learner's* (the target student's) specific misconception or lack of understanding;

(3) The help offered must be at a level of elaboration that corresponds to the level of help requested by the *learner*;
(4) The help must be given in close proximity in time to the *learner*'s request for help;
(5) The *learner* must understand the explanation given;
(6) The *learner* must have an opportunity to use the explanation received to solve the problem or one (or several) analogous problem(s);
(7) The *learner* must use that opportunity.

According to Webb (1989), working in small groups of peers creates a social environment that is particularly beneficial to learning insofar as most of the conditions listed above are satisfied in an almost natural way. Considering that team-mates are about the same age and attain the same developmental level, they share a similar language. Because they are working on the same problem at the same time, those who experience difficulties can benefit from immediate regulation. Conversely, in a collective teaching situation, the teacher's explanations rarely come precisely when the student needs them. Joint learning activity situations — either cooperative group work or peer tutoring — give rise to an additional benefit: those students who do understand can easily identify what their team-mate is struggling with and accurately spot his/her problem, so that their help can be targeted at that specific difficulty.

Webb (1989, 1991, 1996) felt that the third condition listed above is particularly important. This led her to envisage three possible starting points for her model of interactive monitoring.

(1) The *learner* shows substantial difficulty in solving the problem. S/he makes a serious error or asks a high-level question. In this case, it is important that the tutor provides a *highly elaborate response* (i.e. detailed explanations on how to solve the problem). Although the effect of this type of tutoring support is not assured, it is the only possible path toward correct problem solving and thus to a successful learning outcome;
(2) The *learner* may ask for specific information, which comes down to asking a low-level question. In this case, receiving *low-level elaboration* may be enough to lead the tutee to successful problem solving and learning. Low-level elaboration includes correcting the tutee's answer, directly giving the answer to a problem or providing specific information;
(3) The third possible starting point is that the tutee may give no indication of difficulty: making no error and/or asking no question. In this case, the student may be able to find his/her own way to successful problem solving.

After reviewing 19 studies discussing the effects of tutoring interaction on learning, Webb (1989) found that very few among them focused on conditions for effectiveness of the help provided. In most cases, the researchers concentrated on calculating correlations between certain types of behavior on behalf of the tutor and tutee achievement outcomes. Making the most of the results of those studies, Webb drew three provisional conclusions to be confirmed by subsequent research:

(1) When a student experiencing difficulties receives help of a lower level of elaboration than requested, the correlation with achievement is negative. In this way, to directly give the correct answer to a *learner* who asks questions about how to solve the problem seems counter-productive;
(2) When an individual encounters difficulties and receives high-elaboration help, this process is not automatically beneficial. The explanation provided may not have been sufficiently relevant or the *learner* may not have understood it properly. The student may also have failed to sufficiently internalize the explanation received;
(3) Obtaining simple information (low-level elaboration) is consistently correlated with achievement gains between the pre-test and the post-test. Specific help can thus prove to be effective.

In a subsequent literature review, Webb & Palincsar (1996) confirmed that the research results were mixed. A majority of studies showed significant correlations between high-level explanations and achievement outcomes and non-significant correlations between low-level explanations and outcomes (see Webb 1989, 1991; for a synoptic view). Other studies showed a positive relationship between low-level explanations and outcomes (Webb 1992; Webb & Fall 1995; Webb & Farivart 1994). According to Webb & Palincsar (1996), it was not possible with current data to confirm or to refute the hypotheses drawn up by Webb in 1989. It was thus necessary to set up new studies with a closer look into peer interactions. The present study was developed within that scope.

More precisely, the aim of this study was to test Webb's hypotheses in a very structured situation: the tutoring. Again, it was important to distinguish tutoring where partners are forced to dissymmetric interactions from cooperative learning context where symmetric interactions are favored. It was also important to consider that Webb's model was based on two implicit assumptions:

(1) Effective tutoring interaction builds on the initiatives taken by tutees who engage in problem solving. By reacting to the tutee's errors and/or questions, the tutor applies a *retroactive* tactic, i.e. s/he corrects mistakes or contributes to correcting them by giving explanations;
(2) Effective tutoring interaction goes through the explanation of problem-solving approaches, procedures and/or concepts, explanations, particularly when the tutee has important difficulties.

To this reactive or retroactive tactic, one could oppose a proactive tactic, i.e. the teacher (or tutor) could guide the learner's approach step by step so as to avoid that the latter would make errors. In this perspective, the learning process would simply be based on the fact that problem solving would take place under the tutoring supervision of an expert learner or that the latter would solve the problem together with the novice. In this pattern, the expert learner would be less concerned about explaining the reason for the steps than about guiding the novice's steps. The novice would solve problems by acting him/herself, under the expert's guidance and with much less trial and error. It is worth noting that Webb pointed out that low-level elaboration may be sufficient to make tutoring interaction effective.

The aim of the present study was to investigate to what extent peer tutors use retroactive versus proactive tactics and to what extent one approach or to what extent these approaches foster pupils' learning. Before examining those issues, one should find out whether the tutors have actually applied a form of educational guidance.

Method

Sixty-six children from 3 classes of the 5th and 6th grades of primary education (mixed classes, vertical distribution) from the region of Liège took part in this experiment. A majority of the children came from a rather privileged environment. Thirty-three attended the 5th grade and 27 the 6th grade of primary education. Their age ranged from 9 years 10 months to 13 years 2 months. The children's mean age was 11 years 2 months.

A classic pre-test/post-test design was adopted, with a supplementary delayed post-test or retention test.

The experiment lasted 3 weeks, at a rate of one week for each class. It was conducted in February-March. The pre-test was administered collectively in each full class. This instrument included 12 arithmetic problems of the multiplying type:

- 3 scale problems;
- 3 speed problems;
- 3 problems implying a rule of 3; and
- 3 combination problems.

Each problem was graded on a 2-point scale: 1.5 point for a correct equation and 0.5 point for a correct answer. A global mark was computed on a 6-point scale (because there were 3 different problems per type) per child and per type of problem.

Based on the pre-test results, tutor-tutee dyads were set up. All children having obtained 2 points out of 6 or less for a given type of problems were selected as tutees while all children having obtained 5 points out of 6 or more for a given type of problem became tutors.

Once the dyads were set up, the tutoring sessions began. They took place on the second, third and fourth days of the week, in an isolated room. Each session handled one specific type of problem, i.e. a type of problem for which the tutee failed the pre-test whereas the tutor had obtained a good mark (i.e. at least 5 points).

The experimenter briefed the tutor individually before each session. She showed the tutor his/her pre-test form and explained that, considering his/her mastery of a given type of problem, s/he would be asked to assist a team-mate — who failed the pre-test — in solving that particular type of problem. She gave the tutee's name and asked the tutor to review the problems s/he had to explain to the tutee. She read those problems over with the tutor and asked how the latter would go about to solve them. She numbered the problems so that the tutor would present them in a given order. She then showed the tutor the tutee's form and pointed out that s/he should *correct* the tutee's exercises together with him/her. This first part of the session was referred to as the *correction phase*. She then provided the tutor with another form, which contained 3 new problems of the same type as those previously discussed. The aim of those exercises was to provide the tutee with an opportunity of using the help received (condition 6 for Webb). This second part of the session was referred to as the *application phase*. Finally, the experimenter read all three problems aloud and, after each one, asked the tutor how one should solve it. Once the tutor had identified the correct procedure, the experimenter told him/her to go and fetch the tutee in class.

On the last day of the week, all children (30 tutees and 30 tutors) who took part in a tutoring session took a post-test containing three problems of the type covered by the tutoring. One month after the first post-test, a delayed post-test (retention test containing 3 items) was organized, again with the type of problem covered by the tutoring interaction. The post-test items were marked the same way as the pre-test items.

Technique Used for the Analysis of Peer Interaction

All tutoring sessions were videotaped. The analysis of every interaction was based on an observation scheme. This scheme featured separate coding fields for tutor and tutee as well as for the correction and application phases. The observation scheme was structured around five major categories of behavior:

(1) Initial stimulus (e.g. behaviors meant to specify the nature of the task; for example, "*look here, you have a problem you failed, we will do it again together*");
(2) Prompts for action (e.g. behaviors meant to let the other do something; for example, "*try to do it by yourself now*");
(3) Verbal statements (e.g. answers, oral computing, instructions to recall, explanations, argumentations, justifications; for example, "*I multiply 48 by 8 because the tower on the poster is 8 times smaller than in reality*");
(4) Actions or problem-solving behaviors (for example, the child does the multiplication of 48 by 8);
(5) Feedbacks (e.g. behaviors meant to evaluate an action or a verbal statement; for example, "*yes, it is right!*").

Sub-categories mainly corresponded to the scope covered by the different behaviors. Considering the problems that had to be solved, we identified the following objects:

(1) Terms and/or data to be processed;
(2) Approach;
(3) Computation;
(4) Answer to be given;
(5) Phrasing the response;
(6) Argumentation, justification, explanation.

This breakdown based on objects was done in each category, except "Initial stimulus". Besides categorizing pupils' behaviors in terms of the above-mentioned categories and objects, we also categorized them in terms of retroactive and proactive tactics (these groupings are explained in Table 2). A cross-marking reliability index was calculated.

One hundred randomly selected behaviors were marked twice by the same researcher, but at different times (three weeks apart). Consistency between both ratings attained 96%.

Trends in Students' Performances on the Pre-Test, Post-Test and Retention Test

One half of the tutors succeeded all three tests i.e. they obtained 6/6. The scores achieved by a majority of the others slightly fluctuated: they were between 5 and 6. The errors made by tutors were exclusively computations errors, no one error pertained to the process of drawing the equation. Two tutors failed to solve one of the problems given in the retention test and, therefore, got a 4 point score on that test. It appeared legitimate to regard those errors as expressions of slackening attention, since those children had easily succeeded in solving all other problems of the same type.

Five different trend patterns can be identified based on an analysis of tutees' marks.

(1) Tutees who obtained a maximum score for post-test and retention test, i.e. who achieved important progress since the pre-test;
(2) Tutees who gradually improved their score as they passed successive tests: they obtained a mark equal to or lower than 2 for the pre-test, a mark between 3.5 and 4 for the post-test and, finally, a mark close to 6 for retention test;
(3) Three tutees achieved a score close to 6 for post-test 1, but obtained a slightly lower mark for retention test. In other words, their score slightly dropped (by 2 points) from the first post-test to the second;
(4) Three others showed a significant regression (4 points) between both post-tests after having obtained a poor score for the pre-test;
(5) Two tutees stagnated. One got 0 for post-test 1 and 2 for the retention test, while the other got 0 for both post-tests.

The trend of the 15 tutees listed under pattern 1 and that of the 7 tutees under pattern 2 can both be described as positive. That of the three tutees with pattern 3 can be described as intermediate: fluctuations in the scores of these tutees are difficult to interpret to the extent that at the retention test, they succeeded to solve two problems out of three. Trends in the scores achieved by the three pattern 4 students seem to imply that the tutoring session's gains were superficial and therefore failed to resist to erosion by time. Finally, it is clear that tutees of the pattern 5 did not progress as a result of the tutoring sessions.[1] On the whole, the great majority of tutoring sessions proved to be effective.

---

[1] Four dyads were confronted with scale problems: 2 tutees out of 4 achieved some progress before regressing heavily; a third did not benefit from the tutoring sessions at all. Tutee 2 was the only one who improved. This observation suggests that scale problems raised more learning difficulties than the other types of problems.

Role Distribution During Both Phases of the Tutoring Process

Before any further analysis, we verified whether the tutors actually fulfilled their guidance task and, besides, whether the breakdown of the tutoring process into two phases (correction and application) was correctly implemented. Indeed, instructions given to the tutors incited them to steer the tutees' activity during the course of the correction phase before encouraging them to solve problems from the application form as independently as possible. Correct implementation of that canvas inevitably resulted in a corresponding behavioral expression: as far as interaction was concerned, a strong presence was required from the tutors for both phases, particularly for the first one.

Table 1 shows the frequency of behaviors, per generic category and per phase, for tutors and for tutees.

Initial stimuli, prompting for action and feedbacks are peculiar to tutors. Consequently, those types of behavior are produced almost exclusively by tutors. Conversely, actions mostly come from the tutees (605 vs. 265 or 69.5%). Verbal statements are the only type of behavior recorded in close proportion for both partners (407 or 52% for tutors and 380 or 48% for tutees). Clearly, the tutors' and tutees' roles are marked. The tutors initiate the resolution of all problems, prompt for action, formulate all the feedbacks and realize an important part of the verbal statements. By doing this, they actually produce 58% (1389 vs. 1018) of the whole of the interactive behaviors. The tutees produce most of the actions (605 for the tutees vs. 265 for the tutors) and close to one half of the verbal statements (380 vs. 407).

The overall frequency of interactive behaviors generated by tutors is higher than that of the tutees for phase 1, while this ratio tends to reverse for phase 2. This global

Table 1: Overall frequency and mean frequency of behaviors shown by tutors and tutees during the course of the correction phase (C) and the application phase (A).

	Correction		Application		Total		
	Tutor	Tutee	Tutor	Tutee	Tutor	Tutee	Tutor + Tutee
Initial Stimulus	103	0	34	0	137	0	137
Prompts for Action	184	2	115	0	299	2	301
Verbal statements	266	191	141	189	407	380	787
Actions	154	221	111	384	265	605	870
Feedbacks	110	0	133	0	243	0	243
Other	25	21	13	10	38	31	69
Total	842	435	547	583	1389	1018	2407
Mean Frequency	28.07	14.5	18.23	19.43	46.3	33.93	

Note: The mean frequency shown at the bottom of this table is the mean for the 30 dyads and not the average of the different categories of behavior.

observation can be ascribed to verbal statements, for which the ratio switches from 266/191 to 141/189 and, to a lesser extent, to actions (from 154/221 to 111/384). In fact, it was recorded that the number of actions performed by tutors dropped as they switched from phase 1 to phase 2, while the reverse was recorded for tutees.

How Tutors Teach

After a detailed analysis of the observation records, one can draw up an overall picture of the set of teaching practices used by tutors. They initiate the activity by showing the problem to be solved. They steer their tutees' approach by prompting them to read or to write down the terms of the problem, to formulate a problem-solving approach, to make a computation, to produce an answer or correctly phrase a response. The better part of their verbal statements consisted of telling the tutees what they should do and, when the verbal channel appeared to be ineffective, they acted in the tutee's place. Tutors gave far more positive than negative feedback, which leads one to suppose that tutees made few mistakes. In short, everything seems to indicate that tutors preferred proactive guidance, as indicated in Table 2. This table shows categories we consider as proactive and retroactive guidance.

Regulations referred to as *proactive* cover more than 69% of the whole set of interactive behaviors on the tutors' behalf. These are proportionally as important in the correction phase than in the application phase. Retroactive regulations within the scope of which tutors explained, argued etc. cover no more than 16% of the whole of the tutors' behaviors and disapproval cover only 4%. Finally, 88% of the feedback is targeted either at computation (39%) or at the answer (49%).

What Tutees Do

During the tutoring sessions, the tutees' behaviors mainly fell within two categories: verbal statements and actions.

More than two thirds (73.2%) of the tutees' verbal statements focused on computation (36.3%), on the answer (30%) and on phrasing the response (6.9%). The same set covered 37.5% for tutors. Another distinctive feature for tutees was the low frequency of giving an argument, a justification, an explanation, a summary or similarities between problems: 1.6% of such behavior for tutees against 25.1 for tutors. It was also quite rare that tutees formulated the terms of the problem or stated what to look for: 8.4% for the tutees against 34.1% for the tutors. Conversely, they expressed more frequently their understanding or lack thereof (14.2% against 0 for the tutors). In a nutshell, verbal participation by tutees during tutoring interaction was clearly of a different nature than by tutors.

The amount of incorrect verbal statements was much higher for tutees than for tutors: it totals 69 (i.e. 24%) for the former and 2 (i.e. 1.3%) for the latter. However, one should point out that, including for tutees, correct verbal statements occurred more often than incorrect verbal statements. The correct/incorrect verbal statements ratio was three to

Table 2: Proactive and retroactive regulation performed by tutors during the course of the correction (C) and application (A) phases.

	Proactive regulations			
	C	A	Total	%
Shows the problem that must be solved	86	34	120	9.4
Prompts to read the terms of the problems or write out the data	19	13	32	2.5
Prompts to formulate an approach	43	37	80	6.3
Prompts to compute	48	26	74	5.8
Prompts to give an answer or correctly phrase a response	31	18	49	3.8
States what to look for or which data should be processed	100	51	151	11.8
States what approach to set up or what computation to make	61	24	85	6.7
Formulates the answer or phrases the response	43	25	68	5.3
Makes the calculation and/or writes it out	29	14	43	3.4
Writes out or draws the data, the answer or a well-phrased response	51	32	83	6.5
Approval	74	102	176	13.8
Total amount of proactive regulations	**585** **(60%)**	**376** **(50.7%)**	**961**	**69**

	Retroactive regulations			
	C	A	Total	%
Seeks information on tutee's errors or announces the type of problem for which the tutee has encountered difficulties	17	0	17	1.3
Prompts tutee to express his/her understanding or lack of understanding	31	15	46	3.6
Argues, explains, summarizes, synthesizes, underscores similarities	62	40	102	8
Assists the other in computation	20	22	42	3.3
Verifies what tutee has written or drawn	7	3	10	0.7
Total amount of retroactive regulations	**137** **(16%)**	**80** **(15%)**	**217**	**16**
Disapproval	**29**	**28**	**57**	**4**

Note: Percentages are computed in proportion to the total amount of behaviors performed by tutors (cf. Table 1).

one. This goes in the direction pointed out earlier: tutors mainly implemented a proactive regulation mode, which prevented tutees from making a significant number of mistakes.

The proportion of incorrect verbal statements remained just under 25% for tutees. However, this rate does not apply to their actions: tutees performed very few incorrect actions (5.6%).

Besides, more than half of the actions performed by tutees pertained to computation (52%). If, to this figure, one adds the 28% that consist in writing an answer or phrasing a response (5.9%), the result accounts for 85% of the tutees' actions.

Are There Distinct Patterns of Tutoring Interaction?

One cannot rule out that some of the dyads interacted in a distinctive way in relation to the overall pattern shown by the above analyses. For instance, some tutors may have relied more heavily on retroactive regulation, despite the overall trend that appeared to favor the opposite mode. If so, it would be normal to observe in these dyads a higher rate of errors made by the tutee (at the level of both verbal statements and actions), given that trial and error was inherent to the logic of this regulation mode.

To explore this hypothesis, we considered seven parameters, corresponding to the frequency of occurrence, for every single dyad and during each phase, of seven behaviors. Three parameters described tutors' interactive tactics: proactive regulations, retroactive regulations and disapproval. Four parameters concerned tutees' behaviors: correct verbal statements, incorrect verbal statements, correct actions and incorrect actions.

Variability of interactions in relation to the task corresponding to each phase was observed. It was therefore legitimate to suppose the existence of weak correlations between the values observed for the same parameters in the two phases. This was confirmed by the calculations we subsequently performed (see Table 3).

Clearly, the measured frequencies during the correction phase did not allow for any prediction of the frequency of interactions during the second phase.

Were there any relations between the various parameters observed within a same phase? Tables 4 and 5 provide the values of the correlation coefficients that were calculated to answer this question.

Table 3: Correlations between the same parameters as observed in the correction and application phases and corresponding explained variances.

Proactive regulations	Retroactive regulations	Dis- approvals	Correct statements	Incorrect statements	Correct actions	Incorrect actions
0.27	0.26	0.05	0.33	0.28	0.10	0.31
7%	7%	<1%	11%	8%	<1%	10%

Table 4: Correlations between seven interaction parameters during the correction phase.

	Retroactive regulations	Dis- approvals	Correct statements	Incorrect statements	Correct actions	Incorrect actions
Proactive regulations	0.29	0.14	0.30	0.04	0.10	0.01
Retroactive regulations		0.41	0.41	0.45	0.37	0.02
Disapprovals			0.47	0.71	0.33	0.31
Correct statements				0.34	0.46	0.14
Incorrect statements					0.28	0.30
Correct actions						0.61

Table 5: Correlations between seven interaction parameters during the application phase.

	Retroactive regulations	Dis- approvals	Correct statements	Incorrect statements	Correct actions	Incorrect actions
Proactive regulations	0.53	0.08	0.28	0.23	–0.10	–0.01
Retroactive regulations		0.41	0.09	0.48	–0.11	0.09
Disapprovals			0.02	0.68	–0.09	0.65
Correct statements				0.25	0.11	–0.19
Incorrect statements					0	0.29
Correct actions						0

During both phases, the frequency of tutees' incorrect verbal statements was strongly correlated with the frequency of disapprovals (respectively 0.71 and 0.68) and, to a lesser extent, with the frequency of retroactive regulations (respectively 0.45 and 0.48). Logically, there was positive correlation between the frequency of disapprovals and retroactive regulations (0.41 and 0.41). There was also a positive correlation between tutees' correct and incorrect verbal statements (0.34 and 0.25). This last observation contrasts with the idea that tutees who formulated many correct verbal statements produced few errors and vice versa.

Relations between tutees' verbal statements and actions were complex. They were positively correlated during the correction phase but not during the application phase. No overall patterns seemed to emerge from the observation of correlations between tutees' correct or incorrect actions and other parameters during the two phases. For instance, correct and incorrect actions were observed to be strongly interrelated during the correction phase (0.61), but not at all during the application phase. Likewise, correct actions were positively correlated to retroactive regulations, disapprovals, and correct and incorrect verbal statements during the correction phase. During the application phase, there was only a trend into that direction. Ultimately, a single common pattern emerged in this respect: disapprovals were positively correlated with incorrect actions (0.31 and 0.65).

It is easier to interpret correlations between proactive regulations and the other parameters. During both phases, the frequency of proactive regulations was mainly correlated to that of retroactive regulations (0.29 and 0.53) and correct verbal statements (0.30 and 0.28). A discrepancy between phases was nevertheless observed: proactive regulations and incorrect verbal statements were positively correlated during the application phase (0.23), whereas the correlation coefficient was almost zero during the correction phase (0.04).

The most important finding, from our perspective, was the presence of positive correlations, during both phases, between proactive and retroactive regulations (0.29 and 0.53 respectively). Otherwise said, there were not two contrasting interaction modalities: all tutors relied mainly on proactive regulation, resorting only when needed to retroactive regulation.

Let us finally note that it was not possible to distinguish an interactive profile typical of the "efficient" dyads from another one typical of the "inefficient" ones. We found the same tutoring process in dyads where tutees did make achievement progress as well as in the other ones. More precisely, the interaction pattern of dyads 5 and 21 where tutees made little progress was like the other ones.[2]

Discussion

The observations collected during that study offered a clear picture of the tutoring interaction, since they produced a similar profile, with a few exceptions, in all the dyads. Tutors focused strongly on proactive strategies. Moreover, they rarely explained the rationale of the approaches and computations they prescribed. Particularly during the

---

[2] We did not compute correlations between interactive behaviors and tutees achievement because the overall high efficiency of this tutoring process caused small variance.

correction phase of the exercises failed by tutees, all tutors conducted the exchanges. Through their prompts, their questions and/or their solicitations, they guided the tutees' approaches so that the latter were led to the correct answer with few mistakes; the tutors could thus formulate mainly positive feedbacks. Moreover, tutees were limited to perform execution tasks: four-fifths of their actions and close to three-quarters of their verbal behaviors consisted of computations or of producing an answer.

Interaction modes were not deeply different during the application phase. Tutors went on applying proactive strategies rather than on retroactive ones. Tutees' activity nevertheless increased greatly; whereas in the correction phase, the tutors' behavior frequency was almost twice more than the tutees', the ratio was slightly reversed in the application phase. That makes us suppose that the tutees' activity became more autonomous, and thus, that the tutors' guidance was less pregnant during that second phase than during the first one.[3]

Here is another important fact to note: the positive correlation between retroactive and proactive modes as well in the correction phase as in the application mode. This means that the dyads with the greatest number of proactive patterns were also the dyads with most retroactive ones.

What are the implications of our results in regards of the Webb's (1989) model? No doubt they do not corroborate perfectly this model, which assumes that effective tutoring interaction builds on the initiatives taken by tutees and on retroactive tactics and detailed explanations of the procedures by the tutors. According to our observations, it is quite occasional that the tutor takes action based on the tutee's questions or errors. Tutees very rarely express their misunderstanding. But the infrequency of the tutees' questions must be — at least partly — considered as a consequence of the guidance exerted by tutors. As far as they guide step by step the tutees' approaches, it is quite logical that there are few errors and so, that there are few opportunities for tutees to become aware of a possible misunderstanding. In short, we need first to explain the tutors' behavior.

Probably, the interactive profile impulsed by tutors was influenced by the design of our study. The guideline given to tutors was to help tutees to correct some exercises. We think that this guideline had two main aspects. First, the tutor was responsible for his/her peer's progress; secondly, it emphasized improvement of performances rather than progress in the understanding of the concepts. Of course, the experimenter explained that the tutor had to "*help his/her peer to understand the problems he/she missed*", but the aim of enhancing performance was the major part, since the tutor received the tutee's sheet and noted there were some mistakes to correct. The point is thus for the tutor to help the tutee to be able to solve problems. Action prevailed over understanding.

Generally, predominance of proactive patterns seems to be a logical consequence of the tutoring situation. This imposes an asymmetric interactive structure. Partners' parts are clearly defined. The tutor receives the status of the one who knows; he receives the task to help his partner, which has as a consequence to impose him an education

---

[3] Proactive patterns represent 46% of the whole interactions, for tutors and tutees altogether, during the correction phase, and 33% during the application phase. The retroactive patterns represent 11% during the phase 1 and 7% during the phase 2.

responsibility (e.g. to attend to the improvement of his/her peer's performance). And the tutee is put under the supervision of a peer; he/she feels legitimately in a situation of reaction rather than in a situation of initiative).

Otherwise, the effect of the role distribution ascribed by the tutoring scheme is probably reinforced by a cognitive factor. As Nelson-Le Gall's findings showed it (1981), the child's help-seeking process when confronted to a cognitive task, is complex. It needs mainly the perception of a lack, but also a certain confidence in the people around him/her to get relevant help. Another phenomenon, which acts as a brake, is the fear of being mocked. As noted by Webb & Palincsar (1996), this aspect of peer interactions is too often neglected.

In our study, the relevance of a proactive pattern from the tutor was reinforced by the characteristic of the task: the partner had to be led to a concrete result, in the form of correctly completed exercises, and in this aspect, a step-by-step guidance was necessary.

We have indeed to keep in mind that the mainly proactive tutoring guidance appeared to be efficient, at least in relationship with the adopted progress: the success of exercises similar to those that have been discussed during the tutoring session. As we noticed above, the marking of students' answers to post-tests only concerned the result. It did not consist of an assessment of the children's understanding of underlying concepts. In short, it is possible that tutees have learnt to *succeed to solve* some problems without understanding. It is known, since Piaget's *Réussir et comprendre* (1974), that it is possible.

Some other questions can be raised at the end of our study. For instance, it would be useful in future research to understand when and why the tutors use retroactive patterns and what is the specific effect of this tutoring intervention in combination of proactive patterns. Is it correct that proactive tutoring enhances the regulation of procedures for the tutee, and that steps of retroactive regulation contribute to the understanding of concepts and procedures implemented in the situation of problems solving? Finally, even if most tutees made progress in relation to the adopted criterion, it was not the case for all of them. We have thus to wonder: why does a same interactive profile produce effects in most cases, while not producing any in other cases? The data we collected here do not help to answer that crucial question. We can imagine that some tutees needed some more elaborated help. That hypothesis raises undoubtedly several questions for further research. How can tutors diagnose when a peer needs an elaborated explanation? Are they able to make that diagnosis, and if they are, are they able to supply that elaborated explanation? Such educational competences require psychological competences. When and how do children develop such competences?

References

Anderson, J. R. (1983). *The architecture of cognition*. Cambridge, MA: Harvard University Press.
Beaudichon, J., Verba, M., & Winnykamen, F. (1988). Interactions sociales et acquisition de connaissances chez l'enfant. Une approche pluridimensionnelle. *Revue Internationale de Psychologie, 1*, 129–141.

Berzin, C., Cauzinille, E., & Winnykamen, F. (1985). Effets des interactions sociales dans la résolution d'une tâche de combinatoire auprès d'enfants de CM1. *Archives de Psychologie, 63,* 17–42.

Bruner, J. (1996). *Le développement de l'enfant: savoir faire, savoir dire* (5th ed.). Paris: Presses Universitaires de France.

Cohen, P. A., Kulik, J. A., & Kulik, C.-L. A. (1982). Educational outcomes of tutoring. A meta-analysis of findings. *American Educational Research Journal, 19,* 237–248.

Crahay, M. (1999). *Psychologie de l'éducation.* Paris: Presses Universitaires de France.

Crahay, M. (2000). *L'école peut-elle être juste et efficace?* Bruxelles: De Boeck.

Dewey, J. (1900). *The school and society.* Chicago: The University of Chicago Press.

Ellis S., & Rogoff, B. (1982). The strategies and efficacy of child vs. adult teachers. *Child Development, 53,* 730–735.

Freinet, C. (1964). *Les techniques Freinet de l'école moderne.* Paris: Colin.

Kilpatrick, W. H. (1922). *The Project Method: the use of the purposeful act in the educative process.* New York: Teachers College Press.

Logan, C. D.(1985). Skill and automaticity: Relations, implications and future directions. *Canadian Journal of Psychology, 39,* 367–386.

Nelson-Le Gall, S. (1981). Help-seeking: An understudied problem solving skill in children. *Developmental Review, 1,* 224–246.

Piaget, J. (1974). *Réussir et comprendre.* Paris: Presses Universitaires de France.

Radsiszewska, B., & Rogoff, B. (1988). Influence of adult and peer collaboration on children's planning skills. *Developmental Psychology, 24* (6), 840–849.

Saxe, G. B. (1992). Studying children's learning in context: Problems and prospects. *Journal of the Learning Sciences, 2,* 215–234.

Shavelson, R. J., Webb, N. M., Stasz, C., & McArthur, D. (1988). Teaching mathematical problem solving. Insights from teachers and tutors. In: R. Charles, & E. Silver (Eds), *Teaching and assessing mathematical problem solving: A research agenda* (pp. 203–231). Hillsdale, NJ: Lawrence Erlbaum Associates.

Shute R. H., Foot, H. T., & Morgan, M. (1992). The sensitivity of children and adults as tutors. *Educational Studies, 18* (1), 21–36.

Vedder, P. (1985). *Cooperative learning: A study on processes and effects of cooperation between primary school children.* Westerhaven Groningen, Netherlands: Rijkuniversiteit Groningen.

Verba, M., & Wynnikamen, F. (1992). Expert-novice interactions: influence of partner status. *European Journal of Psychology of Education, 7* (1), 61–71.

Webb, N. M. (1989). Peer interaction and learning in small groups. *International Journal of Educational Research, 13* (1), 21–40.

Webb, N. M. (1991), Task-related verbal interaction and mathematics learning in small groups. *Journal for Research in Mathematics Education, 22,* 366–389.

Webb, N. M. (1992). Testing a theoretical model of student interaction and learning in small groups. In: R. Hertz-Lazarowitz, & N. Miller (Eds), *Interaction in cooperative groups: The theoretical anatomy of group learning* (pp. 102–119). New York: Cambridge University Press.

Webb, N. M., & Farivar, S. (1994). Promoting helping behavior in cooperative small groups in middle school mathematics. *American Educational Research Journal, 31,* 369–395.

Webb, N. M., Troper, J. D., & Fall, R. (1995). Constructive activity and learning in collaborative small groups. *Journal of Educational Psychology, 87,* 406–423.

Webb, N. M., & Palincsar, A. M. (1996). Group processes in the classroom. In: R. Berliner, & R. Calfee (Eds), *Handbook of educational psychology* (pp. 841–873). London: Pergamon Press.

Chapter 13

Effects of Explicit Reading Strategies Instruction and Peer Tutoring in Second and Fifth Graders

Hilde Van Keer and Jean Pierre Verhaeghe[1]

Theoretical Background

In both studies presented here we focused on peer tutoring as a powerful learning environment for primary school children's acquisition of metacognitive strategies. More particularly the additional value of peer tutoring on top of explicit instruction in reading strategies and the effects of two types of peer tutoring were investigated.

Learning to read is a crucial learning process in primary school. However, especially with regard to the ultimate goal of reading comprehension many children appear to have persistent problems. Reading comprehension, defined as constructing a mental representation of textual information and its interpretation (Van Den Broek & Kremer 2000), refers to understanding and giving meaning to written words, sentences, and texts (Aarnoutse & Van Leeuwe 2000). Notwithstanding the simplicity of the definition, complex processes are behind it. Expert readers distinguish themselves from novice or poor readers by comprehension-monitoring and regulating activities (Baker & Brown 1984; Dole *et al.* 1991). This implies metacognition, which refers to the awareness of one's own cognitive abilities and activities and to the skills to manage and evaluate these cognitive processes (Baker & Brown 1984). So, proficient readers have a split focus: they are able to concentrate simultaneously on the material and on themselves, monitoring their reading. They are aware of whether they understand what they are reading or not, usually leading to regulation when they encounter difficulties (Dole *et al.* 1991). To that end, they select from a variety of cognitive strategies, which are consciously selected, deployed, and adapted to a variety of texts, purposes, and

[1] The present study was supported by a Research Grant of the Fund for Scientific Research — Flanders.

Powerful Learning Environments: Unravelling Basic Components and Dimensions
© 2003 Published by Elsevier Science Ltd.
ISBN: 0-08-044275-7

occasions (Baker & Brown 1984; Pressley & Allington 1999; Pressley *et al.* 1989). The mastery of cognitive and metacognitive strategies appears critical in becoming a skilled reader. However, not all students develop those strategies spontaneously (Pressley & Allington 1999). Despite convincing research results documenting that explicit strategies instruction effectively promotes students' strategic reading and comprehension (e.g. Brand-Gruwel *et al.* 1998; De Corte *et al.* 2001; Dole *et al.* 1991; Klingner & Vaughn 1996; Palincsar & Brown 1984; Pressley *et al.* 1989), evidence shows that the dominant instructional practice still focuses on evaluating students' understanding performance by questioning them about the content of a text after reading it (Aarnoutse & Weterings 1995; Dole 2000; Pressley *et al.* 1998).

In addition, learning to read appears to be a social process. Research convincingly establishes that interaction among peers about texts promotes comprehension and the application of self-regulation strategies (e.g. Almasi 1996; Brown *et al.* 1996; Dole *et al.* 1991; Fuchs & Fuchs 2000; Fuchs *et al.* 1997; Klingner *et al.* 1998; Mathes & Fuchs 1994; Palincsar & Brown 1984; Pressley *et al.* 1992; Rosenshine & Meister 1994; Simmons *et al.* 1995). Given these findings, one might expect teachers allot a fair amount of reading comprehension instruction periods to peer interaction. Nevertheless, student-centered discussion is anything but common practice (Alvermann 2000).

Among the various ways to encourage task-oriented interaction among students "peer tutoring" appears to be a promising technique, for tutoring increases individualization, time on task, immediate and specific feedback, reinforcement and error correction, as well as frequent opportunities to respond, and academic engagement (Greenwood & Delquadri 1995; Utley & Mortweet 1997). Peer tutoring can be defined as "people from similar social groupings who are not professional teachers helping each other to learn, and learning themselves by teaching" (Topping 1996). This covers a series of practices employing peers as one-to-one teachers to provide individualized instruction and practice and is characterized by specific role taking: someone takes the job of tutor, while the other is in a role as tutee (Topping 1996). Two broad categories can be distinguished based on the composition of the dyads. Cross-age tutoring refers to older students tutoring younger students. In same-age tutoring, children are paired with children from within their own classroom. The specific form in which students regularly change roles is called reciprocal same-age tutoring.

Traditionally peer tutoring was seen as a way to help the less able or the younger students. But with regard to school achievement not only tutees benefit from peer tutoring; the tutors seem to do even more (Topping 1996). This can be explained by the nature of tutoring a peer: tutors are challenged to consider the subject fully from different perspectives, to engage in active monitoring to identify and correct errors, to reorganize and clarify their knowledge, and to elaborate on information in their explanations in order to provide help (Fuchs & Fuchs 2000). With regard to practising strategic reading, peer tutoring invites tutors to focus on the tutee's reading, which allows them to supervise their reading process attentively, to monitor their understanding, and to foster comprehension by having their tutees apply relevant reading strategies. In this respect, tutoring a peer is assumed to create powerful opportunities to acquire metacognitive monitoring and regulation skills with respect to reading and the appropriate use of reading strategies, presumably leading to an improvement in reading comprehension. Because there is less danger for a fading away of the distinction between tutee and tutor roles and because the differences in reading level make the actual reading process less demanding for the tutors, it may become easier for tutors to pay full attention to their monitoring and regulating task in the case of cross-age tutoring. This in turn may lead to a better acquisition of the metacognitive skills involved and — in the end — a larger improvement of the tutor's own reading comprehension achievement. Since in this way they probably will have better tutors, one might also expect tutees in a cross-age tutoring condition to make more progress in reading compared to tutees in same-age tutoring conditions. So far, no peer tutoring research has made an explicit comparison of the effects of cross-age and same peer tutoring. Some indirect indication for the higher effectiveness of cross-age peer tutoring can be found in the meta-analysis by Cohen *et al.* (1982), which shows larger effect sizes for both tutors' and tutees' achievement in cross-age programs.

Unlike other studies exploring the effects of either explicit reading strategies instruction or peer tutoring, the studies presented in this article blend practices from both research fields, trying to find out if practising reading strategies in tutoring sessions provides any surplus value to explicit strategies instruction. Moreover, whereas past studies on tutoring focused on either cross-age or same-age tutoring, the present studies compare both variants. Experimental treatments were implemented in complete regular second- and fifth-grade classes during an entire school year, providing an ecologically valid test of the hypotheses. Finally, long-term effects till six months after finishing the treatments were assessed.

Hypotheses

The major hypotheses of the studies can be formulated as follows:

- Explicit reading strategies instruction, followed by practice in teacher-led whole-class activities or peer tutoring activities, enhances second and fifth graders' reading comprehension achievement, strategy use and self-efficacy perceptions towards reading more than traditional reading comprehension instruction;
- Peer tutoring activities to practice reading strategies generate greater positive changes in second and fifth graders' reading comprehension achievement, strategy use and self-efficacy perceptions towards reading than teacher-led practice during whole-class activities;
- The improvement in reading comprehension, strategy use and self-efficacy perceptions towards reading is larger for second and fifth graders in cross-age tutoring dyads than in reciprocal same-age dyads.

Description of the Experimental Treatments

Depending on the experimental condition, the treatment consisted of explicit reading strategies instruction combined with practice in either teacher-led whole-class, cross-age, or reciprocal same-age tutoring activities. The interventions substituted traditional reading comprehension classes during regular reading instruction periods. A detailed description of the treatments can be found in Van Keer (2003) and Van Keer & Verhaeghe (2003a).

Explicit Reading Strategies Instruction

Experimental treatments focused on acquiring a set of six reading strategies: activating prior knowledge and imagining what the text will be about, predictive reading and verifying story outcomes, distinguishing main issues from details, monitoring and regulating the understanding of words and expressions, monitoring and regulating text comprehension, and classifying types of text and adjusting reading behavior to it. Some of these strategies are cognitive, other ones are metacognitive. For some of them the application requires using one or more "underlying" cognitive strategies. So what is called a "strategy" in some cases consists in fact of a set of strategies in itself. The selection of strategies was based on a review of related research (e.g. De Corte *et al.* 2001; Fuchs *et al.* 1997; Klingner & Vaughn 1996; Klingner *et al.* 1998; Palincsar & Brown 1984). As far as the instructional techniques are concerned, treatments were influenced by studies on transactional strategies instruction (Pressley *et al.* 1992) and reciprocal teaching (Klingner & Vaughn 1996; Palincsar & Brown 1984). Attention was paid to extensive and explicit teacher explanations and modeling of strategic reading. Children were instructed in where, when, and why to use the strategies; as well as in how to adapt them to various situations. A gradual transfer from external teacher regulation to self-regulation of strategy use by the students was striven for. To support this, an assignment card was provided for each strategy. These cards specify the steps to be taken and some questions students should ask themselves. Unlike the content-related questions typically asked by teachers in traditional comprehension activities, those questions are not text specific, but generally applicable to different texts.

Tutor Preparation

Since peer tutoring is less effective when no attention is paid to preparing tutors (e.g. Bentz & Fuchs 1996; Fuchs *et al.* 1994), experimental tutoring treatments included seven 50-minutes preparatory lessons. Explanations, modeling, role plays, discussions, and student practice with teacher feedback represented an important part of the training. Students got acquainted with the tutor tasks and responsibilities; they learned how to show interest, how to give corrective feedback, explanations, and help, and how to offer positive reinforcement.

Peer Tutoring Sessions

While students in the teacher-led condition practised reading strategies during individual seatwork in whole classroom settings, followed by whole classroom discussion, in both tutoring conditions weekly tutoring activities were organized to practice reading strategies. Two variants were studied. In the cross-age condition fifth graders were paired with second graders. In the reciprocal same-age condition second and fifth graders were paired with classmates and students alternated regularly between tutee and tutor roles for an equal amount of time. Tutoring activities were organized class-wide, so all students were paired and worked simultaneously. The regular classroom teachers observed and supported the dyads and provided corrective and instructional feedback. Sessions were organized once or twice a week for 25 to 50 minutes from October till May. On the average a total of 959 minutes were devoted to tutoring sessions. A "sandwich model" was applied in which a teacher-led introduction of a reading strategy was followed by at least one tutoring session in which that strategy was practiced using a text from the teachers' manual. Thereafter that strategy was further practiced in tutoring sessions with books from the class library. This whole cycle, which took about one month, was repeated for every new strategy. At the end a number of sessions was organized in which all strategies came together and students had to select the appropriate strategy themselves. Since a combination of dyadic peer interaction and structured academic activity enhance cognitive gain more than either of both separately (Cohen *et al.* 1982; Fantuzzo *et al.* 1989), the above mentioned strategy assignments cards were used as a vehicle for structuring the tutoring interaction.

Support to the Teachers

Because experimental treatments were implemented by regular class teachers, these teachers were thoroughly supported by the first author. They were provided with a manual (Van Keer 2002) including a description of the rationale, aims, and organization of the interventions, lesson scenarios, and student materials, such as the strategy assignment cards and reading texts. The manual was based on review of related research (e.g. Bentz & Fuchs 1996; Fuchs *et al.* 1997; Klingner & Vaughn 1996; Klingner *et al.* 1998; Palincsar & Brown 1984; Pressley *et al.* 1992).

Method

Design

Two successive quasi-experimental studies with a pretest posttest retention test control group design were executed. In the first study (1999–2000) participating teachers and their classes were assigned to four research conditions. In the strategies-only condition (STRAT) the treatment included explicit reading strategies instruction and practice in teacher-led whole-class settings. The experimental same-age (STRAT + SA) and cross-age (STRAT + CA) tutoring conditions included identical strategies instruction, but strategic reading was respectively practiced in reciprocal same-age and cross-age dyads. The control group was characterized by traditional instruction without explicit strategies instruction nor peer tutoring. All experimental treatments were preceded by a pretest (October). Between the posttest (June) and retention test (six months later, December) no explicit strategies instruction or systematic practice in tutoring dyads was organized.

In a partial replication of the first study a further comparison was made between the control group and the STRAT + SA and STRAT + CA conditions during the school year 2000–2001. Based on the first experiences, the program and some of the materials were slightly modified. The interventions were implemented by the same teachers with a second cohort of students.

Participants

Twenty-five primary schools throughout Flanders participated in the studies. Except for one inner-city school with mainly a low SES and ethnic minority population, the schools' population was comprised mainly of white, Flemish, Dutch-speaking students from middle-class families. Table 1 shows the number of second- and fifth-grade classes and students in each condition for both studies.

Teachers were selected from a group of about 100 volunteering second- and fifth-grade teachers. The selection was based on the geographical distribution of the schools and on the possibility to match experimental and control teachers and classes with regard to teaching experience, class size, students' age, gender distribution, and dominating mother tongue. Teachers were randomly assigned to either the STRAT or one of the two tutoring conditions. Within the tutoring conditions teachers could opt in favor of the STRAT + SA or STRAT + CA condition according to their own preference and the readiness of a colleague to collaborate in cross-age activities. Control classes were selected to match teachers and class groups in the three experimental conditions.

Table 1: Number of participating classes and students in both studies.

	Grade							
	2				**5**			
	Study 1		**Study 2**		**Study 1**		**Study 2**	
Condition	**Classes**	**Students**	**Classes**	**Students**	**Classes**	**Students**	**Classes**	**Students**
STRAT + SA	5	91	6	110	4	101	9	186
STRAT + CA	3	66	8	162	4	69	7	156
STRAT	8	163	—	—	8	177	—	—
Control group	6	124	6	124	6	107	6	107
Total	22	444	20	396	22	454	22	449

Measurement Instruments

Standardized reading comprehension tests and questionnaires assessing students' use of reading strategies and preoccupation with self-efficacy related thoughts were administered at all measurement occasions, within regular class time.

Reading comprehension. Choice of the standardized tests (Staphorsius & Krom 1996; Verhoeven 1993) was based on their well-established psychometric characteristics, the built-in adaptation to different student abilities and the coverage of reading strategies in the experimental program. Each test presents a number of reading texts to the students, each of them followed by a number of multiple choice questions asking what the text (or a particular part of it) is mainly about, what the author or some character in the text intends to communicate or what their attitude with regard to some issue in the text is, what the reason or cause of some action or process is or what the particular meaning of a word or phrase in the context of the text is.

For second-grade tests Cronbach's α for internal consistency ranged from 0.83 to 0.90 (n between 348 and 432). In fifth grade the tests consist of three modules of 25 multiple-choice questions each. All students took the first module. Afterwards they completed the second more easy or third more difficult module, depending on their first results. Sum scores were transposed into an IRT-modeled score. Cronbach's α ranged from 0.66 to 0.82 (n between 31 and 468).

Reading strategy use. Students were asked to report their strategy use before, while or after reading by ticking one of the boxes ("never", "almost never", "sometimes", "very often") following statements as: "Before starting to read I think about what I already know about the topic of the text", "While reading I try to find the meaning of difficult words", "While reading I try to find out what's the story is about". Cronbach's α ranged from 0.70 to 0.87 (n between 275 and 401) revealing acceptable levels of reliability.

Self-efficacy related thoughts. Students' self-efficacy perceptions towards reading were assessed by means of a self-report questionnaire on the incidence of positive or negative thoughts with regard to reading proficiency and accompanying success and failure attributions. Factor analysis revealed that success attributions and positive self-efficacy related thoughts on the one hand and failure attributions and negative self-efficacy related thoughts on the other hand were closely related. Therefore, two scales were constructed. Scores do not represent a direct measure of students' self-efficacy perceptions, but rather an indication of the degree to which a student is preoccupied with self-efficacy related thoughts. In that sense the data are more directly related to (meta)cognitive activity than in the case of more traditional self-concept questionnaires. A high incidence of negative self-efficacy related thoughts can be considered as an indication of a low self-efficacy perception, but the reverse does not hold for a low incidence of positive self-efficacy related thoughts. It only reveals that the student is little preoccupied with thoughts about reading proficiency.

Cronbach's α ranged from 0.62 to 0.75 (n between 322 and 441) for the positive subscale and from 0.76 to 0.86 (n between 297 and 408) for the negative subscale.

Data Analysis

The data of both studies have a clear hierarchical structure with students nested within a smaller number of classes. Moreover, the experimental condition is a group level variable, whereas the dependent variables are measured at the individual level. Hence the use of multilevel analysis is recommended. Since three measurement occasions were used in the studies, a multilevel repeated measures design was used. So, three-level models were built with the measurement occasions (level 1) clustered within students (level 2), nested within classes (level 3). Models were estimated using the iterative generalized least squares (IGLS) procedure in MLwiN (Rasbash *et al.* 1999). Effects of experimental condition on students' evolution from pretest to posttest and from pretest to retention test were tested after having controlled for the potential effects of gender, years behind at school, mother tongue, and (for second graders) reading fluency scores on students' evolutions, as well as for the effects of pretest levels of the criterion variables involved. To test the hypotheses regarding the differential effects of different experimental conditions, pair-wise comparisons were conducted.

Results

In the next section a summary of the main results for both studies will be presented. Statistical details including regression coefficients, standard errors and significance levels for fixed and random effects can be found in Van Keer (2003) and Van Keer & Verhaeghe (2003a, 2003b).

Effects on Reading Comprehension

Table 2 presents the effect sizes for the significant experimental effects on reading comprehension achievement. In study 1 conditions did not differ in how reading comprehension achievement in second grade evolved over time. In study 2, however, STRAT + CA second graders' pre- to posttest increase was significantly greater than in the control group (effect size 0.42 *SD*), but for the whole period from pretest to retention test, the difference was no longer significant. Pair-wise comparisons of the experimental conditions revealed no significant differences at neither post- nor retention test. As concerns short-term effects we can conclude that study 2 yields better results, at least with regard to the STRAT + CA condition. This suggests that teachers' experience with this particular technique may be an important variable. That improvement was particularly found for STRAT + CA students points out the higher potential of this condition for second grade. The absence of long-term effects in both studies shows that for these young students lasting effects are only likely to appear after a substantial continuation of the treatment.

In the first study, fifth graders' progress throughout the school year was significantly higher for the STRAT + CA and STRAT conditions compared to the control group. Effect sizes are 0.36 and 0.31 *SD* respectively. Moreover, students in both conditions

Table 2: Effect sizes for significant experimental effects on second and fifth grade reading comprehension achievement scores for both studies.

	Grade			
	2		**5**	
	Study 1	**Study 2**	**Study 1**	**Study 2**
Effect on evolution from pretest to posttest				
Post*STRAT			0.31*	
Post*STRAT + SA				0.21*
Post*STRAT + CA		0.42*	0.36*	0.28***
Effect on evolution from pretest to retention test				
Retention*STRAT			0.46**	
Retention*STRAT + SA				
Retention*STRAT + CA			0.75***	0.42*

* $p < 0.05$, ** $p < 0.01$, *** $p < 0.001$.

kept growing, resulting in a significantly larger progress from pretest to retention test with effect sizes of 0.75 and 0.46 *SD* respectively. Pair-wise comparisons also indicated that STRAT + CA students made a significantly larger progress from pretest to retention test than STRAT + SA students (effect size 0.56 *SD*). For study 2, Table 2 reveals a significantly higher progress from pre- to posttest for both STRAT + SA and STRAT + CA conditions compared to the control condition. Effect sizes are 0.21 and 0.28 *SD* respectively. But at retention test only STRAT + CA students made significantly more learning gains (effect size 0.42 *SD*). The differential slope of the STRAT + SA condition (effect size 0.28 *SD*) only reached marginal significance. Pair-wise comparison showed no significant difference between STRAT + SA and STRAT + CA students' progress. Generally, study 2 seems to confirm study 1, especially with respect to the positive short- and long-term STRAT + CA effects on fifth-graders reading comprehension. However, effect sizes seem to be smaller in study 2. Presumably, this can be explained mainly by the significantly lower average STRAT + CA pretest score in study 1. This low average pretest score was quite unexpected, since much effort was done to match teachers and classes, based on reading comprehension data from the preceding school year. The results suggest that STRAT + CA students in study 1 were able to catch up during fifth grade and together with the positive effect of the experimental treatment this yielded a quite high effect size. Probably the effect sizes found in study 2 are more realistic. With regard to the STRAT + SA condition, study 2 shows better results, since a positive significant short-term effect was found.

To summarize: for both second and fifth grade significant positive effects on students' reading comprehension achievement were found for the STRAT + CA condition, indicating that the combination of explicit reading strategies instruction and cross-age peer tutoring for practising the reading strategies yields a significant improvement of students' reading comprehension for both tutors and tutees, with moderate effect sizes. In fifth grade smaller but still significant positive effects were also found for both other experimental conditions. This was not the case for second grade. Only in fifth grade significant positive long term effects were found, more particularly for the STRAT + CA condition and for the STRAT condition.

Effects on Reading Strategy Use

With regard to students' reports of strategy use, similar models were built. Both studies yield quite similar results. Only for second graders significant effects were found (Table 3). So, we will only discuss results for second grade.

Compared to the beginning of the school year, control group students reported significantly less frequent strategy use at post- and retention test. On the contrary, students in all three experimental conditions reported more frequent strategy use at the end of second grade. Differences with the control group students were significant. Effect sizes ranged from 0.33 to 0.45 SD in study 1, with the highest effect size for the STRAT + CA condition. In study 2 effect sizes were 0.42 SD for STRAT + SA and 0.71 SD for STRAT + CA. Only for the second study's STRAT + CA condition the difference with the control group remained significant at the retention test (effect size 0.62 SD). Pair-wise comparisons of experimental conditions revealed a significant difference between the STRAT + SA and STRAT + CA condition in study 2. The increase in the reported use of reading strategies was significantly larger in the STRAT + CA condition,

Table 3: Effect sizes for significant experimental effects on second grade measures for use of reading comprehension strategies for both studies.

	Study 1	Study 2
Effect on evolution from pretest to posttest		
Post*STRAT	0.33*	—
Post*STRAT + SA	0.39*	0.42**
Post*STRAT + CA	0.45**	0.71***
Effect on evolution from pretest to retention test		
Retention*STRAT		—
Retention*STRAT + SA		
Retention*STRAT + CA		0.62***

$* p < 0.05$, $** p < 0.01$, $*** p < 0.001$.

both at post- and retention test (effect sizes 0.29 and 0.31 *SD* respectively). In general, results for study 2 appear to confirm those of study 1. The higher effect sizes in the latter study and the appearance of a retention effect for the STRAT + CA condition even show an improvement of the treatment effects compared to study 1, especially for the STRAT + CA condition.

Effects on Self-Efficacy Related Thoughts

Significant effects were found for the incidence of second graders' positive self-efficacy related thoughts in study 2 and the incidence of fifth graders' negative self-efficacy related thoughts in both studies (Table 4).

While throughout the school year a significant decrease was found for the control group, the incidence of positive self-efficacy related thoughts remained more or less stable from pre- to posttest for the STRAT + SA and STRAT + CA conditions in study 2, resulting in significantly different slopes (effect sizes 0.44 and 0.56 *SD* respectively). For the pre- to retention test evolution, these differences were no longer significant. A pair-wise comparison revealed no significant difference between both tutoring conditions.

Table 4: Effect sizes for significant experimental effects on measures of positive (for 2nd grade) and negative (for 5th grade) self-efficacy related thoughts in both studies.

	Grade			
	2 (Positive SE related thoughts)		5 (Negative SE related thoughts)	
	Study 1	**Study 2**	**Study 1**	**Study 2**
Effect on evolution from pretest to posttest				
Post*STRAT				
Post*STRAT + SA		0.44*		0.40*
Post*STRAT + CA		0.56***		
Effect on evolution from pretest to retention test				
Retention*STRAT				
Retention*STRAT + SA			0.36*	
Retention*STRAT + CA				

* $p < 0.05$, ** $p < 0.01$, *** $p < 0.001$.

In fifth grade, the incidence of negative self-efficacy related thoughts reported by the control group students remained stable from pre- to post- and retention test. In study 1 a decrease in preoccupation with negative self-efficacy related thoughts from pretest to retention test was observed for STRAT + SA students resulting in significant differences with the control group students (effect size 0.36 *SD*). In study 2 a similar significant effect was revealed at posttest for the STRAT + SA condition, with an effect size of 0.40 *SD*. Moreover, pre- to posttest evolution in the STRAT + SA condition was also significantly different from the STRAT + CA condition (effect size 0.29 *SD*). At retention test, however, the difference with the control condition became only marginally significant and the difference between the STRAT + SA and STRAT + CA conditions disappeared. The common finding for 5th grade in both studies is that "positive" effects were only found for the STRAT + SA condition, but whereas study 1 shows a long-term effect without any short-term effect preceding it, study 2 shows mainly a short-term effect, followed by a marginally significant long-term effect.

Discussion

During two successive school years two similar large-scale quasi-experimental studies were conducted to investigate the effects of reading strategies instruction combined with practice in either teacher-led whole-class settings, or in same-age, or cross-age peer tutoring activities on regular second and fifth graders' reading comprehension achievement, strategy use, and self-efficacy perceptions towards reading.

Effects of Explicit Instruction in Reading Strategies

As concerns the first hypothesis, about the effects of explicit reading instruction, no general conclusion can be formulated. Therefore, results are discussed for the three dependent variables separately.

Effects on reading comprehension. Findings generally accord with previous research, emphasizing the educational benefits of explicit strategies instruction (e.g. Brand-Gruwel *et al.* 1998; Fuchs *et al.* 1997; Klingner & Vaughn 1996; Palincsar & Brown 1984; Pressley *et al.* 1989) and peer-led interaction about texts (e.g. Almasi 1996; Fuchs & Fuchs 2000; Fuchs *et al.* 1997; Klingner *et al.* 1998; Mathes & Fuchs 1994; Palincsar & Brown 1984; Pressley *et al.* 1992; Simmons *et al.* 1995) in promoting comprehension achievement. Contrary to other studies, significant results were found on standardized instead of experimenter-designed tests, which underlines the value of the experimental treatments.

For second graders, the results basically document the feasibility of explicit strategies instruction with practice in cross-age tutoring activities. No similar effects were detected for practice in teacher-led or reciprocal same-age activities. The absence of significant extra learning gains for the latter two conditions parallels the findings of Rosenshine & Meister's (1994) review of reciprocal teaching, revealing significant effects from grade four onwards, but non-significant effects for younger students. In other studies reporting significant same-age tutoring effects in a variety of age groups including second graders (Fuchs *et al.* 1997; Simmons *et al.* 1995), no separate analyses were done on second-grade data. As to cross-age tutoring, it can be hypothesized that the significant findings for second grade are attributable to two elements of the treatment, namely individualized assistance and the quality of the support that could be offered by the fifth graders. In both other conditions, these two essential elements are not present simultaneously. The strategies-only condition is characterized by proficient teacher support, but no individualized tutoring is offered; the same-age tutoring condition supplies individualized assistance, but it can be assumed that second graders are not yet able to tutor reading strategy use effectively.

For fifth graders, the results confirm that explicit strategy instruction, supplemented with teacher- or peer-mediated practice, fosters comprehension achievement more than traditional comprehension instruction. The effect sizes, in particular of the strategies-only (teacher-mediated practice) and the cross-age condition, compare favorably with the effects on standardized tests reported in Rosenshine & Meister's (1994) review of reciprocal teaching. Moreover, except for the same-age condition, the treatments' effectiveness is particularly corroborated by significant long-term effects, with moderate to large effect sizes.

Effects on reading strategy use.   With regard to students' strategy use, the findings only reveal significant second-grade effects, with significantly higher reports of strategy use after explicit strategies instruction. The results for second grade are congruous with previous studies, applying strategies tests, questionnaires, or interviews (e.g. Brand-Gruwel *et al.* 1998; De Corte *et al.* 2001; Klingner & Vaughn 1996; Klingner *et al.* 1998; Palincsar & Brown 1984; Pressley *et al.* 1989). When comparing the effects' magnitude and maintenance, being a tutee in a dyad with a fifth-grade tutor seems most effective in accomplishing this effect, even in the long term.

Contrary to the expectations, no significant results were recorded for fifth graders. A possible reason might be that the questionnaire that was applied is not appropriate for this age group, perhaps because it elicited a tendency to social desirability.

Effects on self-efficacy related thoughts.   As concerns students' thoughts about their reading proficiency, different results favoring the experimental conditions were found for each age group, with effects on the incidence of positive self-efficacy related thoughts in second grade and effects on the incidence of negative self-efficacy related thoughts in fifth grade.

In second grade the experimental groups' pretest scores were not equivalent to the control group's scores, which imposes some threat to the internal validity of the results. In addition, a decrease in reported positive self-efficacy related thoughts does not necessarily mean that students' self-esteem grows worse. Strictly spoken, it merely indicates being less preoccupied with thoughts about one's own reading proficiency.

For fifth grade, a significant decrease in negative self-efficacy related thoughts was shown in the reports of students in the same-age tutoring condition, either at the end of the school year (study 2) or at the time of the retention test (study 1). Since it can be assumed that high scores for negative self-efficacy related thoughts indicate the presence of low self-esteem, these results indicate that opportunities to alternate between the roles of tutor and tutee in same-age dyads have a positive impact on fifth graders' self-esteem and perceived competence in reading. The non-significant effects for the cross-age condition are rather surprising. Since generally a positive relationship is found between self-efficacy perceptions and achievement, one would have expected that the significant positive (meta-)cognitive effects for the cross-age peer tutoring condition would have gone hand in hand with similar effects on self-efficacy related thoughts. Clearly, additional research is necessary to shed light on these ambiguous results. Again, stimulated recall techniques or thinking-aloud protocols in response to exposure to comprehension tasks with divergent levels of difficulty could be an interesting supplement to assess students' occupation with self-efficacy related thoughts while reading.

Additional Effects of Peer Tutoring

The second hypothesis regarding the surplus value of practising strategic reading in tutoring dyads in comparison with practice in teacher-led activities was addressed by the first study with three experimental groups. Contrary to the expectations based on the literature stressing the importance of peer-led interaction on reading activities (e.g. Almasi 1996; Fuchs & Fuchs 2000; Fuchs *et al.* 1997; Klingner *et al.* 1998; Rosenshine & Meister 1994), this hypothesis was not confirmed. No statistically significant differences were found between the second- and fifth-grade strategies-only condition on the one hand and the same-age or cross-age condition on the other hand. Attention should, however, be drawn to the fact that for some measures no significant results were found for the strategies-only condition in comparison with the control condition, while the same-age or cross-age condition actually did yield significant effects, which provides some indication that peer tutoring does have an additional value. Unfortunately, no comparisons can be made with previous research. Previous studies investigating the impact of peer tutoring or peer-led interaction about texts only equate the innovative instructional technique to a control condition, characterized by traditional instruction without any form of experimental treatment.

Surplus Value of Cross-Age Peer Tutoring over Same-Age Peer Tutoring

Unlike other studies exploring the effects of peer tutoring, the present studies' design allowed testing the third hypothesis stating a surplus value for cross-age over same-age peer tutoring. It was investigated whether effects of practising strategic reading in cross-age dyads differ from effects of practice in reciprocal same-age dyads. This design is unique compared to other studies, which focus on only one tutoring variant. In the present studies pair-wise comparisons of the same- and cross-age conditions generally did not reveal statistically significant mutual differences. Three exceptions to this global finding could however be registered. First, there is the significant difference with regard to fifth graders' retention test reading comprehension achievement in study 1 which confirms the hypothesis. Second, the significant difference with regard to second graders' reported strategy use at posttest in study 2 also confirms the hypothesis. Third, but opposite to the hypothesis, study 2 indicated that at the end of fifth grade, children in the same-age condition were significantly less occupied with negative self-efficacy related thoughts than students in the cross-age condition.

Moreover, when setting the significant and non-significant effects side by side and comparing the effect sizes of both conditions, some other results also point in the direction of the hypothesis. For second graders' comprehension achievement, for example, the results solely revealed a significant effect for the cross-age peer tutoring condition. Taken into account the magnitude of the effect sizes and the long-term effects, it can be concluded that fifth graders also seem to profit more from participating in cross-age than in same-age dyads. This is especially noticeable since cross-age tutors are working with texts on second-grade level. Nevertheless, their learning gains outperform other fifth graders' growth and they effectuate the most persistent long-term progress. A possible explanation relates to the nature of tutoring a younger student in connection to the opportunity to practice and acquire metacognitive monitoring and regulation skills. The tutoring task requires tutors to focus on the tutees reading, to superintend their reading processes attentively, to monitor their understanding, and to endeavor to foster comprehension by applying relevant reading strategies. The fact not having to read themselves makes it easier for the tutors to give full attention to these metacognitive skills. In other words, it may be easier to practice the metacognitive skills by monitoring and regulating someone else's reading, more particularly if this is a younger student with a lower reading level. So, functioning as a tutor for a younger student can be a powerful learning environment for the acquisition of metacognitive skills leading to a higher reading comprehension achievement.

In sum, it can be concluded that there are some indications that confirm the hypothesis of the surplus value of cross-age tutoring for both tutors and tutees in comparison with reciprocal same-age tutoring. In this respect, future more qualitatively oriented systematic research should try to elucidate the differential effects of practising strategic reading in same-age or cross-age dyads. Therefore detailed in-depth observation and analysis of the content, the nature, and quality of students' interactions in either teacher-led whole-class discussions, cross-age, or reciprocal same-age dyads will be necessary.

Finally, the reported studies exhibit some limitations. First, although a start was made with comparing the effects of different ways of practising reading strategies, the design did not allow to draw strong conclusions about the relative contribution of the different constituent components of the treatments (e.g. the focus on the selected strategies; the explicit teacher explanations, modeling, and a gradual transfer from teacher to student regulation; the regular opportunities to practice strategic reading; . . .). From former studies, it can be assumed that the combination of elements accounts for the observed positive effects. However, this is only an assumption. A convincing explanation requires a detailed component analysis to clarify what components are essential.

A second restriction relates to the instrument used to assess students' reading strategy use. Especially for fifth graders the findings were not consistent with the results revealed on comprehension achievement. As mentioned before, the non-significant results with respect to strategy use in fifth grade may be attributed to the inappropriateness of the questionnaire. It can be assumed that fifth graders have a tendency to social desirability in answering the questionnaire. Self-report questionnaires have the disadvantage of being an indirect measurement, which entails that children's reportage of strategy use is not necessarily consistent with their actual reading behavior (Veenman & van Hout-Wolters 2002). In this respect, future research should substitute the use of the questionnaire by more objective measures. Thinking-aloud protocols, behavior observations, and retrospective techniques, like stimulated recall, can offer opportunities to shed light on students' reading strategy use, and metacognitive functioning in different formats and contexts.

A third shortcoming relates to the total amount of time teachers spent on reading comprehension instruction and practice. In this respect, no differences between the research conditions were intended. However, since the studies were executed in natural class settings, variations between teachers could not be totally excluded. To control for those variations, all teachers were asked to pass information on the total amount of time they spent on reading comprehension instruction. They relayed information about the fixed scheduled instruction periods, but no information was supplied on reading activities outside these planned teaching periods. The data teachers provided revealed that in all conditions similar amounts of time were allocated to comprehension instruction, but large differences were found between the classes within each condition. Surprisingly, the total amount of time spent on comprehension instruction did not significantly influence second or fifth graders' achievement or any other response variable. This is a rather unexpected finding, possibly attributable to the fact that the data do not give a real overall picture of the total amount of time spent on reading, including for example reading activities within social studies. Subsequent research should try to assess this potential explanatory variable more precisely, for example by means of teachers' logs.

Finally, it is important to gather information on how well the treatments have been implemented. In the present studies regular discussions with the teachers took place and class observations were executed. Still, quality of implementation data were not collected systematically. In addition, it was practically impossible to perform in-depth analysis of reading activities in the control classes. Subsequent research should strive to collect good quality data on the characteristics of the control group's comprehension instruction and the treatment integrity of the interventions. In this respect, the use of a structured checklist by double-blind observers could be useful.

References

Aarnoutse, C. A. J., & Van Leeuwe, J. F. J. (2000). Development of poor and better readers during the primary school. *Educational Research and Evaluation, 6*, 251–278.

Aarnoutse, C. A. J., & Weterings, A. C. E. M. (1995). Onderwijs in begrijpend lezen [Education in reading comprehension]. *Pedagogische Studiën, 72*, 82–101.

Almasi, J. F. (1996). The nature of fourth graders' sociocognitive conflicts in peer-led and teacher-led discussion of literature. *Reading Research Quarterly, 30*, 314–351.

Alvermann, D. E. (2000). Classroom talk about texts: Is it dear, cheap or a bargain at any price? In: B. M. Taylor, M. F. Graves, & P. Van Den Broek (Eds), *Reading for meaning. Fostering comprehension in the middle grades* (pp. 170–192). New York: Teachers College Press.

Baker, L., & Brown, A. L. (1984). Metacognitive skills and reading. In: P. D. Pearson, R. Barr, M. L. Kamil, & P. Mosenthal (Eds), *Handbook of reading research* (pp. 353–394). New York: Longman.

Bentz, J. L., & Fuchs, L. S. (1996). Improving peers' helping behavior to students with learning disabilities during mathematics peer tutoring. *Learning Disability Quarterly, 19,* 202–215.

Brand-Gruwel, S., Aarnoutse, C. A. J., & Van Den Bos, K. P. (1998). Improving text comprehension strategies in reading and listening settings. *Learning and Instruction, 8,* 63–81.

Cohen, P. A., Kulik, J. A., & Kulik, C. C. (1982). Educational outcomes of tutoring: A meta-analysis of findings. *American Educational Research Journal, 19,* 237–248.

De Corte, E., Verschaffel, L., & Van De Ven, A. (2001). Improving text comprehension strategies in upper primary school children: A design experiment. *British Journal of Educational Psychology, 71,* 531–559.

Dole, J. A. (2000). Explicit and implicit instruction in comprehension. In: B. M. Taylor, M. F. Graves, & P. Van Den Broek (Eds), *Reading for meaning. Fostering comprehension in the middle grades* (pp. 52–69). New York: Teachers College Press.

Dole, J. A., Duffy, G. G., Roehler, L. R., & Pearson, P. D. (1991). Moving from the old to the new: Research on reading comprehension instruction. *Review of Educational Research, 61,* 239–264.

Fantuzzo, J. W., Riggio, R. E., Connelly, S., & Dimeff, L. A. (1989). Effects of reciprocal peer tutoring on academic achievement and psychological adjustment: A component analysis. *Journal of Educational Psychology, 81,* 173–177.

Fuchs, L. S., & Fuchs, D. (2000). Building student capacity to work productively during peer-assisted reading activities. In: B. M. Taylor, M. F. Graves, & P. Van Den Broek (Eds), *Reading for meaning. Fostering comprehension in the middle grades* (pp. 95–115). New York: Teachers College Press.

Fuchs, L. S., Fuchs, D., Bentz, J., Phillips, N. B., & Hamlett, C. L. (1994). The nature of students interactions during peer tutoring with and without prior training and experience. *American Educational Research Journal, 31,* 75–103.

Fuchs, D., Fuchs, L. S., Mathes, P. G., & Simmons, D. C. (1997). Peer-assisted learning strategies: Making classrooms more responsive to diversity. *American Educational Research Journal, 34,* 174–206.

Greenwood, C. R., & Delquadri, J. C. (1995). Classwide peer tutoring and the prevention of school failure. *Preventing School Failure, 39,* 21–25.

Klingner, J. K., & Vaughn, S. (1996). Reciprocal teaching of reading comprehension strategies for students with learning disabilities who use English as a second language. *The Elementary School Journal, 96,* 275–293.

Klingner, J. K., Vaughn, S., & Schumm, J. S. (1998). Collaborative strategic reading during social studies in heterogeneous fourth-grade classrooms. *The Elementary School Journal, 99,* 3–21.

Mathes, P. G., & Fuchs, L. S. (1994). The efficacy of peer tutoring in reading for students with mild disabilities: A best-evidence synthesis. *School Psychology Review, 23,* 59–80.

Palincsar, A. S., & Brown, A. L. (1984). Reciprocal teaching of comprehension-fostering and comprehension-monitoring activities. *Cognition and Instruction, 1,* 117–175.

Pressley, M., & Allington, R. (1999). What should reading instructional research be the research of? *Issues in Education, 5,* 1–35.

Pressley, M., El-Dinary, P. B., Gaskins, I., Schuder, T., Bergman, J. L., Almasi, J., & Brown, R. (1992). Beyond direct explanation: Transactional instruction of reading comprehension strategies. *The Elementary School Journal, 92*, 513–555.

Pressley, M., Johnson, C. J., Symons, S., McGoldrick, J., & Kurita, J. (1989). Strategies that improve children's memory and comprehension of text. *The Elementary School Journal, 90*, 3–32.

Pressley, M., Wharton-McDonald, R., Hampston, J. M., & Echevarria, M. (1998). The nature of literacy instruction in ten grade–4/5 classrooms in upstate New York. *Scientific Studies of Reading, 2*, 159–191.

Rasbash, J., Browne, W., Goldstein, H., Yang, M., Plewis, I., Healy, M., Woodhouse, G., & Draper, D. (1999). *A user's guide to MLwiN*. London: Institute of Education.

Rosenshine, B., & Meister, C. (1994). Reciprocal teaching: A review of research. *Review of Educational Research, 64*, 479–530.

Simmons, D. C., Fuchs, L. S., Fuchs, D., Mathes, P. G., & Hodge, J. P. (1995). Effects of explicit teaching and peer tutoring on the reading achievement of learning-disabled and low-performing students in regular classrooms. *The Elementary School Journal, 95*, 387–408.

Staphorsius, G., & Krom, R. (1996). *Toetsen Begrijpend Lezen* [Reading Comprehension Tests]. Arnhem, The Netherlands: Cito.

Topping, K. J. (1996). The effectiveness of peer tutoring in further and higher education: A typology and review of the literature. *Higher Education, 32*, 321–345.

Utley, C. A., & Mortweet, S. L. (1997). Peer-mediated instruction and interventions. *Focus on Exceptional Children, 29*, 69–92.

Van Den Broek, P., & Kremer, K. E. (2000). The mind in action: What it means to comprehend during reading. In: B. M. Taylor, M. F. Graves, & P. Van Den Broek (Eds), *Reading for meaning. Fostering comprehension in the middle grades* (pp. 1–31). New York: Teachers College Press.

Van Keer, H. (2002). *Een boek voor twee. Strategieën voor begrijpend lezen via peer tutoring* [A book for two. Reading comprehension strategies through peer tutoring]. Antwerp, Belgium: Garant.

Van Keer, H. (2003). *Fostering reading comprehension in fifth grade by explicit instruction in reading strategies and peer tutoring*. Manuscript submitted for publication.

Van Keer, H., & Verhaeghe, J. P. (2003a). *Effects of explicit reading strategies instruction and peer tutoring on second and fifth graders' reading comprehension and self-efficacy perceptions*. Manuscript submitted for publication.

Van Keer, H., & Verhaeghe, J. P. (2003b). *Strategic reading in peer tutoring dyads in second- and fifth-grade classrooms*. Manuscript submitted for publication.

Veenman, M. V. J., & van Hout-Wolters, B. H. A. M. (2002, May). *Het meten van metacognitive vaardigheden* [Measuring metacognitive skills]. Paper presented at the Onderwijsresearchdagen 2002, Antwerp, Belgium.

Verhoeven, L. (1993). *Lezen met begrip 1* [Reading with comprehension 1]. Arnhem, The Netherlands: Cito.

Author Index

Subject Index